> . . . it is not the task of the writer to defend or criticize one or another mode of distributing the social product, or to defend or criticize one or another form of government organization. The task of the writer is to select more universal and eternal questions, the secrets of the human heart and conscience, the confrontation of life with death, the triumph over spiritual sorrow, the laws of the history of mankind that were born in the depths of time immemorial and that will cease to exist only when the sun ceases to shine.

SOLZHENITSYN
Appendix to *Cancer Ward*, pp. 554-55

EDWARD E. ERICSON, JR.

SOLZHENITSYN
The Moral Vision

FOREWORD BY MALCOLM MUGGERIDGE

GRAND RAPIDS
WILLIAM B. EERDMANS PUBLISHING COMPANY

Copyright © 1980 by Wm. B. Eerdmans Publishing Co.
255 Jefferson Ave. S.E., Grand Rapids, Mich. 49503

Reprinted, January 1982

Library of Congress Cataloging in Publication Data

Ericson, Edward E
  Solzhenitsyn, the moral vision.

    1. Solzhenitsyn, Aleksandr Isaevich, 1918–
Religion and ethics.   I. Title.
PG3488.04Z646   891.73'44   80-15533
ISBN 0-8028-1718-1

FOR JAN

CREDITS

ACKNOWLEDGMENTS

I have lived with the works of Aleksandr Solzhenitsyn for more than a decade by now; they have become an integral part of my mental furniture. But my ruminations on those writings would never have found their way into print in this volume without the encouragement and assistance of many friends, colleagues, and auditors. It would be a sin of omission to neglect naming the chief among them.

Milorad Drachkovitch of the Hoover Institution may be surprised to learn that his words of approval several years ago helped bear this fruit. In recent years my friendship with Vladislav Krasnov, who has now published his own (splendid) book on Solzhenitsyn (and Dostoevsky), has been of immeasurable aid. Krasnov read the manuscript and spared this American commentator more than one embarrassing misstep. My senior colleague and admired friend Richard R. Tiemersma, of Calvin College's English Department, brought to this work the editorial expertise which those who know him know that only he can bring. My former secretary Barbara Drake provided, as usual, an immaculate typescript. To my friend Kay Dull I am again indebted for a superb job of indexing. The good folks at the Wm. B. Eerdmans Publishing Co., especially Jon Pott, were wonderfully supportive and patient as I struggled to find spots of working time amid my ongoing tasks of teaching and administration and the disruption caused by a traumatic broken leg (which my friends and I know as The Fall) and the six subsequent operations. Also, I appreciate the enthusiasm of students of mine in five classes (one at Northwestern College and four at Calvin College) in which Solzhenitsyn's works were the featured attraction. But no assistance can begin to compare with that daily benevolence breathed into my life by my family: wife Jan, to whom this book is dedicated, and blessing-bringing good sons Ed and Bill.

My work has been enhanced by small but strategically targeted grants from two institutions at which it has been my pleasure to serve in recent years: Northwestern College in Orange City, Iowa, and Calvin College (through the Calvin Foundation) in Grand Rapids, Michigan.

Finally, I note the recent receipt of Solzhenitsyn's *The Oak and the Calf*, now, at last, available in English. These memoirs reached me only after my book had been set in type. Had I received it earlier, I would have altered an occasional statement of mine about the author's actions and intentions. My consolation is that the changes would have been few and minor. Solzhenitsyn's account of his struggles with the Soviet literary establishment causes me to think that on the whole I have understood my subject aright. For any errors I ask his indulgence. Solzhenitsyn, the weak, unprotected calf, has butted up against the apparently immovable oak of the Soviet establishment. Who is to say if the calf or the oak is stronger? Time—perhaps a long time—will tell. One commentator, however, has recently suggested that the battle between the Soviet authorities and Mr. and Mrs. Solzhenitsyn was altogether unfair: that the Soviets never had a chance.

Grand Rapids, Michigan, U.S.A.
July 1, 1980

CONTENTS

FOREWORD

by Malcolm Muggeridge

I cannot think of any more worthwhile study for any student on any campus today than to go carefully through all the writings and discourses of Aleksandr Solzhenitsyn available in English translation—which is practically his whole corpus. For a variety of reasons, one of which is the sheer greatness of the man in face of afflictions and dangers which otherwise would have destroyed him long ago, he speaks out more bravely and understands more clearly what is going on in the world than any other commentator. I see him as being in the same category as, in the words of the psalmist, one of the holy prophets which have been since the world began; like the great Isaiah, he writes and speaks splendid words of encouragement and hope to people in darkness and despair.

All the same, it has to be admitted that Solzhenitsyn's writings are by no means easy to read. For those of us—the great majority—who do not know Russian, they have to be read in translations of varying quality. They were for the most part produced in conditions of clandestineness and danger without any of the appurtenances of a writer's life—as, for example, quiet, available works of reference, a sympathetic publisher, and the companionship of supportive fellow writers. In the latest of his works to be published in English translation, *The Oak and the Calf*, he describes the conditions under which he went on writing in the USSR, and what he achieved seems like a miracle. Take, for example, the Gulag books—apart from anything else, an invaluable document of our times—and imagine the difficulties presented by having to collect thousands of testimonies relating to life in the prison camps, collate them, guard them from prying eyes when discovery would have been disastrous, and get the manuscript abroad for safekeeping and ultimate publication. Let it be remembered, too, that he undertook this hazardous work in the interest of historical truth and for the sake of all the millions who were still suffering in the camps. In all the annals of literature, I cannot think of a more heroic and disinterested endeavor. How splendidly it stands out in contrast to the wretched Gorky, who allowed himself to be used as an apologist for the cruelty and oppression of the regime in return for a villa in Italy and V.I.P. treatment in the Kremlin!

Given the difficulties in reading Solzhenitsyn, a guide is clearly useful for a tour of his writings, and this is precisely what Professor Ericson provides. His book takes the reader systematically through all Solzhenitsyn's works—not by any means with a view to saving people the trouble of reading them, but rather to make it possible for people to read them to maximum advantage. Furthermore, it has the great merit of taking full account of the role of Christianity and of Solzhenitsyn's own Christian faith in all his thinking about life and the contemporary world. This is something that the media have slurred over or ignored, since it does not fit their concept of dissidence and dissidents in communist countries. Solzhenitsyn insists that he came to understand what freedom was only in his prison camp, when, humanly speaking, he had lost it; to fulfil the media's requirements, he should have felt liberated when, as an enforced exile, he found himself living amidst the squalid lawlessness and libertinism that in the western world passes for freedom. What amazing perceptiveness on his part to have realised straight away, as he did, that the true cause of the West's decline and fall was precisely the loss of a sense of the distinction between good and evil, and so of any moral order in the universe, without which no order at all, individual or collective, is attainable.

So, instead of pleasing the media by saluting the new-found Land of the Free, Solzhenitsyn sees western man as sleep-walking into the selfsame servitude that in the Soviet Union has been imposed by force; of his own free will, choosing to be enslaved, creating his own consensus or party line, and voluntarily subjecting himself to it, making straight the way to his own Gulag. On the campuses and the TV screen, in the news-papers and the magazines, often from the pulpits even, the message is being proclaimed—that Man is now in charge of his own destiny and capable of creating a kingdom of heaven on earth in accordance with his own specifications, without any need for a God to worship or a Savior to redeem him or a Holy Spirit to exalt him. How truly extraordinary that the most powerful and prophetic voice exploding this fantasy, Solzhenitsyn's, should come from the very heartland of godlessness and materialism after more than sixty years of the most intensive and thorough-going indoctrination in an opposite direction ever to be attempted!

It is from this point of view that Professor Ericson surveys Solzhenitsyn's writings and polemical utterances, fitting him as a literary figure into the great tradition of Tolstoy and Dostoevsky, and as a Christian into the mystical tradition of a Berdyaev and a purified Russian Orthodox Church. In my time at Cambridge, now well over half a century ago, to be admitted to the university we were required to satisfy examiners that we were familiar with Paley's *Evidences of Christianity*. Doubtless nowadays it is the other way round: entrants are required to have a nodding acquaintance with the attacks on Christianity mounted by Nietzsche and Bertrand Russell. There is little chance, I fear, of getting Solzhenitsyn's works made required reading for admission to our groves of academe. But let me conclude by saying that any serious student, whatever his discipline, could not fail to benefit from a preliminary reading of Solzhenitsyn, whether as a writer of fiction, as an historian, or as a polemicist, and that he would be greatly assisted in so doing by keeping Professor Ericson's book within convenient reach.

1

INTRODUCTION:

A Single Vision

Never in the history of world literature has there been a story quite like that of Aleksandr Solzhenitsyn.[1] Less than a decade after his first being published, he was hailed in various corners as the world's greatest living writer, as one of the great writers in the rich history of Russian literature, even as one of the giants of all world literature. He has already been anthologized in texts of world masterpieces. At the same time, he has been vilified in the strongest terms. In the Soviet Union he has been highly praised and roundly condemned. In the West he has been highly praised, roundly condemned, and damned with faint praise.

The strong reactions to Solzhenitsyn are not, of course, prompted by and directed toward his literary craftsmanship alone—or even primarily. It is the man—a man burning with ideas and beliefs, a man with a sensational life history—who has elicited such strong feelings. Indeed, the force and volatility of the reactions to Solzhenitsyn are a kind of mirror image of his own single-minded intensity.

It is usually difficult for literary critics to distill a consensus of a writer's aesthetic achievement. It is exceptionally difficult in the instance of Solzhenitsyn. His life and the setting against which it has been lived have ineluctably plunged him, once an unknown small-town high school teacher of physics and mathematics, into the vortex of current world affairs of a highly charged and controversial nature. Just how great a writer is Solzhenitsyn? Although this book makes abundantly manifest my profound admiration for both the man and his writing, I do not write to answer that question. Given that we his contemporaries cannot yet disentangle ourselves from the controversies which have enveloped him, and given that he has not yet finished his work—including especially the work which he has always considered would be his masterpiece—we had best leave to the readers of the twenty-first century the judgment of his literary worth.

In the meantime, what we can do is try to get straight what it is that Solzhenitsyn is saying. He is clearly a man driven by a mission. He has a vision of life which permeates all of his writing. It is to the explication of that vision that this book is devoted. I would not, as a professor of English literature and as one without the Russian language, have had the temerity to write this book if I thought that the heart and main body of this vision were being perceived accurately. The fact is that I think that Solzhenitsyn has for the most part been misinterpreted, misunderstood. So I write. I write primarily for the general reader—in the hope, of course, that such still exists today. I have in mind especially, but certainly not exclusively, those in the general readership who share Solzhenitsyn's Christian faith. I have also tried to keep in mind those specialists in Slavic language and literature to whom will fall the major burden of mediating Solzhenitsyn to future generations of readers. For I write in the conviction that he has much to say to those readers.

The main impediment, in my opinion, to understanding Solzhenitsyn has to do with the spirit of the times. Although Solzhenitsyn is thoroughly conversant with the currents of thought which prevail in his own day, he chooses to stand largely opposed to them. For instance, in his art, as one critic put it,

"Solzhenitsyn takes for granted an absolutely direct and open connection between literature and morality, art and life. . . . In the West today such an assumption about the relationship between art and morality is distinctly unfashionable."[2] Even more important, though not unrelated, is the fact that in a day when secular humanism flourishes among the cultural and intellectual elite, he holds fast to traditional Christian beliefs. And, specifically, in a day when politics has a kind of primacy as the category for understanding human problems and seeking their solution, he relegates politics to a secondary status.

This last is of utmost importance. It is easy enough to understand that among those for whom political affairs are of supreme interest and importance everything will be viewed through the prism of politics. It is equally easy to see that there is much in the writing of Solzhenitsyn which would encourage readers with such predilections to view him through that prism. He writes, after all, of Soviet prison camps and Russian history; he draws portraits of Stalin and Lenin; he makes nonliterary pronouncements on world affairs.

Nevertheless, to view Solzhenitsyn through the political prism is to distort his image. For Solzhenitsyn is ever the writer about moral issues. Furthermore, he is a religious man, a Christian. And it is his Christian vision of life and of the nature of man which always undergirds and provides the context for his moral judgments. To make a distinction between a primarily moral and religious writer and a primarily political writer is to make no mean, or false, distinction. Certainly, Solzhenitsyn sees a relationship between a religious view of life and the sphere of political action; properly, a religious person sees a relationship between his religious view of life and every sphere of human activity. Solzhenitsyn writes, of course, of man in action in the cauldron of the twentieth-century world, a world on which politics impinges in an especially vital way, but always of moral man in action, always of man created in the image of God and thus endowed with moral responsibility toward others and for himself. What this means for an accurate understanding of his work is elaborated in every chapter of this book.

At least since 1972, when Solzhenitsyn made public his commitment to Christianity, his religious faith has been widely acknowledged—though sometimes only to dismiss him as old-fashioned, as if it were quite apparent that a Christian could have nothing to say to the twentieth century. What has not been widely enough acknowledged is the importance that his Christian convictions have for his writings—for all of his writings, even the earliest ones. For 1972 did not mark his embrace of Christianity but only the time of his "going public" about it. It was back in the 1940's, in his first year or so of imprisonment, that he moved from Marx to Jesus.

That his "conversion" was well considered and intentional Solzhenitsyn himself has told us (see the closing section of my chapter on *The Gulag Archipelago*). That he fully understood what this most cataclysmic change in his life meant for his art is less clear. In a most fascinating article, written in 1970—that is, before Solzhenitsyn's going public—Alexander Schmemann, whom I consider the best commentator on Solzhenitsyn (though he has written only two brief essays on him), explicated his work in terms of the *"triune intuition of creation, fall, and redemption."*[3] Conceding that he did not know whether Solzhenitsyn "accepts or rejects Christian dogma, ecclesiastical ritual, or the Church herself," Schmemann insisted that he found in Solzhenitsyn "a Christian writer,"[4] that is, one who has "a deep and all-embracing, although possibly unconscious perception of the world, man, and life, which, historically, was born and grew from Biblical and Christian revelation, and only from it."[5] In an unusual response Solzhenitsyn wrote, ". . . his article about me . . . was also very valuable to me. It explained me to myself. . . . It also formulated important traits of Christianity which I could not have formulated myself. . . ."[6] Without my having known it from the beginning, then, this book apparently is an elaboration of Schmemann's theme (though with not much emphasis on the intuition of redemption).

Schmemann's use of the world *intuition* is intriguing. This theologian knows that Solzhenitsyn is no theologian; few Christians are. And this Russian Orthodox priest aligns the writer not with Russian Orthodoxy in particular but with Christianity in general. Both perceptions are, I think, correct. Solzhenitsyn's "triune intuition" is not explicit in his work; it is implicit, available only to those, like Father Schmemann, who have eyes to see and ears to hear. To others it needs to be explained.

What else needs to be explained is the consistency of vision in Solzhenitsyn's work. (Here the "conversion" date is an important datum.) Some Western critics praised him in the 1960's and criticized him in the 1970's. But the change was not in him. If Solzhenitsyn must eventually succumb to the literary critics' penchant for marking into discrete periods the career of an author, such dissection cannot properly be done on the basis of a change in outlook.

The goal of demonstrating the remarkable continuity in the vision of Solzhenitsyn is one reason for the considerable quoting from the author which characterizes this book. Another reason is that heavy quoting has a cumulative effect of showing the centrality of those themes which this study declares to be central. Citation is perhaps most extensively deployed in the final chapter, since the nonliterary utterances of Solzhenitsyn are the ones most widely misunderstood.

Also, there is some repetition of argument from chapter to chapter, which may annoy those who read this book straight through. My only excuse is that I have tried to keep in mind those readers of a book or two by Solzhenitsyn who may wish to peruse only those chapters on the works which they know; I have wanted each chapter to be readable as a self-contained unit. So on a few occasions, but only a few, I have included key citations in more than one chapter.

My greatest hope and wish is that those who pick up this book will be encouraged to read the books by Solzhenitsyn himself. I am confident that they will be more than amply rewarded. So shall I.

2

APPRENTICE UNDER HEAVEN:

the *Nobel Lecture*

Much of the confusion about Solzhenitsyn would be eliminated if his theory of art were understood. He took the occasion of his winning the Nobel Prize in Literature in 1970 to enunciate that theory. Although he did not go to Stockholm to receive the prize in person, because the Soviet authorities would not guarantee him reentry into his homeland, he did follow the standard practice of preparing a speech for the occasion. As its final sentence summarizes, this *Nobel Lecture* both calls the writers of the world to a high sense of mission and provides the basis for understanding the author's own work. The latter is the primary concern of this chapter, which will analyze the lecture in detail, section by section.

The first section is the most important one, for in it Solzhenitsyn establishes the religious basis for his literary work. True art, he explains, is premised on two fundamental concepts: that truth is absolute and that reality is objective. Both ideas grow organically from Solzhenitsyn's belief that there is a personal God who created and sustains the world. Art, then, is a gift from

God; it entails the exercising of a God-given ability. Artists may misuse this gift, "but Art is not profaned by our attempts, does not because of them lose touch with its source."[1] Thus, art is grounded in the objective reality of God's created order, not in an individual's subjectivity; and this fact is so whether or not a given artist acknowledges it.

Solzhenitsyn elaborates this point by contrasting two kinds of artists. One kind "imagines himself the creator of an independent spiritual world . . ." (p. 4). This attempt is doomed to failure, because man is not an autonomous being, in art or in any other realm. "Just as man, who once declared himself the center of existence, has not been able to create a stable spiritual system" (p. 4), so neither can the artist successfully create his own reality. A novel must conform to the same moral laws that govern ordinary human life.

This point Solzhenitsyn's second kind of artist understands. He "acknowledges a higher power above him and joyfully works as a common apprentice under God's heaven . . ." (p. 4). And the acknowledgment of his creatureliness serves to enhance his sense of responsibility, for he is answerable to the one who created and gives direction to the world. This artist works in "a world about whose foundations he has no doubt" (p. 5). His task is "to sense more keenly than others the harmony of the world, the beauty and the outrage of what man has done to it, and poignantly to let people know" (p. 5).

"The harmony of the world" refers to the orderliness of God's original creation. "The beauty and the outrage of what man has done to it" refers to the effects of the Fall; man remains capable of both good ("beauty") and evil ("outrage"). And "poignantly to let people know" refers to the artist's calling to tell the truth about this dual nature of man. These universal matters, best explicated in the Christian schema of Creation and Fall, are the artist's primary subject. As Solzhenitsyn said elsewhere,

> . . . it is not the task of the writer to defend or criticize one or another mode of distributing the social product, or to defend or criticize one or another form of government organization. The task of the writer is to select more universal and eternal

questions, the secrets of the human heart and conscience, the confrontation of life with death, the triumph over spiritual sorrow, the laws of the history of mankind that were born in the depths of time immemorial and that will cease to exist only when the sun ceases to shine.[2]

In later sections of the *Nobel Lecture*, Solzhenitsyn makes certain pronouncements on social and political matters. Yet he has denied that such subjects are the primary material of art. There is no contradiction here. The "universal and eternal questions" are played out by finite man in his daily activities, not excluding his social and political activities. A religious outlook, far from precluding one's commenting on social and political matters, demands that he do so. For the religious mind sees life as indivisible: it sees the eternal and the temporal as inextricably intertwined, and it does not abandon the affairs of this world. In Solzhenitsyn's words, "The transference of values is entirely natural to the religious cast of mind: human society cannot be exempted from the laws and demands which constitute the aim and meaning of individual human lives."[3] Furthermore, this "transference of values" is simply a human thing to do; all men bring their whole selves to bear on any matter under consideration.

> But even without a religious foundation, this sort of transference is readily and naturally made. It is very human to apply even to the biggest social events or human organizations, including the whole state and the United Nations, our spiritual values: noble, base, courageous, cowardly, hypocritical, false, cruel, magnanimous, just, unjust, and so on. Indeed everybody writes this way, even the most extreme economic materialists, since they remain after all human beings.[4]

The relationship for Solzhenitsyn between the eternal and the temporal, or, more specifically, the religious and the political, is a crucial one, since much commentary has viewed him through political eyes. *The Gulag Archipelago* provides an illuminating case study. In a book thick with political detail, he asserts early, "So let the reader who expects this book to be a political exposé slam its covers shut right now."[5] He proceeds immediately to set the terms in which this book, and all of his works, should be read:

> If only there were evil people somewhere insidiously committing evil deeds, and it were necessary only to separate them from the rest of us and destroy them. But the line dividing good and evil cuts through the heart of every human being. . . . During the life of any heart this line keeps changing place; sometimes it is squeezed one way by exuberant evil and sometimes it shifts to allow enough space for good to flourish. One and the same human being is, at various ages, under various circumstances, a totally different human being. At times he is close to being a devil, at times to sainthood. But his name doesn't change, and to that name we ascribe the whole lot, good and evil.[6]

While the opening section of the *Nobel Lecture* contrasts two kinds of artists, underlying that contrast is one between two competing views of human nature. One, nurtured by the long history of the Judaeo-Christian tradition, posits the subordination of man to God. The other, of much more recent vintage, places man at the center of reality and declares that man is ultimately responsible for himself. It is difficult for adherents of the latter to comprehend proponents of the former, for their world-views diverge at the very starting point.

The second section of the *Nobel Lecture* offers a not insignificant tribute to Dostoevsky, a writer with "the gift of seeing much, a man wondrously filled with light" (p. 8). Dostoevsky had once said that beauty would save the world. This notion initially puzzled Solzhenitsyn. But now he thinks he understands. In a world inured to the abstract claims of Truth and Goodness, in a world in which lies and evil often have their way, perhaps that beauty resident in the concretions of art will have its effect. There is a kind of art whose "artificial, strained concepts do not withstand the test of being turned into images; they fall to pieces, turn out to be sickly and pale, convince no one" (p. 7). But there is also a kind of art which carries a con-

viction which "is absolute and subdues even a resistant heart"
(p. 7). Such a work of art "contains its verification in itself
. . ." (p. 7). So perhaps the beauty of genuine art can be an effective antidote to ideology and prejudice and, "in fact, help the
modern world" (p. 8).

The third section opens with a passage reminiscent of the public
prayer Solzhenitsyn circulated two years later, in 1972, but which
David Burg and George Feifer, in their biography of Solzhenitsyn, declare was written in 1962, when he first attained public
recognition.[7] In any case, the sentiments are similar. The passage reads as follows:

> To reach this chair from which the Nobel Lecture is deliv-
> ered—a chair by no means offered to every writer and offered
> only once in a lifetime—I have mounted not three or four
> temporary steps but hundreds or even thousands, fixed, steep,
> covered with ice, out of the dark and the cold where I was
> fated to survive, but others, perhaps more talented, stronger
> than I, perished. (pp. 8-9)

The prayer reads as follows:

> How easy it is to live with You, O Lord.
> How easy to believe in You.
> When my spirit is overwhelmed within me,
> When even the keenest see no further than the night,
> And know not what to do tomorrow,
> You bestow on me the certitude
> That You exist and are mindful of me,
> That all the paths of righteousness are not barred.
>
> As I ascend into the hill of earthly glory,
> I turn back and gaze, astonished, on the road
> That led me here beyond despair,
> Where I too may reflect Your radiance upon mankind.
>
> All that I may reflect, You shall accord me,
> And appoint others where I shall fail.[8]

Here Solzhenitsyn acknowledges both his creatureliness—his subservience (even as an artist) to divine providence,
and his representativeness, as he seeks to speak for those "mute

inglorious Miltons"[9] who shared his hard fate in the Soviet concentration camps and from whom the world has heard nothing: "A whole national literature is there, buried without a coffin ..." (p. 9). He catalogues the dismay of his fellow prisoners when the outside world seems to invert all proper human values. No reckoning of Solzhenitsyn can divorce his art from his *zek* (prisoner) experience, for it was in the camps that he came to his settled, mature views on life. However, he always sees his role as representative voice of the zeks as synchronous with his calling to speak the truth in a world in which all men, including himself, are subordinate to God's ultimate sovereignty over human affairs. He speaks always on behalf of fellow human beings, not merely on behalf of fellow zeks.

Solzhenitsyn's later writings continue to elaborate his understanding of the fundamental importance of a sense of creatureliness. Witness this excerpt from his 1978 commencement address at Harvard University:

> ... in early democracies, as in American democracy at the time of its birth, all individual human rights were granted because man is God's creature. That is, freedom was given to the individual conditionally, in the assumption of his constant religious responsibility. ... Subsequently, however, all such limitations were discarded everywhere in the West; a total liberation occurred from the moral heritage of Christian centuries with their great reserves of mercy and sacrifice. ... The West ended up by truly enforcing human rights, sometimes even excessively, but man's sense of responsibility to God and society grew dimmer and dimmer.[10]

In a world created by God, each individual creature is duty bound to develop a global consciousness; this subject, which dominates the second half of the *Nobel Lecture*, is introduced in section four. Solzhenitsyn introduces here, then elaborates later, two foci: individuality and community. Both are important to him.

First, he calls on us to judge for ourselves and not to accept blindly others' (even leaders') standards of judgment. "As the Russian proverb puts it, 'Don't trust your brother, trust your own bad eye' " (p. 12).

This is dangerous advice, and Solzhenitsyn knows it; the eye is bad. We could easily become provincial and "confidently judge the whole world according to our own domestic values" (p. 14). Also, what is close to home affects us more directly than what is far away, thereby shaping our perceptions. "What in one country seems a dream of improbable prosperity in another arouses indignation as savage exploitation . . ." (p. 15).

The problem here is one of differing scales of value. Sixty-six million died in the Gulag Archipelago;[11] yet some Westerners who read Solzhenitsyn's account of this unspeakable horror claim to find it dull and boring, not gripping and chilling. "The heart is especially at ease with regard to that exotic land about which nothing is known . . ." (p. 16). What would be the outcry if a quarter of America's population were liquidated? Is there not a gross difference in the scale of values which we apply to the pains of the world?

Solzhenitsyn's obvious answer to this ethnocentrism is to call for one scale of moral values to be applied worldwide. (His answer is obvious unless, that is, one takes seriously the charges by certain Westerners that Solzhenitsyn is a Russophile chauvinist.) The Christian doctrine of creation insists upon the unity of mankind, and this teaching underlies the thought here: "Given six, four, or even two scales of values, there cannot be one world, one single humanity: the difference in rhythms, in oscillations, will tear mankind asunder. We will not survive together on one Earth, just as a man with two hearts is not meant for this world" (p. 16).

If all of this seems far afield from a theory of art, we must recall the ever-present interconnection for Solzhenitsyn between art and life, art and morality.

Section five extends and refines the call for global consciousness. Humanity is divided into nations. What agency can surmount national boundaries to coordinate separate scales of value?

"Who will give mankind one single system for reading its instruments . . . ?" (p. 17).

Solzhenitsyn's answer is art (meaning, always, primarily literature). Literature, even that clearly colored by a given national experience, has "the marvelous capacity of transmitting from one nation to another—despite differences in language, customs, and social structure—practical experience, the harsh national experience of many decades never tasted by the other nation" (p. 18).[12] But, just as the unity of mankind extends across time as well as space, literature can speak from generation to generation as well as from nation to nation. It "thus becomes the living memory of a nation" (p. 19).

Here Solzhenitsyn takes an unpopular stance. In the very passages in which he advocates global consciousness, he praises national distinctives. As nations comprise different individuals, so the world comprises different nations, and this is as it should be. Rejecting the notion of "various peoples disappearing into the melting pot of contemporary civilization" (p. 19), he trumpets instead: "Nations are the wealth of humanity, its generalized personalities. The least among them harbors within itself a special aspect of God's design" (p. 19). Global consciousness and national loyalty are not, he holds, inherently mutually exclusive, but can and should be naturally related and mutually reinforcing.

It is not surprising, then, that Solzhenitsyn decries the refusal to publish Anna Akhmatova and Evgeny Zamyatin in their homeland. Interfering with the natural flow of literature risks "stopping up the nation's heart, carving out the nation's memory. The nation loses its memory; it loses its spiritual unity—and, despite their supposedly common language, fellow countrymen suddenly cease understanding each other" (pp. 19-20). And, since no nation is an island, this silencing of a national literature can imperil us all, "when HISTORY as a whole ceases to be understood because of that silence" (p. 20).

The focus of section six turns to the writer, not the writer in a vacuum—he or she is never in a vacuum—but rather, the writer

in the world of modern social reality. Solzhenitsyn depicts a
fearsome world in which the writer must move. Yet, he insists,
the writer cannot escape a social responsibility. He must not,
of course, be a servile mouthpiece for any regnant ideology; he
must be a truth-teller. Solzhenitsyn places himself squarely in
the Russian literary tradition, in which is "ingrained" the "notion that a writer can do much among his own people—and
that he must" (p. 21). Such a writer can become, in the words
of Shelley, an "unacknowledged legislator of the world."

Sadly, there is that all-too-common other kind of writer
(see the first section) who, while "retreating into a world of his
own creation or into the vast spaces of subjective fancies"
(pp. 21-22), can be harmful to his world. Lacking mission and
moral commitment, "he CAN deliver the real world into the
hands of self-seeking, insignificant, or even insane people" (p. 22).

The twentieth century is a diabolically difficult time for
genuine writers. It "has turned out to be more cruel than those
[centuries] preceding it, and all that is terrible in it did not come
to an end with its first half" (p. 22). Solzhenitsyn's examples
raise some hackles. Many youths are in "SLAVERY TO HALF-
COCKED PROGRESSIVE IDEAS" (p. 24). Terrorists such as air-
plane hijackers signal "their determination to shake civilization
apart and to annihilate it," and "they may very well succeed"
(p. 23). The "spirit of Munich" is "a disease of the will of pros-
perous people," and "the intimidated civilized world has found
nothing to oppose the onslaught of a suddenly resurgent fang-
baring barbarism, except concessions and smiles" (p. 24). The
spirit of the times has dictated that even the United Nations,
that ostensible bearer of international good will, turns as immoral as the times, becoming "not a United Nations but a United
Governments, in which those freely elected and those imposed
by force and those which seized power by arms are all on a par"
(p. 26). So our times, progressive though some say they should
be, nurture "the same old caveman feelings—greed, envy, violence, and mutual hate, which along the way assumed respect-
able pseudonyms like class struggle, racial struggle, mass
struggle, labor-union struggle . . ." (p. 22).

In such a setting what should the writer's stance be? Of course, he should not give in to ephemeral ideas. But, still, what should he do? In the midst of this (abbreviated) list of social ills, Solzhenitsyn turns at once to abiding religious concepts. He urges a belief in those "fixed universal concepts called good and justice" (p. 22). Better than modernity's passing whims are "the steadfastness of good" and "the indivisibility of truth" (p. 27). What writer, given these realities, can reject Solzhenitsyn's imperatives? What writer can accept the role of "bystander" or "sideline judge"? What writer has the "impudence" to announce that he, too, is "not responsible for the sores of the world today"? (p. 28).

The seventh and final section pulls together all the preceding themes, especially the call for global consciousness and a mystical reverence for the power of the word. The section opens with a statement of optimism—this, from a writer frequently charged with pessimism. Solzhenitsyn announces that he is "encouraged by a keen sense of WORLD LITERATURE as the one great heart that beats for the cares and misfortunes of our world . . ." (p. 28). He insists (doubtless to the surprise of many) that the idea of a world literature is not today "an abstraction or a generalized concept invented by literary critics, but a common body and common spirit, a living heartfelt unity reflecting the growing spiritual unity of mankind" (p. 30). Again optimistically, Solzhenitsyn sees world literature in a salutary role: "I think that world literature has the power in these frightening times to help mankind see itself accurately despite what is advocated by partisans and by parties" (p. 31).

Although it may appear unusual that a Russian provincial, until recently unknown, be a spokesman for world literature, Solzhenitsyn is acutely aware that the "almost instantaneous reciprocity" between writers and readers of various nations is what gave him quickly "a responsive world readership" (p. 29), quite possibly even saving his life later. And he acknowledges here that it was François Mauriac and other French writers who nominated him for the Nobel Prize, not his own countrymen who constitute the Soviet Writers Union.

But what he also understands is that the universal access made possible by modern means of communication imposes on the writer a universal responsibility; all are now citizens of the world. It is possible now to realize existentially that ancient Christian teaching: the spiritual unity of mankind. Isolation is an indefensible posture, whether of the individual or of the nation, and therefore ". . . no such thing as INTERNAL AFFAIRS remains on our crowded Earth. Mankind's salvation lies exclusively in everyone's making everything his business . . ." (p. 30). Ultimately, of course, this is an individual matter; we must, each of us, develop "our own WORLD-WIDE VIEW" (p. 32). And this supremely Russian writer, who generally writes for a Russian audience, has given more than lip service, especially since his exile to the West, to his position statement by sounding various warnings to the West, however irritating some Westerners might find them. These comments are, he feels, part of his endeavor to develop a global consciousness and to speak as part of a *world* literature.

This final section, focusing as it does on the writers and artists of the world, nevertheless concludes on the same note of the absoluteness of truth with which the lecture opened. It is the very note which Solzhenitsyn sounded before he was exiled, in his parting statement, "Live Not by Lies!"[13] But the world's writers and artists can do more: ". . . they can VANQUISH LIES! In the struggle against lies, art has always won and always will. . . . Lies can stand up against much in the world, but not against art" (p. 33). So he concludes with the clarion call, for all men, but especially writers: "ONE WORD OF TRUTH OUTWEIGHS THE WORLD" (p. 34).

Solzhenitsyn's own career is eloquent testimony to the rightness of his estimate of the power of the word spoken on behalf of truth. Whenever he speaks, the world listens. His 1978 Harvard commencement address, after some years of public silence, is recent proof. How do we explain his enormous impact? His own explanation would begin, I think, with the concepts

enunciated in this *Nobel Lecture*. His is an art which is loyal
to absolute truth, which is grounded in concrete, objective reality. He works as one who is ever conscious that he bears within
himself the image of God and that he is an apprentice beneath
God's heaven.

3

GENESIS:

Prose Poems and Stories

Solzhenitsyn had done some writing during both World War II and his imprisonment thereafter. We cannot be sure how much of this work, probably mostly poetry, he committed to memory before he felt it necessary, for safety's sake, to destroy the manuscripts. His narrative poem *Prussian Nights* is an example of a work originally composed early in his career. What we can be sure of is that shortly after the end of his years of incarceration he had penned a handful of stories and a series of brief vignettes, or meditations—prose poems, as they are called. In any case, we can safely take these sixteen prose poems and six stories, later gathered into a volume entitled *Stories and Prose Poems*, as the work of Solzhenitsyn's early apprenticeship.[1]

The importance of the delicate prose poems is twofold. First, they show us a side of Solzhenitsyn not readily guessed by readers of his more recent polemical pronouncements: the pensive, reflective, even gentle side. Second, they introduce many of the primary themes of his later, long works; and thus they help us to appreciate the exceptional continuity of perspective which

18

marks the author's whole writing career. They provide a kind of microcosm of his central ideas; they show us Solzhenitsyn is genesis. Already he deals in concretions; he has escaped from ideological abstractions. He thirsts after what is true and good and beautiful. He knows that he is a creature under God's heaven. And all this, more than a decade before he is cerebral about these matters in the *Nobel Lecture*.

We may best understand these meditations as Solzhenitsyn's first halting efforts to rediscover that beloved Mother Russia from which he had been cut off for eleven years. There surfaces periodically a contrast between enduring Russia and the recent efforts by the Soviets to deface and to erase it. Already this early, Solzhenitsyn sees the Soviets as only temporary conquerors who cannot finally ruin the landscape and the abiding spirit of Russia.

And, when he lauds old Russia, prominent in his thinking always is the beneficent permeating presence of the Russian Orthodox Church. If his religious references are seldom overt in the prose poems, his later spiritual affirmations nevertheless provide the best context for a coherent reading of these early works.

We shall examine the prose poems according to the following schematic organization of themes:

1. Joy in the beauty of nature and man's place in it.
2. Respect for simple peasant ways.
3. Appreciation of old Russian towns and their mystic harmony with nature.
4. Despiritualization of modern man.
5. Recognition of the life urge at all levels.
6. Judgment of the scarring effects of the Soviet system.

The first prose poem, "Freedom to Breathe," expresses both joy in nature and the author's reveling in his return to "this air steeped in the fragrance of flowers, of moisture and freshness" (p. 197). This simple "freedom to breathe freely, as now I can," he finds "the single most precious freedom that

prison takes away from us" (p. 197). He cannot savor too much
the countryside, often on bicycle. When he visits the town and
cottage of Sergei Yesenin, he marvels at the "thunderbolt of
talent the Creator must have hurled . . . into the heart of that
quick-tempered country boy" (p. 210) to enable him to write
such moving nature poetry. The unaffected naturalness of this
reference to God is typical of even the early Solzhenitsyn. And
while much of his joy in nature has a Wordsworthian tone, he
can also enter into Byron's pleasure in the grand, even harsh
aspects of nature: thunder and lightning, for example, as in "A
Storm in the Mountains." Here, too, however, his is a religious
sensibility. As he participates in "a primal world in creation
before our eyes" (p. 213), the power of nature reminds him of
human finitude. And, again, biblical images are ready at hand:
thunder is "like the arrows of Sabaoth" (p. 213).

Solzhenitsyn's respect for peasant ways is epitomized in
"The Kolkhoz Rucksack," with its praise of a "tough, roomy
and cheap" woman's basket (p. 211). A similar eye for detail is
seen in "Matryona's House" and "Zakhar-the-Pouch." Especially with Zakhar, we see Solzhenitsyn's awareness that the
peasants, though often only with partial comprehension, yet
have a natural piety which reveres the spirituality of old Russia.
Zakhar knows that the Kulikovo Field, which he guards, marked
the place where "Holy Russia" fought off a heathen invasion.
Solzhenitsyn, the historical scholar, yearns for deeper historical
meaning, seeking to trace, as he will in *August 1914*, the buried
meaning of Russian history which lies beyond simple Zakhar's
ken. Nevertheless, the peasants' instincts are almost always
good ones, and Solzhenitsyn values that folk wisdom.

For instance, peasants share the author's valuing of the
old Russian towns, on sites selected first for "good, drinkable
running water" and next for "beauty" (p. 201). But what mainly
gives these towns their "soothing effect" (p. 214), as they and he
know, is those old domed churches. They link mystically the
old Russia and the new, so that "you are never alone" (p. 214).
And, as though by Providential dispensation, the Byzantine dome
of St. Isaac's, in "The City on the Neva," is situated so that no

"wedding-cake skyscraper" or "five-story shoebox" can mar the effect (p. 205).

This effect was not merely architectural or aesthetic; it was always deeply spiritual: ". . . the Angelus [bell] . . . reminded man that he must abandon his trivial earthly cares and give up one hour of his thoughts to life eternal" (p. 215). This simple tolling of the bell, surviving now only in a popular song, "raised man above the level of a beast" (p. 215). The "middle state" of man, between angel and beast, a staple of Christian reflection through the ages, is a familiar theme in Solzhenitsyn. His repeated criticism of Soviet society is that it treats men and women like animals.

Similarly, the despiritualization of modern man is an important theme in these early prose poems. This process of despiritualization, readily evident all about him, Solzhenitsyn must, for himself, resist. Already at this stage he seemed to sense some mystical objective for his life and work. In the finely wrought "Reflections" he sees himself in transit, on a spiritual odyssey, moving toward some as yet unknown end—the kind of thought which, as we have seen, recurred in his *Nobel Lecture* and public prayer. It is in the nature of life that we see through a glass darkly, or as if through "the restless kaleidoscope of water" (p. 204). How, even when writing these lines, could Solzhenitsyn have predicted the strange peregrinations of his life still to come? Yet "if so far we have been unable to see clearly or to reflect the eternal lineaments of truth, is it not because we too are still moving towards some end—because we are still alive?" (p. 204).

For life is of the soul as well as of the body. Yet our materially oriented age, one in which "no one is surprised if people cherish their bodies patiently and attentively every day of their lives" (p. 216), is an age in which people "would be jeered at if they paid the same regard to their souls" (p. 216). The striking "At the Start of the Day" depicts thirty young people outdoors and moving in such a way that from a distance one might think that they were saying morning prayers. But no, the piece concludes curtly, "these people are not praying. They are doing their morning exercises" (p. 216).

The story "Easter Procession" also shows the despiritualization of modern man. The contrast is between the outnumbered faithful in procession at the patriarchal church of Peredelkino and the rabble who interfere with the rite—a majority, it is wryly observed, whose "right not to believe in God is safeguarded by the constitution" (p. 103). The harassment of the believers is bad enough; but, worse, the mob's jeering "amounts to an insult to the Passion of Christ" (pp. 103-04). What will come to a people who have raised a godless generation? "The truth is that one day they will turn and trample on us all. And as for those who urged them on to this, they will trample on them too" (p. 106).

The simple joy of living and the urge to live are also important matters to this ex-prisoner. _Cancer Ward_ explicates this theme. So does "The Duckling." Solzhenitsyn stands in awe before even God's simple creatures. The achievements of modern technology do not begin to compare. We may soon fly to Venus, he says; and we could plough up the whole world in twenty minutes if we pooled our efforts. "Yet, with all our atomic might, we shall never—never!—be able to make this feeble speck of a yellow duckling in a test tube; even if we were given the feathers and the bones, we could never put such a creature together" (p. 200). Another animal, "The Puppy," shows us the most important thing about being alive. He shuns the offer of chicken bones for the simple joy of running loose, unrestrained. We are back to the "Freedom to Breathe." Even the plant kingdom displays the urge to life. "The Elm Log" tells of a tree which had been sawn down and cut up. But a year later the stump had sprouted the beginnings of a new branch, even a whole new tree. With reverence, we must leave it alone; "its urge to live was even stronger than ours" (p. 203).

Even modern man shares in this urge to live. But his materialistic ideology distorts this natural matter. For one thing, he neglects the proper, respectful honoring of the dead; death is part of the natural process. For another, he cannot accept the inevitability of his own death; his materialistic world-view has no place for it: *"We Will Never Die."* This prose poem, which demonstrates how at odds are the Marxist ideology and those rhythms of life and death which the religious man is able to accept, is one of Solzhenitsyn's best.

The prose poems do not provide a definitive catalogue of the themes of Solzhenitsyn's later works. His thinking has been enriched and deepened along the way. Yet even a cursory examination of these literary miniatures shows the direction in which he is headed. His essential view of life is, at this early date, already firmly in place.

The three stories next to be discussed—"Matryona's House," "An Incident at Krechetovka Station," and *For the Good of the Cause*—saw the light of published day in 1963, following hard on the heels of the spectacular public success in late 1962 of *One Day in the Life of Ivan Denisovich*. The first two of these three stories are superb; the third, which is long enough to have been published separately as a short novel,[2] is aesthetically mediocre though thematically interesting. All three stories are set, as usual, in the Soviet Union, from World War II on. All three concentrate on moral, not political, themes, though political machinations lurk, ever present, as the background for the moral actions and judgments of the foreground. All three have discernible religious references but, like the prose poems, few directly Christian statements.

At this point, one may wonder how much during this period Solzhenitsyn was influenced by his passionate desire to be published in the U.S.S.R. Certainly, he never wrote anything to suit the literary (socialist-realist) or religious (atheist) tastes of the Kremlin masters. His praise for the spiritual traditions of old Russia, as contrasted with the sterility of the Soviet system, is never camouflaged. Yet even in the Khrushchev era he had to know that the authorities would allow him to be published only if they (who, he had to presume, did not always have eyes to see or ears to hear) considered his work to be anti-Stalinist (which it was), rather than anti-Soviet (which it also was). As

a result, these early stories suggest that Solzhenitsyn was playing a clever, if dangerous, cat-and-mouse game with officialdom.
The fact that Solzhenitsyn's Christian convictions were settled
well before this period and have become pronounced in some
of his recent statements is ample warrant for watching for covert, or semi-covert, intimations of them already at this stage
of his career.

"Matryona's House" is narrated by a character, Ignatich, strikingly similar in life story to Solzhenitsyn himself.[3] After a "delay" of ten years (eight for Solzhenitsyn), the ex-soldier wishes
just "to creep away and vanish in the very heartland of Russia"
(p. 1)—to find peace and, if possible, to teach mathematics. He
finds lodging with an old woman, a person whom he early likes
but later comes to revere as almost a saint—and as a kind of
personification of that spirit of old Mother Russia for which he
has been yearning.

   Actually, we learn very little of Ignatich's life. Unlike
other Solzhenitsyn alter egos, he does not figure prominently in
the action. He is mainly an observer. But it is his moral judgment which permeates the story, and the reader finds himself
ineluctably drawn into sharing his viewpoint. The story turns,
as all do, on conflict—primarily between the saintly Matryona
and her selfish relatives and neighbors, secondarily between the
heroine and the heartless Soviet bureaucracy.

   The plot—never Solzhenitsyn's strong point and never
complex—is a simple one, admirably suited to this brief work.
Greedy relatives, too impatient to wait for her to die, persuade
the guileless but reluctant Matryona to let them tear down the
small structure adjacent to her very modest house (the "out-
house," as the translator would have it) and move the boards to
a new building site. And the kindly lady finally consents, against
her better judgment. In the newly fallen snow the rickety sledge
drops its load on the railroad tracks. As part of the clean-up
crew, Matryona, though always deathly afraid of trains, is struck
and killed by two unlighted engines. And few genuinely mourn;

most, scavenger-like, simply want to pick up the remaining pieces of her meager belongings.

How are we to judge the characters in this story? Matryona's husband had been dead twelve years, but garbled book-keeping on the collective farm obstructs the deciphering of the pension to which she was entitled. Although she herself had worked on the farm for a quarter of a century, she was listed as her husband's dependent, and it was his records which were not in order. So she got nothing. And although she was not deemed ill enough to be certified as disabled, she was clearly too infirm to work on the farm. Even so, at peak working times she was forced to labor on the collective farm—for nothing. Good Russian folk are clearly ill served by the new Marxist system. From each according to his ability, to each according to his need? Both ability and need are ignored. The already hard lot of the Russian peasant is only exacerbated by the new overlords.

However, the chief antagonists in the story are not the cold, bumbling bureaucrats but Matryona's fellow peasants. They are, in the main, a grubbing, heartless lot. Whereas Ignatich may have hoped to find a kind of folk wisdom among the Russian peasants—and does in Matryona—Solzhenitsyn in no way idealizes the rural peasantry.

Matryona's own relatives are the worst. With no sense of her quality of person, they want from her only something material. To validate their claim to a parcel of land, they must build on it. But wood is scarce. So they coerce Matryona into letting them dismantle part of her humble shack, even before she is dead, to get the needed wood. The women distill moonshine vodka. The men drink up. And off they go, through the snow, to the climactic crash on the railroad tracks.

The mourning for Matryona is insincere and perfunctory. Not only do the relatives absolve themselves of any guilt for her death, but they actually place the blame on Matryona herself. Even the closest of her acquaintances thinks only of acquiring her shawl. The cold-blooded plunderers which are her family will soon pick over the few pitiful pieces she has left behind. Food, clothing, and shelter circumscribe their vision of life; there is no room for spiritual matters. The moral judgment made against them is set in terms of their attitude toward Matryona.

Matryona herself is a poor, sick, lonely sixty-year-old woman, long widowed, who has had to rely on herself to eke out a mere subsistence. Though simple and unimaginative, she "had an infallible means of restoring her good spirits: work" (p. 10). She would drop her own work to help a neighbor dig potatoes and then exclaim to Ignatich: "It was a pleasure to dig them up. I didn't want to stop, honest" (p. 14). A perfect candidate, it would seem, for honor in a "worker's paradise"!

But Matryona's virtue extends far beyond her joy in work. She exudes an unthinking natural piety which for Solzhenitsyn exemplifies old Russia at its best. She is at one with nature, respecting the life-giving earth and loving animals, especially her lame cat. She accepts injustices with equanimity; rancor never touches her; and, equally important, she does no one harm.

Ignatich looks for a connection between her moral actions and some religious belief, but he is not sure that he finds it.

> I never once saw her say her prayers or cross herself. Yet she always asked for God's blessing before doing anything and she invariably said "God bless you" to me whenever I set off for school in the morning. Perhaps she did say her prayers, but not ostentatiously.... There were ikons in the cottage. (p. 18)

Her righteousness, which Ignatich readily grants, grows not from observing external religious forms but from an easy and natural intimacy with the created order.

The story concludes with a paean of praise for Matryona in which Solzhenitsyn's mind runs readily to biblical allusion.

> Misunderstood and rejected by her husband, a stranger to her own family despite her happy, amiable temperament, comical, so foolish that she worked for others for no reward, this woman, who had buried all her six children, had stored up no earthly goods. Nothing but a dirty white goat, a lame cat, and a row of fig plants.

> None of us who lived close to her perceived that she was that one righteous person without whom, as the saying goes, no city can stand.
> Neither can the whole world. (p. 42)

Values, whether spiritual or material, dominate the story. Solzhenitsyn pictures here what he has stated directly in later statements: that evil is innate in human nature. Persons who give in to human depravity have no room in their outlooks for spiritual values, thus limiting themselves to material ones. We might expect to see this limitation in Soviet figures formally committed to a materialistic philosophy of life, and we do. But the same materialistic myopia is seen in those who could have been heirs to the spiritual heritage of Holy Russia, the peasants. Through each human heart runs a line dividing evil and good, and sometimes it presses toward one side and sometimes toward the other. When it presses toward the other, we get a Matryona. If Russia's spirituality is now stunted, it is not extinct. And it is that spirituality which must be cultivated.

"An Incident at Krechetovka Station" is slighter than "Matryona's House" but is likewise based on the author's first-hand knowledge. It is the only Solzhenitsyn story set in World War II (autumn of 1941). In this case, there is no authorial alter ego; instead, the author takes us directly inside the mind of the main character, Lieutenant Vasya Zotov. The time span is only a few hours.

The pivotal incident takes the last third of the narrative; the first two-thirds give the flavor of wartime behind the front, in a slice-of-life style almost Chekhovian. Throughout, the delineation of Zotov's character is paramount; it is always character, not plot, language, or even theme, which fascinates Solzhenitsyn the fictionist.

Zotov, second in military command at the railroad station at Krechetovka, is depicted as a responsible and serious soldier and citizen, the very flower of Soviet manhood, the best of humanity Soviet ideology can spawn. He seeks in all ways to help his nation's war cause, and he is ashamed that he is not at the front ready to take the ultimate risk for the cause in which he believes. Although his wife is behind enemy lines, he turns down two offers of sex, instead spending his nights reading *Das Kapital* and memorizing it in order to become "invincible, invulnerable, irrefutable in any ideological combat" (p. 156).

Still, the war was going so badly that "he wanted to howl out loud" (pp. 137-38). Why? And "where was the revolution all over Europe?" (p. 138). Yet surely the cause was right and his thoughts cowardly. They constituted "blasphemy," an "insult to the omniscient, omnipotent Father and Teacher [Stalin] who was always there, who foresaw everything" (p. 139). Solzhenitsyn finds the religious phraseology appropriate, since Communism espouses a world-view which claims to explain man's ultimate concerns and demands of its adherents the same kind of faith demanded by traditional religions. Zotov keeps the faith, even when shaken.

For his sense of commitment, Solzhenitsyn gives him credit; he draws him sympathetically. Nevertheless, no strength of commitment can undo the life-debasing nature of ideology to which he pledges allegiance. And this means that Zotov's values are inevitably warped. So, when a young sentry shoots a hungry returnee from the war front for trying to pilfer some flour, Zotov approves; anything for the good of the cause.

The climactic incident highlights the morally corrupting effect on Zotov of his ideology. An actor, Tveritinov, who is passing through, delights Zotov by his refined bearing. But when he asks Zotov what the name of Stalingrad was before it was changed, the suspicion which the system has ingrained in the devotee resurfaces, and Zotov arrests the actor as a possible spy, perhaps a White émigré.

At first, Zotov is sure of his decision. Then his humane impulses cause him to doubt. When he tries to find out what ever became of Tveritinov, all that he can pry out of the security officer is, "Your Tverikin's been sorted out all right. We don't make mistakes" (p. 193). This penultimate sentence of the story is most effectively ironic, since the officer has gotten the name wrong.

The story's last line is, "After that, Zotov was never able to forget the man for the rest of his life" (p. 193). The security officer presumably forgets immediately. Zotov's basic decency will not allow him to do so. Still, this gross violation of human dignity does not cause him to doubt the ideology which precipitated it; the light does not penetrate that far. The simplistic ethic on which he has been reared leaves no room for the moral ambiguity which he has confronted. It enforces a subordination of humaneness in even the best of men.

For the Good of the Cause has a contemporary setting—in Khrushchev's time, not Stalin's. Solzhenitsyn's contribution to the debate of that time about the remaining influence of Stalin, the story presents his view that many "little Stalins" perpetuate Stalinism. Even here the conflict is not between competing political philosophies; ". . . it was a clash of right and wrong" (p. 85), of creative, humane instincts and destructive, dehumanizing ones. And when right and wrong collide "head-on," "wrong is more brazen by its very nature" (p. 79). Still, the topicality of this subject makes this Solzhenitsyn's most overtly political work. And while it is not an unsuccessful effort, it is aesthetically less pleasing than most of his work. It is difficult to say if there is a connection between these two points. The subject matter does seem to allow for less play of his spiritual imagination.

As in most of his long works, Solzhenitsyn here draws a large gallery of characters, giving a rough cross section of Soviet life. In relatively short works—*The Love Girl and the Innocent* is another example—the large cast is not strategically effective; it swamps the work. In this case, the many students named early are necessarily left undeveloped.

Solzhenitsyn also employs characters as spokesmen for conflicting points of view. But in this short novel, characterization is somewhat sacrificed to direct thematic interests. For instance, the teacher Lidia, the most interesting person, is prominent early in the story but reappears only sporadically and all too briefly as the story approaches its climax. The most interesting scenes are those early ones between Lidia and her students. The second half features bureaucrats; this arrangement may be vital to the theme but is a narrative letdown. Also, characters are more clearly lined up as good or bad than is typical in Solzhenitsyn's novels. Instead of dramatizing that line which runs through every human heart dividing good and evil, this work tends to draw the line between good people and evil people. That life is not that simple is a point Solzhenitsyn himself has frequently made.

The plot, straightforward as usual, is about a technical school housed in cramped quarters. The nine hundred teenaged students and their teachers work a whole year without pay to construct a new building for their school. Then some purblind bureaucrats decide whimsically to take their building away from them and turn it into a research center. Economically, this decision is stupid; the four-million-dollar structure will cost almost half that much more for remodeling. But worse, this is a morally unconscionable treatment of the school's students and staff. The school principal's compelling arguments are met with obstinate deafness on the part of the state and party authorities.

The title states the central thematic issue. In a state governed in the name of the people, what action, in a concrete case, is "for the good of the cause"? The voluntary work of the students embodies the highest ideals of Communist theory. Yet the self-serving response of those who rule in the name of the people perverts these proclaimed ideals into their very opposite.

The chief protagonist, the young teacher Lidia Georgievna, is not yet thirty. She works on the new building, never bossing her students around, never asking them to do something that she herself is unwilling to do. Students readily acknowledge her moral authority; this natural hierarchy is at a far remove from the arbitrary hierarchy of the official system. Her students, "being young . . . responded to everything genuine. You only had to take one look at her to know that she meant what she said" and that "she never lied" (pp. 17, 25). Her chastising of the Party Secretary for not being staightforward with the students about the decision to take their building away from them represents

Solzhenitsyn's own passion for truth: "They'll think we're afraid to tell them the truth—and they'll be right! How will they ever respect us again?" (p. 74).

Lidia, who teaches Russian language and literature at this technical school, promotes those humanistic principles which are the heartbeat of Solzhenitsyn's outlook. (She is in some ways a prototype of Professor Andozerskaya of *August 1914*.) With her philosophy of liberal education she denigrates television, which lasts "just for a day," and advocates books, which "last for centuries" (p. 22). She is critical of those state-approved productions which pass for literature. Fearing intellectual indifference among her students, she is pleased when she hears them arguing ideas: "People who argue are open to persuasion" (p. 26).

The school principal, Fyodor Mikheyevich, is similarly humane. As a leader, he has a goal of "bringing together people who trusted one another and could work together harmoniously" (p. 34). Even a technical education, he believes, should seek to build character. But his valiant efforts to save the new building for the school go for naught. One good man in a corrupt system is inevitably overwhelmed.

Ranged against Fyodor and Lidia are a host of party and government functionaries. The most odious is the "little Stalin," district committee supervisor Victor Vavilovich Knorozov. His boast is that he never goes back on his word: "As it had once been in Moscow with Stalin's word, so it was still today with Knorozov's word. . . . And though Stalin was long dead, Knorozov was still here" (p. 83). As his name implies, Victor inevitably wins the unequal contest between bureaucrats and mere human beings. While Solzhenitsyn later attacks Marxist-Leninist ideology head-on, in this early work the critique is that the likes of Knorozov do not begin to approximate in their deeds those ideals which they profess.

Solzhenitsyn was to draw many portraits of intransigent, obstructive officeholders, not sparing even Stalin and Lenin. This one of Knorozov is less memorable and less effective than most. There are no moral shadings in his character; he is unrelievedly evil. An instructive contrast is with Rusanov, who is the spokesman of the official line in *Cancer Ward*, yet who has his personal doubts at times. Although Solzhenitsyn's basic viewpoint does not change, his art does ripen.

The only official who shows vestiges of a moral sensibility is Grachikov. But he is ineffectual, and his strivings toward justice are feeble and occasional. The mindless grinding of the system is too much for the likes of him.

The story ends with little room for hope. The school principal dreams of starting all over to erect a new building. But will the defeated young students share his steadfastness? The decency and integrity resident within the Russian citizenry must, the principal believes, prevail. In this story they do not. It ends with rage and frustration at a state of affairs which violates the proper moral order.

Although *Prussian Nights* is not a part of *Stories and Prose Poems* and did not appear in print until more than a decade after the other pieces treated in this chapter, it belongs to a very early period of Solzhenitsyn's writing career, having been composed in the author's head during his years of imprisonment. It is a narrative poem set during the Russian incursion into Germany in World War II. While translation of poetry makes aesthetic judgments problematic, this poem seems more important as a human document than as a piece of art.

The poem, with its tense, highly charged rhythm, sticks close to narrative throughout; nevertheless, the work abounds with implicit moral judgments. The Russian soldiers, proud in their conquering, still are in awe of the foreignness they find: steep-pitched roofs, cleanliness throughout. It is the same territory which swallowed up Samsonov and his troops a war earlier (see *August 1914*). Yet those bestial passions which war inevitably lets loose get a grip on the soldiers. So they loot, pillage, and kill, sublimating all pangs of conscience.

The narrator, an officer who is a reflective soul plagued by "the worm of self-analysis,"[4] tries for a while to resist the animal urges which he sees swirling about him. But a set of high-quality pencils, such as he has never known at home, first ·

seduces him. It is not long before this captain, who had shortly earlier been shocked at the incivility of some of his troops, finds himself, albeit furtively and guiltily, raping a young German woman. As soon as he is finished with her, she pleads that he just not shoot her. But he, stricken with remorse, can only think, "Another's soul is on my soul . . ." (p. 105). And so the poem ends.

This war poem assiduously avoids any attention to the political or military rights and wrongs. Even this early, Solzhenitsyn's focus is squarely on the basic moral issues of human nature in action. All of the episodes, but chiefly the climactic one, show that good and evil struggle against each other in every truly human heart. It is a perennial Solzhenitsyn theme.

4

HUMANITY *IN EXTREMIS*:

One Day in the Life of Ivan Denisovich and
The Love-Girl and the Innocent

The short novel *One Day in the Life of Ivan Denisovich* is a very important work, both for Solzhenitsyn's artistic reputation and for the unfolding story of his career. The play *The Love-Girl and the Innocent* is considerably less important on both scores. What links them together is their setting in similar (not identical) hard-labor prison camps; they reflect on the same general period and experiences of Solzhenitsyn's life. Both were composed shortly after the author's release into freedom.

The story of the publication of *One Day in the Life of Ivan Denisovich* is one of the exciting literary stories of our time. When, in 1961, Solzhenitsyn hoped that the Soviet cultural climate might possibly have thawed enough to allow his novel to be published, he sought to get it through to Alexander Tvardovsky, editor of *Novy Mir*. His middleman was Lev Kopelev (the real-life model for the character Lev Rubin in *The First Circle*). Solzhenitsyn knew that he risked his life in seeking to be published. He knew also that if any Soviet periodical would publish his story, _Novy Mir_ would be the one. Tvardovsky stuffed this work by a total unknown into his briefcase and took it home; and, as was his wont, he propped himself up comfortably in his bed to page through newly received manuscripts. He opened _One Day_. The work immediately overwhelmed him: "I realized at once that there was something important, and that in some way I must celebrate the event. I got out of bed, got fully dressed again in every particular, and sat down at my desk. That night I read a new classic of Russian literature."[1]

Anticipating the knee-jerk response of the Soviet literary establishment to this searing indictment of Stalin's prison camps, Tvardovsky, the supreme literary diplomat, using his powerful position and connections, went right to the top and sought from Nikita Khrushchev permission to publish the novel. Khrushchev apparently decided that this novel would help him consolidate his base of power, which he was building partly on a denunciation of Stalin's corruption of total control. Khrushchev's fellow members of the Politburo felt that they had little choice but to allow _Novy Mir_ to publish the controversial novel.[2]

It appeared in the November 1962 issue, in an overrun of 95,000 which sold out immediately. A separate run of nearly a million copies also sold out quickly. An unknown small-town teacher was, at one stroke, on the center stage of Russian literature. The whole world took note. For his "liberalism" Khrushchev was praised widely.

Early reviews, even in the most orthodox of Soviet sources, were overwhelmingly favorable. _Pravda_ remarked on Solzhenitsyn's "profound humanity, because people remained people even in an atmosphere of mockery."[3] Zhores Medvedev, who was later to write _Ten Years after Ivan Denisovich_, emphasized the artistry of the novel. But most responses, in keeping with Khrushchev's motivation for allowing publication, centered on the book's political significance. Importantly, most Western reviews also emphasized the political dimension; the book's publication was viewed as an event illustrating the increasing thaw within the Soviet Union, thus auguring well for future East-

West relations. So from the beginning Solzhenitsyn's work was viewed through the wrong lens.

A political approach does not penetrate to the heart of *One Day*. The novel is not, in its essence, about Stalin's inhumanity to man; it is about man's inhumanity to man. Stalin is not some aberration in an otherwise smooth progression of humaneness in history. The evil of the human heart is a universal theme: this is Solzhenitsyn's approach.

Perhaps never has the political appropriation of a work of art by state authorities backfired so dramatically and totally as in the case of *One Day*. Once having been catapulted into the limelight of world attention, Solzhenitsyn would not be silent. Now he had a platform, and his sense of duty urged him on. Khrushchev had let out of the bottle a genie which his successors could not put back in. The high visibility afforded by Khrushchev's decision provided Solzhenitsyn with all the protection of world opinion which he needed in order to escape the brutalities which almost certainly would otherwise have been visited upon him for saying what he went on to say.

Despite the fact that some critics consider *One Day in the Life of Ivan Denisovich* the best piece Solzhenitsyn ever has written, he seems to have felt that he was still at a kind of apprenticeship stage. He had already laid plans for much larger novels; first he had to perfect his craft by working in units of smaller scope.

One Day nevertheless has many traits in common with one or more of the longer novels. Of course, it keeps its eye on those universal issues of human suffering, of good and evil, of life and death. Like *The First Circle* and *Cancer Ward*, it is based on persons and events which Solzhenitsyn experienced and observed in his own life. It has Solzhenitsyn's characteristically tight setting in time—one day in this case. It has a large number of characters, giving us something like a cross section of Soviet society—another Solzhenitsyn trait.

If *One Day* was part of a period of apprenticeship, it stands near the end of that period. The author was about to embark on those long novels of his maturity. And this novel is a piece of such consummate artistry that to call it the work of an apprentice seems ultimately inadequate. Had Solzhenitsyn written nothing after *One Day*, his reputation as an author of note would have been secure. With this short novel he had arrived, whatever his further ambitions. His literary situation at this stage is interestingly parallel to that of Milton: had Milton written nothing after "Lycidas," he would still be an anthologized poet; but he went on to *Paradise Lost, Paradise Regained,* and *Samson Agonistes*.

The novel depicts a single day in the life of a simple peasant, Ivan Denisovich Shukhov, who has been unjustly thrown into a prison camp.[4] While we see many of his fellow zeks, the focus remains rather tightly fixed on Shukhov. It is a day in which not much, certainly nothing momentous, happens. The zeks eat their pitifully inadequate gruel, work hard as bricklayers and foundrymen (Solzhenitsyn himself worked as both), are counted and recounted, and finally retire—to prepare for another day, and other days, of the same.

Solzhenitsyn shows great respect for his title character. Shukhov is not at all an authorial alter ego, as are Oleg Kostoglotov in *Cancer Ward* (somewhat) and Gleb Nerzhin in *The First Circle* (considerably). The clearest sign of respect is in the mere naming of the hero. The combination of given name (Ivan—significantly, the most common of Russian names) and patronymic (Denisovich—son of Denis) is a polite form most readily used for persons of high station or intrinsic importance. Solzhenitsyn applies it to a simple peasant. The author deems his character worthy of the respect usually reserved for "important" people.

The most memorable technical trait of *One Day* is its understatement. The novel depicts horrors which might well elicit white-hot anger—or, if not that, a kind of sentimentality over the suffering of innocents. The novel makes no such explicit claim on our emotions. Rather, it describes the day of Shukhov and his fellows as not too bad, as almost a good day.

The final passage of the novel, capped by a brilliantly conceived final sentence, highlights the device of understatement:

> Shukhov went to sleep, and he was very happy. He'd had a lot of luck today. They hadn't put him in the cooler. The gang hadn't been chased out to work in the Socialist Community Development. He'd finagled an extra bowl of mush at noon. The boss had gotten them good rates for their work. He'd felt good making that wall. They hadn't found that piece of steel in the frisk. Caesar had paid him off in the evening. He'd bought some tobacco. And he'd gotten over that sickness.
>
> Nothing had spoiled the day and it had been almost happy.
>
> There were three thousand six hundred and fifty-three days like this in his sentence, from reveille to lights out.
>
> The extra ones were because of the leap years. . . .[5]

This concluding passage also allows us to check on the important technical matter of narrative point of view. It is a matter handled delicately but consistently in this novel. The author is always telling the story; Shukhov is always in the third person. Yet, by a clever sleight of hand, the author keeps making his readers feel as if they are inside the mind of the main character; truly, Ivan Denisovich is the one who thinks that this is not the worst of days. Readers are left with the impression that they see and experience Shukhov's day through his own eyes, though in technical fact they never do. In this, Solzhenitsyn has shown considerable skill as a fiction writer.

As is typical of Solzhenitsyn's works, *One Day* shows us suffering humanity *in extremis*. But because of Shukhov's limited perspective, suffering here is depicted as primarily physical. In *The First Circle* the more sophisticated Gleb Nerzhin shows that suffering is also psychological and even spiritual. Yet both of these novels—in contrast with *Cancer Ward*, which deals with the *mystery* of suffering—treat a suffering the perpetrator of which is no mystery at all. Still, even in *One Day* the suffering of the body takes on a metaphysical dimension—through the mediation of the author, who can go beyond the ken of the main character. The inhospitably cold climate becomes a symbol of the inhumane setting for human life in general, and the reader comes away feeling moral outrage rather than mere vicarious physical pain. When a medical assistant finds the feverish Ivan not ill enough to exempt from the day's work, the author queries, "How can you expect a man who's warm to understand a man who's cold?"[6] It is one of those microcosmic remarks from which ray out large symbolic meanings. The warm man is the one open to perpetrating injustice. Solzhenitsyn devotes his life to making warm men feel the cold.

Any such "big" thoughts are as far beyond Shukhov as they are beyond the prison guards. Shukhov, now yearning after a handful of oats that once he would have fed only to his horses, thinks, as he gets his pittance of food for the day, "This was what a prisoner lived for, this one little moment" (p. 169). But even here the stomach is cheated and the soul, thereby, troubled. And what do these guards of the "animals" care? "Every ration was short. The only question was—by how much? So you checked every day to set your mind at rest, hoping you hadn't been too badly treated" (p. 27).

The arbitrariness of the life of the zeks is all-governing. The guards are not allowed to recognize the diversity and unpredictability of life; only two zeks may be sick per day; only two letters per zek may be mailed out per year. "Soviet power," Solzhenitsyn satirizes, has decreed that the sun stands highest in the sky not at noon but an hour later. Being dehumanized entails being denatured.

Given the collectivist ideology of the Soviets, an ironic effect of their prison regimen is that it breaks down the sense of human solidarity. Solzhenitsyn, who speaks consistently on behalf of individual dignity, always speaks with equal consistency on behalf of human solidarity. So he laments that in a zek's mind it is another zek who is one's worst enemy. Occasional displays of solidarity, which should be a natural outflowing of the zeks' common humanity and their shared plight, usually succumb to the camp attitude, "You croak today but *I* mean to live till tomorrow."[7]

Nevertheless, however much the grim environment and the need to adapt somehow to it may reduce the basic humanity of the zeks, such pressures can never eradicate the human essence. To be sure, Shukhov is constantly and instinctively concerned with self-preservation. When he was accused, absurdly, of high treason for surrendering to the Germans with the intention of betraying his country, he coolly calculated: "If he didn't sign, he was as good as buried. But if he did, he'd still go on living a while. So he signed" (p. 76). But there is more. A man will assert his wants as well as his needs. For instance, he wants to smoke; it is an unnecessary small pleasure, but he will find a way. Then, there is satisfaction in work. Ivan works poorly only when given meaningless tasks. Laying bricks well pleases him, even if in prison. Constructive work brings out in him the ennobling quality of self-validation through creative effort. And what truly human being can remain forever silent when he is treated as mere flesh and bones? When, on the way to work, Ivan is frisked by the camp guards, he thinks, "Come on, paw me as hard as you like. There is nothing but my soul in my chest."[8] The camp system would grant him the status only of an animal, a workhorse. It is up to him to insist, however inarticulately, that he is more than that, that he is spiritual, too, and not only material.

The greatest of all human capacities demonstrated by Ivan Denisovich is his capacity to absorb pain and yet to endure with at least some vestiges of humanity intact. This enduring humanity is one of Solzhenitsyn's most important themes, and it is his great consolation as he weeps for mankind. The best efforts to reduce humanity to the level of the animal are never entirely successful; and, by definition, a process of dehumanization which is not totally successful is a failure: some humanity remains. "There's nothing you can't do to a man . . ." (p. 140)—except that you cannot do away with his humanity altogether. Longsuffering, Solzhenitsyn thinks, is a peculiarly strong trait of the Russian peasantry. The peasant may be patient, but he is also durable; and ultimately he will overcome.

Ivan Denisovich's attitude toward religion is much like

Matryona's in "Matryona's House." Both show little interest in formal religion, either ecclesiastical or credal. Yet both breathe a kind of natural piety, and religious references pepper their everyday talk. Ivan's ready response to his tribulations in prison is, "As long as you're in the barracks—praise the Lord and sit tight."[9] At day's end, grateful that he is not in the cells and thinking that it is not "so bad sleeping here," he murmurs, "Thank God" (p. 195). When he forgets until the last moment before he is frisked that he has a hacksaw blade on him, he almost involuntarily prays as "hard as he could": "God in Heaven, help me and keep me out of the can!" (p. 149). Afterwards, however, this down-to-earth peasant "didn't say a prayer of thanks because there wasn't any time and there was no sense in it now" (p. 150).

Ivan's faith is naive and unreasoned, and includes a sizeable dose of superstition. He believes in God: "When He thunders up there in the sky, how can you help believe in Him?" (p. 128). He also believes, as folk in his village do, that each month God makes a new moon, because he needs the old one to crumble up into stars: "The stars keep falling down, so you've got to have new ones in their place" (p. 129). Atheistic rulers may curtail the growth of religion ("The Russians didn't even remember which hand you cross yourself with" [p. 15]), but it is beyond their power to shake the faith of the Matryonas and Ivans.

While Solzhenitsyn clearly admires Ivan's faith, Ivan does not represent his religious ideal. A character who comes closer to doing so is Alyosha (or Alyoshka) the Baptist. It is intriguing that Solzhenitsyn, who has returned to his ancestral Russian Orthodox Church, gives the deepest religious sentiments in this novel to a character who is hostile to Orthodoxy. This depiction is of a piece with the novel's high praise of two Estonian zeks— and this from an author sometimes called chauvinistic and nationalistic. The fact is that the author is simply being faithful to the quality of the persons whom he knew in the camps. In addition, Solzhenitsyn's handling of Alyosha shows that his primary religious concerns are not with the particularities of Orthodoxy but with those central aspects of the Christian faith held in common by all Christians.

The climactic conversation of the novel is between Ivan and Alyosha.[10] Alyosha's prominence here has been prepared for by frequent earlier depictions of him as a good worker and kind person. Alyosha's faith does not incapacitate him for survival. On the contrary, it is a source of the inner strength that so often characterizes Solzhenitsyn's little heroes, the small people who somehow are able to withstand everything that a soulless bureaucracy inflicts on them. While he allows anyone to order him about, he is still clever enough to have hidden his New Testament in a chink in the wall so that it has survived every search. The regular Sunday fellowship of Alyosha and his fellow Baptists allows them to cope with the hardships of camp life "like water off a duck's back" (p. 49). He is sustained by biblical passages of consolation: "Yet if any man suffer as a Christian, let him not be ashamed; but let him glorify God on this behalf" (p. 28).

The climactic conversation begins when Alyosha, reading his Bible, overhears Ivan's routine, day's end prayer and says, "Look here, Ivan Denisovich, your soul wants to pray to God, so why don't you let it have its way?" (p. 195). Ivan, the naive Orthodox, associates this Baptist with high devotion and thinks that Alyosha's eyes glowed "like two candles" (p. 195). But Ivan, for whom camp experience is a microcosm of all of life, doubts the efficacy of praying: ". . . all these prayers are like the complaints we send in to the higher-ups—either they don't get there or they come back to you marked 'Rejected' " (p. 196). Alyosha scolds Ivan for not praying "hard enough," and adds, "if you have faith and tell the mountain to move, it will move" (p. 196). This bold confidence is too much for literal-minded Ivan, who has never seen a mountain move (though he then allows that he has never seen a mountain at all!). For his part, Ivan, unlike those zeks who have lost their capacity for compassion, pities the Baptists as "poor fellows": They were in no one's way, and "all they did was pray to God"; yet "they all got twenty-five years . . ." (p. 196). On the question of mountain-moving, Alyosha asserts the supremacy of the spiritual realm over the material, since of all physical things, the Lord commanded them to pray only for their daily bread; beyond that, "We must pray about things of the spirit—that the Lord Jesus should remove the scum of anger from our hearts. . . ."[11]

Ivan does not want to be misunderstood. Although disillusioned by a bad priest, he insists that he believes in God. "But what I don't believe in is Heaven and Hell" (p. 198). The afterlife, after all, is not open to empirical verification, as are monthly new moons and falling stars. When he prays, he says, it will be for something real, like release from prison. This attitude scandalizes Alyosha, who consciously suffers for Christ. He counters, "What do you want your freedom for? What faith you have left will be choked in thorns. Rejoice that you are in prison. Here you can think of your soul" (p. 198). This spiritual focus, which Solzhenitsyn elsewhere asserts in his own person, affects Ivan: "Alyosha was talking the truth. You could tell by his voice and his eyes he was glad to be in prison" (p. 199).

Solzhenitsyn admires the Baptist's ability to give a positive meaning to his prison experience; Alyosha is the only character in the novel who can do so. Ivan admires that, too. But it just will not do for him. "It was Christ told you to come here, and you are here because of Him. But why am *I* here? Because they didn't get ready for the war like they should've in forty-one? Was that *my* fault?" (p. 199).

Although he cannot believe everything Alyosha can, Ivan's actions are as good as anyone's. Considering Alyosha impractical, always giving and never getting, Ivan gives him a biscuit, though that gesture leaves the giver with nothing for himself. Solzhenitsyn comments, "We've nothing but we always find a way to make something extra."[12] Ivan gives the cup of cold water, though not always knowingly in God's name. If Alyosha has the best words, no one has better deeds than Ivan.

Ivan and Alyosha are brothers under the skin. Both are models of humanity in the midst of inhumanity; both care for others as much as for themselves. Ivan represents the best possible from a man without an articulated faith; a man can act

very well without faith in a transcendent reality. Such a one is
in no position, however, to explain the mystery of suffering.
This crucial matter, which Ivan deeply needs, is what Alyosha
can add. Without Alyosha, the novel would be much diminished. Ivan, as good as he is, needs Alyosha's insight to complete
the picture.

The Love-Girl and the Innocent is one of Solzhenitsyn's two
published plays, neither of which ranks among his top literary
successes. In this case, the large cast of characters in a brief
work is especially problematical (fifty-seven individuals, plus
others in groups—in a play of 133 pages). It shares with *One
Day in the Life of Ivan Denisovich* the setting of a prison camp,
though this time a mixed camp of "politicals" and thieves. It
also shares the themes of suffering, injustice, and dehumanization. Campland, that "invisible country," is the place "where
ninety-nine men weep while one man laughs."[13]

The two memorable characters are the title characters:
Lyuba Nyegnevitskaya, the love-girl, and Rodion Nemov, the
newly arrived innocent. Her view is that all men are "only after
one thing" (p. 29). So she adapts. She, a so-called kulak from a
land-owning family, had been married off at fourteen years of
age. Nemov, not the adapter Lyuba is, feels "sorry for everyone"
(p. 44) in the cruel camp setting. He carries within him the
staple Solzhenitsyn conviction that conscience is more important and valuable than life itself. Formerly a cavalry captain,
Nemov upon his arrival there is named production chief of the
camp. But quickly the professional thieves, whom Stalin considered "social allies,"[14] persuade the camp commandant to get
rid of this circumspect man and to replace him with a man of
their own ilk, the engineer Khomich. Lyuba, despite her com-
promises, has enough insight to know a good man when she
sees one, and she feels sorry for Nemov; she recognizes that he
is not camp-wise.

After Nemov is demoted to foundryman, he and Lyuba
discover a strong mutual attraction. They live for a week in a
courtship-like arrangement. But the camp doctor, Mereshchun,

wants Lyuba for his live-in "camp wife." Now in love with Nemov, she suggests that he and the doctor share her; she can manage that much. But the idealistic Nemov cannot tolerate such an arrangement.

Shortly thereafter, Nemov is struck on the head by a falling lump of coal. First word is that he is dead, but it turns out that he is not. The final scene shows Lyuba returning to the doctor's cabin, sad but reconciled to her demeaning fate.

This drama, especially given Solzhenitsyn's elaborate stage directions, would probably be better in the playing than in the reading. The background, picturing Stalin and flowers and children, as well as posters ("Work ennobles man," "He who does not work does not eat," and later "People are the most valuable capital—J. Stalin"), provides a striking contrast with the foreground and its unmitigated misery and injustice.

The Love-Girl and the Innocent shows as clearly, if not so effectively, as *One Day in the Life of Ivan Denisovich* the dehumanization of the Soviet camps. Little of Solzhenitsyn's religious outlook comes through in this play, although his moral vision remains constant. In that light, this play could be seen as the most directly anti-Stalinist, or anti-Soviet, of all Solzhenitsyn's full-length works—the others always rising rather clearly to more universal themes. Still, the dual vision of human nature, with good and evil warring in each human heart, remains prominent. The struggle is seen more sharply in Lyuba than in any other character.

It is possible to read this play allegorically, though care must be exercised here, since Solzhenitsyn's writings generally do not invite such an interpretation. Yet it is easy enough to see Lyuba as Mother Russia, who submits unhappily to the demeaning yoke of servitude; repressing her best moral instincts, she turns her back, regretfully, on the high but hard way—to private freedom within public bondage—offered by the example of Nemov.

5

THE LIGHT WITHIN:

Candle in the Wind

I t was in 1973 that the second of Solzhenitsyn's two plays, *Candle in the Wind*, was published. By the author's own reckoning it was not a great artistic success.[1] Yet it is an extremely important work for any who wish to understand Solzhenitsyn's basic view of the world and man. The main contrast is between the traditional Christian view of human nature and of man's place in the world and the substitute viewpoint ushered into the history of thought by the Enlightenment. It is the same contrast introduced, regarding two kinds of artists, in the first section of the *Nobel Lecture*.

The central issue is whether man is autonomous in this world or whether he operates under and is to be subordinate to an all-governing God. It is an issue which looms large in Solzhenitsyn's later writings, most clearly in his nonfiction essays of the 1970's—and nowhere more emphatically than in his 1978 Harvard commencement address. Virtually all critical commentary on this play has acknowledged that a Christian vision of reality informs it.[2] Christopher Moody describes this work as "a thesis play" which "presents in almost abstract form the moral ideas which Solzhenitsyn develops in human terms in his novels."[3] If moral concerns remain the dominant ones in even this play, it is strikingly clear that religious, specifically Christian, values provide the context within which these moral issues are to be understood.

All of this would not be so remarkable if the date of publication were also the date of composition. The fact is that *Candle* was written in 1960, some thirteen years before its translated appearance.[4] In other words, *Candle* belongs roughly to the same period as those works we have already examined. It is safe to assert that the authorial vision of life which informs this work also informs such works as *Stories and Prose Poems*, *One Day in the Life of Ivan Denisovich*, and *The Love-Girl and the Innocent*. While those works may lack the explicit religiosity of *The Candle in the Wind*, their rough contemporaneity of composition reinforces the interpretation given to them in the preceding chapters. In retrospect, it is surprising how few critics have observed that the religious context for Solzhenitsyn's works was present from the beginning. Only in the seventies, especially after his public prayer, his letter to Archpatriarch Pimen on the craven subservience of the Russian Orthodox Church to the authority of an atheistic state, and his joining of the church, have critics begun adequately to recognize Solzhenitsyn's religious faith. Even now, the bugaboo of a political reading haunts his works and provokes considerable misunderstanding.

Candle in the Wind was originally entitled *The Light That Is within Thee*, a borrowing from Luke 11:35: "Take heed therefore that the light which is in thee be not darkness." Aunt Christine (a kind of Christ figure, as her name clearly implies) reads this passage to the hedonist, Maurice, who is on his deathbed. The revised title contrasts the opposing world-views—the candle of an individual's religiously inbred conscience as explicated by a traditional Christian view of man and the fierce wind of a twentieth-century, post-Enlightenment view of human nature which would snuff out that candle of conscience in the name of human autonomy.

This play is the only one of Solzhenitsyn's belletristic works which is not set in the Soviet Union. One can only speculate on any congruence between this fact and its generally acknowledged artistic inferiority. The writer who says of his homeland, "I listen only to its sadness, I write only about it,"[5] here writes a drama "to present the moral problems of society in the developed countries, independently of whether they are socialist or capitalist."[6]

Notwithstanding the vague setting in place (intentionally international) and the vague setting in time (contemporary, in any case), the author's first wife insists that many characters are based on persons she and her husband knew firsthand[7]—par for Solzhenitsyn. Indeed, the main character, Alex, is a namesake of the author, and in the play Alex regularly speaks lines which echo what we have come to recognize as the author's own point of view. For instance, Alex declares, "There are moments when I say, 'God bless you, prison!' " (p. 26). It was in prison that both Alex and Aleksandr matured morally and spiritually. (One thinks, also, of the authorial alter ego of *The First Circle*, Gleb Nerzhin.) Alex also says, "Suffering is a lever for the growth of the soul" (p. 128). Alex had spent three years at the battle front, nine years in prison, and five years in exile, returning to freedom at age forty—a history not dissimilar from the author's own. Also, both are mathematicians, teaching in remote locations.

The play may be described as a debate between two views of human life and its meaning. One view values the individual soul, or conscience. Alex states it, but it takes on its fullest significance in the context of Aunt Christine's spiritual faith. (And here she approximates the outlooks of Matryona and of Aunt Styofa in *Cancer Ward*: both old-woman, Mother-Russia figures of which Solzhenitsyn is fond.) If Alex does not articulate as much of religious substance as Aunt Christine does, the two are nonetheless allies. The other view asserts human autonomy, denying man's need to rely on that transcendent sphere in which God reigns.

Candle offers two variants of this Enlightenment perspective which is opposed to both Alex and Aunt Christine. One trumpets a scientific utopianism in which a rational solution exists for all human problems. The other advocates a life of sensual indulgence, since this life is all there is. The two views are ultimately congruent. Both posit immanence and eschew transcendence; both are philosophically materialistic; both disallow all God-ward motions. Scientism and hedonism are kindred. Both depart from Solzhenitsyn's traditionalist, spiritual point of view.

As the key question in *Cancer Ward* is "What do men live by?", so here Alex asks, "Why are we alive?" (p. 112). The play is about nothing less than the very purpose of human existence. Scientists deal with the "how" but not the "why" of life. One of their number resents Alex's getting "dear little God mixed up" in their discussions (p. 112). Another concurs in the "generally accepted" view that "religion's ridiculous" (p. 112).

Of the two God-denying views which this play seeks to counter, Solzhenitsyn devotes the greater space to scientific utopianism. However, he hints at a semblance of balance by opening and closing the play, envelope-like, with a treatment of hedonism.

The primary exponent of hedonism is Alex's seventy-year-old uncle, Maurice Craig, three times married and always to eighteen-year-old girls. His current wife, Tillie, thirty years younger than he, makes a fetish of powerful automobiles; one son, now eighteen, desires all the gear necessary for waterskiing.

Once an authority on the ethereal art of music, Maurice now has descended to be a subscriber to *Gastronomic News*. He still, Alex sees, "has moments of impulse when he is capable of being a magnificent person" (p. 65). But he has so perverted his intrinsic human quality that he can no longer understand Alex's spiritual outlook. What can Alex know when he advocates keeping shoes until the soles wear out or when he derides television for interfering with "a real communion between souls" (p. 63)?[8]

Only on his deathbed does Maurice repent. He tells his daughter, Alda (a major figure in the play, as we shall see), that everything he has done in his life has been wrong. To this daughter, whom in his heyday he had not appreciated, he commiserates: ". . . the moment when it's terrible to feel regret is when one is dying. . . . How should one live in order not to feel regret when one is dying?" (p. 132).

At his dying request, Alda now plays Schubert's *Die Winterreise*, "old music . . . not modern music" (p. 24). Maurice hears for the last time that classical music which represents those perennial values on which, in his pursuit of fleeting physical gratification, he had turned his back.

As Maurice Craig is the exemplar of hedonism, so Philip Radagise represents a dehumanizing scientism. Significantly, in his first appearance he delivers a panegyric on motorboats and other appurtenances of the good life. Hedonism and scientism grow from the same philosophic stock: both are materialistic. Philip finds conscience only "a conditioned reflex" and "a feeling that's optional," since it is "too im - mat - er - ial to live by in the twentieth century" (pp. 79-80). And, for him, "what is not material is non - ex - ist - ent! Let's drink!" (p. 108). Philip, echoing one of the important prose poems, "We Will Never Die,"[9] insists that "there is no life after death! We have only *one* life, *this* one!" (p. 79). Philip considers a work by Beethoven, the kind of "old" music which puts Solzhenitsyn in mind of the spiritual sustenance of the Great Tradition, "sheer dope" (p. 141). His view of medieval Gothic architecture is similar. He calls it "that old junk" and announces, "We'll pull all that down and build again from scratch with plastics and glass" (p. 109).

Science is never a villain in this play; scientism is. When Alex and Philip argue about science, it is really the elevation of science to scientism that is at stake. When Alex asks, "*What is science for?*" (p. 52), he immediately discounts egotism and human material wealth. After some give and take, Philip gets to the real issue between the two debaters. Recklessly, he barks that Alex should "go down on your knees before it! You should worship science!" (p. 53). This pitch opens the door for Alex's stinging rebuttal: " 'Oh, great science!' That's the same as saying, 'Oh, we great minds!' or even more precisely, 'Oh, great

me!' People have worshiped fire, the moon, and wooden idols—
but I'm afraid that worshiping an idol is not so painful as worshiping oneself" (p. 53).

Philip's intriguing reply shows that he understands the
real terms of the debate. He calls Alex "a real obscurantist" and
asks, "You mean we should worship dear little God?" (p. 53).
The clash between the traditional, God-oriented view of human
nature and the Enlightenment-influenced, man-oriented view
is head-on. Philip understands full well that the only real counter
to his materialistic philosophy of life is one grounded in a belief
in God.

In the same vein, Alex argues for absolute truth and absolute morality; Philip and another colleague, Sinbar, argue
against such archaic notions. And, as Sinbar explains, their view
rules out any idea of "an internal moral law," or conscience
(p. 119). Both sides of the debate, of course, are logically consistent. The main point here is that, in all of his works, when
Solzhenitsyn speaks of conscience, morality, truth, and the like,
he is operating within the same religious world-view which is
adumbrated in this play.

The "progressive" Philip wants to hand on to the twenty-
first century "the light, the meaning, and the interest of life"
(p. 54) embodied in the new science. Alex's choice of baton is
"the flickering candle of our soul" (p. 143). Alex elaborates: "Let
them do whatever they want to it in the twenty-first century.
Just so they don't blow it out in our century, in our century of
steel and the atom, of space, electric power, and cybernetics
. . ." (p. 143).

The two points of view come into direct conflict in the
case of Alda, daughter of Maurice and cousin of Alex. Flighty
and scatterbrained, always "afraid that somewhere they're plan-
ning to do something bad to me" (p. 58), she is the "ideal subject" (p. 74) for the new neuro-stabilization procedures in which
Philip's laboratory specializes. Skittish, she submits only after
reassurances from Alex, who has agreed to work with his old
schoolmate, Philip.

Alex has his own doubts. He says to Philip, "She's a little

candle, Philip! She's a little flickering candle in our terrible
wind! . . . Don't blow her out! Don't harm her!" (p. 92). The title
images (candle = soul, modern science = wind) recur throughout the play.

Sadly (but only temporarily), Alda, whom Philip patron-
izingly calls "our creation" (p. 141), is now "not afraid of anything" (p. 114). But she speaks "in a measured and indifferent
manner, sometimes suggesting tiredness" (p. 113). Even when
she sees a bus run over a dog, she feels no emotion.

For his part, Alex is horrified at the results. He tells Philip,
"We took a marvel of nature and turned it into a stone! And I
can already hear officers' boots stamping down the corridors!
Permit me to be—free!!" (p. 130). Witness Solzhenitsyn's ready
linkage between the abuse of science and the state's tyrannical
power; both dehumanize. Then think of the Soviets' internment
of some dissidents in psychiatric hospitals.

Fortunately, Alda is "knocked completely out of her sta-
bilization interval" (p. 130) by word of the impending death of
her father. Predictably, Philip is beside himself, and Alex is glee-
ful. The moods quickly change as Alda returns for a new oper-
ation. Wind is hard on candles.

The most enigmatic character in the play is Terbolm, a
young sociologist. The difficulty in interpreting him arises not
because he is a well-realized character but either because he is
simply an underdeveloped figure or, possibly, because the author has a deep-seated ambivalence toward him.

Some critics have found Terbolm a "positive character";
Gleb Zekulin calls him that, explaining that for Solzhenitsyn
he "represents the best qualities of the modern scientist."[10] Similarly, Christopher Moody says, "Terbolm is stating Solzhenitsyn's own view that the development of science, but under the
direction of moral conscience, is essential if man is to have a
future."[11] It is true that Terbolm allows for conscience and wishes
for a humaneness in science which is not present with Philip
and Sinbar. He has grown through suffering (a serious, long-
lasting physical ailment). His interest in trying to predict the
global future sounds like that of the Club of Rome, to which

Solzhenitsyn has made favorable references. The strongest piece of evidence for a positive reading of Terbolm is that Alex, the alter ego, leaves Philip's laboratory to go to work for him.

On the other hand, Terbolm considers religion ridiculous. His approach to human problems is a collectivist one. His method is to take the principles of biocybernetics and to apply them to the whole of society. While his immediate purpose is "to help people foresee their social future" and "not to lead humanity down false paths," it is part of his "working out rules for the transition to an ideally regulated society" (p. 106). He asks Alex, "Why should we refuse the collective—society—the principles of information, coordination, and feedback which are possessed by every individual human organism and every collective of living cells?" (p. 101). And Alex's agreement to work with Terbolm comes only after much struggle, and even then with considerable ambivalence. Thinking of Alda, Alex challenges Terbolm: "Here we've taken just *one* human being—and what have we done? And you want us to take millions of people at once!" (p. 106). He explains to Philip that his joining with Terbolm comes "not in hope, but in terror! In fear of success! I'm going to join them in order to prevent their eventually becoming another Leviathan, this time an electronic Leviathan" (pp. 148-49).

Terbolm's final words in the play make a favorable impression on Alex: "Science is needed not only by our intellect, but also by our soul. Perhaps it's just as necessary for us to understand the world and to understand mankind as it is to . . . have a conscience! Yes, that's my hypothesis: we need science also as a conscience!" (p. 147). Alex's desire to be involved in the problems of the world is a tribute to him; he wishes to be the salt of the earth which seasons the whole lot. Battered as he has been, he has reason enough to withdraw into privatism. However, his good intentions do not guarantee a correct decision. He has been wrong before, in joining Philip. At the very least, although the treatment of Terbolm is never sharply negative, Terbolm clearly does not speak the familiar Solzhenitsyn language. Still, Solzhenitsyn is assuredly not anti-scientific. He is himself a student and teacher of science, and he consistently has high praise for engineers. Let us conclude, then, that Terbolm remains enigmatic. His instincts are certainly good. The channel into which he pours them are suspect enough to leave us, and perhaps the author, in a quandary of what to think. Modern science is a powerful tool; Solzhenitsyn knows that, and he must try to come to grips with it. But he seems not quite sure what final verdict to render; so he ends by leaving the question open.

We are on much surer ground when we come to the character of Aunt Christine, the old woman who represents in purest form in this play the author's Christian convictions. Here Solzhenitsyn is not at all ambiguous. Whatever a scientist like Alex should do with his life, he must remain within the context of that spiritual understanding embodied in Aunt Christine.

Christine's only appearance is at the deathbed scene of Maurice the hedonist. Her appearance, unmotivated dramatically as it is, constitutes a *deus-ex-machina*, doubtless a theatrical flaw. After making the sign of the cross over Maurice and lighting the customary candle, she reads from St. Luke (11:33, 11:35, 12:19, 12:20). These verses, read without comment, carry their own message and provide the author's own commentary on the lives depicted in the play:

> No man, when he hath lighted a candle, putteth it in a secret place, neither under a bushel, but on a candlestick, that they which come in may see the light.
>
> Take heed therefore that the light which is in thee be not darkness.
>
> And I will say to my soul, Soul, thou hast much goods laid up for many years; take thine ease, eat, drink, and be merry.
>
> But God said unto him, Thou fool, this night thy soul shall be required of thee: then whose shall those things be, which thou hast provided? (p. 136)

Even apart from introducing Aunt Christine, Solzhenitsyn is clear in this play about the religious context in which his moral vision is couched. Aunt Christine the Christian is icing on the cake, or the underlining of a crucial point.

6

VOICES FROM HELL:

The First Circle

W hereas *One Day* and *Love-Girl* are set in harsh Siberian prison camps, *The First Circle* is set in a scientific institute outside of Moscow. Still, this place is every bit as much a part of the Gulag Archipelago. It is a *sharashka,* the Mavrino, a place where prisoners with scientific and technological expertise are brought together to do experimental work for the state authorities. The state allows these zeks a few comforts unheard of in the camps, but only to get from them more valuable service.

Both in the title and in early pages of the novel, Solzhenitsyn uses imagery from Dante's *Inferno* to explain the true nature of this Mavrino sharashka. When one new zek arrives there from a camp, he is amazed by the contrast. Noting the availability of bread and books, the freedom to shave, the freedom from beatings, he marvels, "What kind of great day is this? What kind of gleaming summit? Maybe I've died? Maybe this is a dream? Perhaps I'm in heaven."[1] A Mavrino veteran (and a loyal Communist, at that) sets him straight: "No, dear sir, . . . you are, just as you were previously, in hell. But you have risen to its best and highest circle—the first circle" (p. 9). The speaker expounds at some length on the parallel between the sharashka and the first circle of hell, which Dante invented as the place for putting enlightened pagans. Another veteran explains the meaning of the sharashka more tersely: "You need only remember the newspaper piece that said: 'It has been proved that a high yield of wool from sheep depends on the animals' care and feeding' " (p. 10).

Thus, at the outset Solzhenitsyn provides a framework for understanding the whole of this long novel. The Dantean allusions provide a religious context; they are supplemented by the many religious references which dot the novel. And by speaking of this hell on earth, Solzhenitsyn works a telling inversion of the Marxist promise of a paradise on earth. Not only is the prison system hellish, but, as *The Gulag Archipelago* shows explicitly, *First Circle*'s scenes outside the sharashka demonstrate that the Gulag's germ of dehumanization infects the whole of Soviet society. The animal imagery highlights the novel's concern for the development of human dignity even in an inhospitable setting.

Solzhenitsyn's choice of setting once again demonstrates the principle of understatement. In *One Day* Ivan Denisovich judged his day to be almost a good day. In *First Circle* the prison could be almost a good prison. Solzhenitsyn knows his aesthetic problem: how to sensitize to horror the imaginations of those who have not suffered the horrors. The problem is ever present in *The Gulag Archipelago*. Understatement is his approach in *The First Circle*: "Descriptions of prisons have always stressed their horror. Yet isn't it even more appalling when there are no horrors? When the horror lies in the gray methodology of years? In forgetting that your one and only life on earth has been shattered?" (p. 232). It is against such a soulless background that the characters are called upon to make themselves truly human beings. That many fail is no surprise. The wonder is that any succeed.

The making of a human being—the theme of the novel can be no more narrowly circumscribed than that. Every character is judged by how well he does in that venture. So, as always with Solzhenitsyn, the central formal fictional element is character. This chapter is organized accordingly.

Solzhenitsyn began writing *The First Circle* in 1955 while in exile in Kazakhstan. He finished it in 1964.[2] He has done some revising since then and professes to prefer the revised version, though it is not yet in print.[3] The book was first published in the West in 1968.[4] Solzhenitsyn's method of composition, working on many works simultaneously and continually revising them, undercuts any attempt to divide his works into separate periods so as to chart changes in his point of view; in any case, since early prison days his view of life has remained strikingly constant.

Again, like all of Solzhenitsyn's novels, *The First Circle* has a tightly compressed time span: four days, December 24-27, 1949. The Christmastide setting is perfect for featuring the conflict between *homo religiosus* and *homo Sovieticus*. Also, the bulk of the novel has a compressed setting in space: the sharashka, though a limited number of scenes occur on the outside. (A parallel structure is found in *August 1914*, with most chapters set at the war front but some behind the front.) So plot, the unfolding of episodes in time and space, is a minor factor. Instead, what dominates is the inspection of the many characters which the novel offers: a large gallery which gives a cross section of Soviet society from top to bottom. Dialogue, not narrative, impels the novel.

This tactic gives the novel a kind of kaleidoscopic quality. Characters, as different centers of consciousness, emerge, overlap, submerge, and later reemerge. As the novel skips from one character to another, it lacks the smooth transition from chapter to chapter expected by many readers of fiction. The interconnections between lives become clear only well along into the novel. But piece by piece the mosaic falls into place. The thematic strain of striving for genuine humanity is the glue which holds the whole together.

The best example of the appearance, disappearance, and reappearance of a center of consciousness is Innokenty Volodin.

After appearing in the very first chapter, he disappears until Chapter 55 (in a novel of 87 chapters), then reappears for his major scene in Chapter 78. It is gradually revealed that the life of this government functionary is intimately enmeshed with the lives of the Mavrino zeks. In the first chapter Innokenty has learned that an old family friend, Dr. Dobroumov, is in danger of entrapment by Soviet authorities. The doctor, in the name of science, plans to share a new medical discovery with Westerners on an upcoming visit to Paris. When Innokenty learns that doing so would get Dobroumov in trouble, he phones his house to warn him, though aware of the personal risk involved. The attempt to help is unsuccessful, but his voice has been recorded. The tape is turned over to those zeks at Mavrino who are working at detecting voiceprints. The detective element of the novel involves the zeks' trying to discover who made the phone call.

The bitter irony here is that the efforts of the collectivist state to gain totalitarian control over its citizens focus on that very individuality which collectivism in theory rejects. Phonoscopy, the reading of sounds as one would read fingerprints, aims at "discovering what makes a human voice unique" (p. 23).

Innokenty is wracked by the fear of being caught in his humane act of warning Dr. Dobroumov. The fear which governs the lives of prisoners penetrates throughout Soviet society. Yet, as Innokenty reflects, "If one is forever cautious, can one remain a human being?" (p. 4). At the very beginning of the novel, then, Solzhenitsyn highlights its main theme.

The occasional appearances of Innokenty are part and parcel of the author's overall novelistic strategy, which Solzhenitsyn himself has described as "polyphonic." In a 1967 interview with Pavel Licko, he declared that he found the most interesting genre to be "a polyphonic novel strictly defined in time and space. A novel without a main hero. If a novel has a main hero the author inevitably pays more attention to him and devotes more space."[5] Solzhenitsyn carefully defines polyphony:

> Each person becomes the main hero as soon as the action reverts to him. Then the author feels responsible for as many as thirty-five heroes. He does not accord preferential treatment

to any one. He must understand every character and motivate
his actions. . . . I had employed this method in writing two
books and I intend to use it in writing a third.[6]

A polyphonic novel will, by its nature, feature interaction
between characters as representatives of differing world-views;
and it will respect the integrity of each. Given a compact time
span, it will not feature the development of characters; it can,
however, show some of that development in two ways: by having a personal crisis fall within the novel's short time setting
and by flashing back (either via the character's memory or via
the omniscient author's commentary) to earlier times in the
character's life.

While the polyphonic principle means that no character
will be on center stage considerably longer than all others, it
obviously does not mean that all characters will be found equally
appealing. It means only that their world-views will be adequately and accurately depicted. The reader may well find a
given character's outlook quite appalling. The clear example
here is Stalin. He is given four consecutive chapters. Only three
or four characters receive greater space. Solzhenitsyn means to
be correct in portraying him. Yet it is scarcely conceivable that
any reader will approve of Stalin's opinions. The author's goal
is that readers will evaluate each character according to the
intrinsic worth of his world-view.

Similarly, the polyphonic principle does not mean that
the author himself cannot prefer one character (and his point of
view) over another. Clearly, as we know (from external evidence
if no other), Solzhenitsyn prefers Gleb Nerzhin to anyone else.[7]
It is not surprising that Nerzhin has been widely viewed, by
commentators unaware of Solzhenitsyn's polyphonic principle,
as the main character of the novel, even though the fact is that
at least one other character receives as many pages as he. Solzhenitsyn's hope is that if readers prefer Nerzhin to all others,
it will be because of the persuasiveness of his world-view. And
what is intriguing here is that some commentators have found
another character, Lev Rubin, equally appealing. Probably, this
says something about the commentators' perspective; surely, it

says something about Solzhenitsyn's success in employing polyphony.

In the polyphonic structure of *The First Circle*, Solzhenitsyn establishes three major points of view, represented by three leading characters, on the meaning of human life. Amidst a large gallery of characters, Lev Rubin, Dimitri Sologdin, and Gleb Nerzhin are prominent because of their arguments about what it means to be truly and fully human. Each has a clearly articulated position. Lev Rubin, ever the loyal Marxist, propounds a consistently collectivist position: the individual must always be subordinate to the social whole. Sologdin, in reaction against this regnant Soviet view, asserts uncompromisingly that great individuals make human history, that collectivist doctrine is a snare and a delusion. Gleb Nerzhin takes a middle way. Learning much from Sologdin, he nonetheless stops short of extreme individualism. He acknowledges the primacy of developing a personal world-view, but he sees this process as issuing naturally into a sense of community with one's fellows. How the individual is related to the rest of humanity is a key point of argument among these three spokesmen.

All three fictional characters are based on real-life personages. Lev Rubin is based on Lev Kopelev; Dimitri Sologdin, on Dimitri Panin; and Gleb Nerzhin, on Solzhenitsyn himself. Kopelev and Panin have now published a book apiece on life in Soviet prisons.[8]

The fact that all three of these zeks have written books suggests a key difference between *The First Circle* and *One Day*. Whereas the suffering of Ivan Denisovich was primarily physical, here it is psychological and even spiritual. These sharashka zeks are intellectual men, and their debates move this novel to a level of abstract speculation beyond the scope of the other works which grow out of Solzhenitsyn's personal experiences. Comparison of their own books with Solzhenitsyn's fictionalizing of these two men shows that Solzhenitsyn took certain liberties, presumably to sharpen a contrast of points of view. Particularly, Panin exhibits a greater religious sensibility than is allotted to Solzhenitsyn's character Sologdin—a sensibility, indeed, not unlike Solzhenitsyn's own. Panin himself, without wishing to be disparaging, finds some factual fault with Solzhenitsyn's depiction of him as Sologdin and of the Panin-Kopelev arguments.[9] This is not to say that the fictional creations are literarily false: they have their own intrinsic coherence.[10] Rubin and Nerzhin receive more space than any other characters; Sologdin is, by comparison, somewhat slighted. We shall examine first these three figures, then pan out over some of the supporting host.

Lev Rubin is a Russian Jew who remains loyal to Communism, even though he recognizes that the Soviet system has (inadvertently in its vigilance) unjustly treated him as an enemy. A philologist with a strong interest in history, he is depicted sympathetically as a Marxist with humane instincts, a worthy debating antagonist for Nerzhin. Indeed, their debates are somewhat like an internal struggle within Solzhenitsyn—before and after his abandonment of Marxist ideology. As the self-appointed "spokesman for progressive ideology in the sharashka," Rubin felt that he "couldn't allow himself to lose even one argument" (p. 441). It is an uneasy role for a capacious soul. As one zek reprimanded, "You claim to be a materialist, but you keep cramming people with spiritual stuff" (p. 8). This best of ideologues has to admit, "No matter how violently he refuted Sologdin's statements they hurt because he knew there was some justice in them" (p. 482). He refuses to write denunciations of other prisoners and finds distasteful the servility toward Stalin of a former Chief of Special Communications for Beria and his secret police. He even writes verses on biblical subjects and is described as "a man with the thick black beard of a Biblical prophet" (p. 11).

But how does a compassionate man explain "numbers on human beings?" (p. 6). This is the challenge to Rubin. And how can he retain the thrill of what he thinks is the founding of the new science of phonoscopy when all that his boss, General Oskolupov, wants is to catch a "criminal"? When Rubin and a colleague, Roitman, think they have the suspects for Innokenty

Volodin's fateful phone call down to two, Oskolupov, a little
Stalin whose style of leadership "descended directly from *Him*,"
bellows, "We'll arrest both the sons-of-bitches!" Rubin exclaims, "But one of them is not guilty!" Oskolupov's wide-eyed
response is, "What do you mean, not guilty? Not guilty of anything at all? The security organization will find something
. . ." (pp. 591-92).

Not only the author but even the character himself sees
his plight as tragic, and tragic "in the Aristotelian sense":

> He had been dealt the blow by the hands of those he loved the
> most. He had been imprisoned by unfeeling bureaucrats be-
> cause he loved the common cause to an improper degree. And
> as a result of that tragic contradiction, in order to defend his
> own dignity and that of his comrades, Rubin found himself
> compelled to stand up daily against the prison officers and
> guards whose actions, according to his view of the world, were
> determined by a totally true, correct, and progressive law.
> (p. 475)

The conflict between the humanity and ideology of Rubin
which colors his entire characterization is illustrated with painful clarity when he first hears the tape of Innokenty's call to Dr.
Dobroumov. Rubin senses at once the caller's humaneness. And
for a man who, "having long since lost all hope of personal
success," has "lived the life of all mankind as if it were his own
family life" (p. 225), the doctor's desire to share universally a
new medical discovery is only laudable. But then ideology surfaces: ". . . objectively that man who had wanted to do what
seemed to him the right thing had in fact attacked the positive
forces of history" (p. 226). In Rubin, faith in Marxism's laws of
history always overwhelms personal urges toward human solidarity; that personalism which Nerzhin so assiduously culti-
vates is precisely what must be shunned.

Nevertheless, even his debating opponents recognize the
genuineness of Rubin's conflict between humane instincts and
ideological loyalty. Nerzhin may scoff at Rubin's vaunted claim
of objectivity, exclaiming, "I've never in my life known a person
as lacking in objectivity as you" (p. 40). Nerzhin may find ab-

solutely pigheaded and obtuse Rubin's stubborn view that Stalin is the most intelligent man alive in Russia. But the two always remain friends, and at the end of the novel they part with affectionate endearments. Both of them always understand that their differences have to do with disagreements about those fundamental issues which constitute competing world-views.

The epitome of Rubin's efforts to fuse his humanism and his ideology comes in Chapter 67, "Civic Temples," in which Rubin speculates on how to infuse a moral approach to living within citizens of a secular, collectivist state. Momentarily freed from the incubus of ideology, he concedes that the people have "lost their feeling for beautiful moral action" (p. 483). Then, with ideology quickly reasserting itself, he calls for "raising still higher the already high morality of the population" (p. 483). Rubin's Civic Temples would dominate the landscape the way the old Russian Orthodox churches still do. Rituals would be developed for state holidays and for such rites of life as marriage, naming the newborn, entering adulthood, and mourning the dead. In Rubin's mind, "the key to the success of the whole project lay in establishing throughout the nation a corps of authoritative attendants who enjoyed the love and trust of the people because of their own irreproachable, unselfish, and worthy lives" (p. 484). Rubin's concern is that his projected temples not be perceived merely as "Christian temples without Christ" (p. 484); yet that, of course, is exactly what they are. The morality of traditional Christianity has great appeal for him. However, any appropriation of it by him must pull it loose from its moorings and attach it to his own (religious or quasi-religious) world-view.

Dimitri Sologdin's views are sharply different. Yet both men are generally depicted sympathetically, as should not be unexpected in a polyphonic novel. Sologdin delights in reciting to Rubin all the evils of the Soviet system, thus making Rubin squirm. Arguments between the two sometimes devolve into personal nastiness, something which does not happen when Nerzhin and Rubin argue.

In defiant reaction against the class analysis of collectivism, for which Rubin is the best advocate, Sologdin swings to the opposite extreme of a thoroughgoing individualism. He belittles the vaunted concept of "the people" as only "an over-all term for a totality of persons of slight interest, gray, crude, preoccupied in their unenlightened way with daily existence"— people whose "multitudes do not constitute the foundation of the colossus of the human spirit" (p. 449). Sologdin prefers the individual—in particular, the great individual who moves beyond being one of the people and becomes a kind of superman: "Only unique personalities, shining and separate, like singing stars strewn through the dark heaven of existence, carry within them supreme understanding" (p. 449). His view is that "great ideas are born only in a single mind" (p. 199). Not surprisingly, he likes Dostoevsky, a suspect writer in Soviet eyes. Sologdin says of Dostoevsky's characters, "They are as complex and incomprehensible as people in real life! . . . That's why Dostoevsky is so great. And literary scholars imagine they can illuminate a human being fully. It's amusing" (p. 442).

Sologdin's efforts to become such a superman result primarily in his being an eccentric. He refuses to use what he calls "bird words," or words of foreign derivation, speaking instead what he calls "the Language of Maximum Clarity" (p. 155). But the chief quirk of this quirky man is "to utter some nonsensical, utterly wild opinion on every question, such as that prostitution is a moral good . . ." (p. 156).

While Sologdin is of major importance as a spokesman for one view of human reality, he is of equal importance as an influence on "the author's hero," Gleb Nerzhin. In his desire to think for himself, Nerzhin finds Sologdin's independence of thought an invaluable stimulant. A major lesson for Nerzhin is the lesson of growth through suffering, and he comes to recognize that he has "acquired some of Sologdin's unhurried comprehension of life; how in particular it was Sologdin who had first nudged him into thinking that a person shouldn't regard prison solely as a curse, but also as a blessing" (p. 158). Sologdin also nurtures Nerzhin's desire to write about history, and he approves when Gleb exclaims that "the grief I have felt within

me and which I see in others is enough to illuminate my speculations about history" (p. 159). Another important lesson—and
we may be seeing the results in Solzhenitsyn's passion to revise
and even to seek good translators—comes in Sologdin's exposition of the rule of the Final Inch:

> The work has almost been completed, the goal almost at-
> tained, everything seems completely right and the difficulties
> overcome. But the quality of the thing is not *quite* right. Fin-
> ishing touches are needed, maybe still more research. In that
> moment of fatigue and self-satisfaction it is especially tempt-
> ing to leave the work without having attained the apex of
> quality. Work in the area of the Final Inch is very, very com-
> plex and also especially valuable. . . . In fact, the rule of the
> Final Inch consists in this: not to shirk this crucial work. Not
> to postpone it, for the thoughts of the person performing the
> task will then stray from the realm of the Final Inch. And not
> to mind the time spent on it, knowing that one's purpose lies
> not in completing things faster but in the attainment of per-
> fection. (p. 161)

Sologdin serves yet one other important role in the novel:
he is a foil to Nerzhin. Both men face two kindred temptations;
and in both Nerzhin succeeds where Sologdin fails. For each,
the lesser temptation is illicit sex; the greater is to submit one's
scientific know-how to the uses of the authorities.

When Larisa, wife of a Chekist, offers herself to Sologdin,
suggesting that in his fidelity he is robbing his wife of her youth
and that he ought to let her live her life on her own, he initially
objects. And he offers a tribute to the wives of zeks which surely
reflects Solzhenitsyn's own thinking: "There is a special class
of women, Larisa Nikolayevna. They are the companions of the
Vikings, the bright-faced Isoldes with diamond souls. You have
been living in vapid prosperity and could not have known them"
(p. 211). Even so, his need for a woman overwhelms his idealism; and he submits to Larisa's charms, all the while chastising
himself as weak, even sinful.

Similarly, Sologdin caves in to the temptation to parlay
his technical expertise into personal gain: possible freedom. The
Mavrino zeks are all at work on voice coding; on his own, So-

logdin has developed a device which a canny old professor, when Sologdin shows it to him, is sure will be the best of the lot, probably good enough to serve as a passport out of prison. Sologdin leaves his chat with the professor knowing that he will try to exchange his invention for his freedom. But he is not elated; for he realizes that by so doing he is giving the despised authorities what they want. "He had come into this room a free contender. And now he left it as a burdened victor. He was no longer the master of his own time, intentions, or labor" (p. 204). A man of high principles is still flawed.

Gleb Nerzhin is the most autobiographical of all Solzhenitsyn's characters. Of the favored figures of Solzhenitsyn's three novels of the sixties which are based on his own personal experiences, Ivan Denisovich of *One Day* is much too unsophisticated to resemble the author, and Oleg Kostoglotov, while sharing cancer with the author, ends up somewhere between Ivan and Gleb in the depth of his ponderings about human fate. Both Nerzhin and Solzhenitsyn are thirty-one in 1949. Both are trained in mathematics and science. Both are allied with a chemistry student named Nadya. Both have had early difficulty accepting official versions of history, and so both study history for themselves. Both had been born in December—Solzhenitsyn on the eleventh and Nerzhin on the twenty-fifth. Even the physical description of Nerzhin resembles that of Solzhenitsyn. Finally, both come to similar views about the world and the nature of man.

Yet the parallelism between the two is not essential to the interpretation of the character of Gleb Nerzhin and of the novel as a whole. Any compelling power of Nerzhin comes not from external imposition but from the role he plays with other characters within the novel. Certainly, Solzhenitsyn is not trying to idealize himself through his portrait of Nerzhin. In fact, Panin asserts that in Nerzhin Solzhenitsyn gives an extraordinarily truthful and accurate picture of himself.[11] Though generally admirable, Nerzhin is not without frailties and limitations. In the same vein, Solzhenitsyn has been very open about confessing his own shortcomings, especially in *The Gulag Archipelago*.[12]

Nevertheless, it is not improper to see in Nerzhin an alter ego of the author.

Like his creator, Gleb Nerzhin finds in his imprisonment that period of time when he learns to think for himself. He had always tended to do so. Now, in the sharashka and among other keen intellects, he senses a great urgency about the duty to think things out. The coherent patterns of thought of Rubin and Sologdin are the primary ones with which he must come to grips. Yet he can adopt neither Rubin's totalitarian-excusing collectivism nor Sologdin's elitist individualism. Where can he turn?

He thinks of going to the people, meaning the peasants— a notion which both Rubin and Sologdin scorn. Gleb, too, soon realizes that there is no help for him in that quarter. The peasants are no more stoic, no firmer of spirit, no more foresighted than he; and they are more susceptible to the tricks of informers and the blandishments of the bosses.

Gleb's only alternative is to "be himself," to develop his own "personal *point of view*" which is "more precious than life itself" (p. 451). He attains a level of spiritual independence and a maturity which allows him to assert, "Everyone forges his inner self year after year. One must try to temper, to cut, to polish one's soul so as to become *a human being*" (p. 452).

However, lest one think that Nerzhin has simply rejected Rubin's collectivism and opted for Sologdin's individualism, Solzhenitsyn immediately has Nerzhin append the line, "And thereby become a tiny particle of one's own people" (p. 452). Gleb's personalism separates him from a monolithic collectivism, but it equally separates him from an isolated individualism. When, he suggests, one comes truly to know himself, he will know that he is also a social being and that fullness of selfhood results in compassion and community. First—and this is in keeping with the spirit of the *Nobel Lecture*—he will sense a belonging to a nation; then, beyond that, a belonging to all mankind. Individual identity is no more a deterrent to national loyalty than is national loyalty to global consciousness. Individual dignity and a sense of community are not, then, to be seen as conflicting values. Rather, they reinforce each other. This is what Nerzhin, but neither Rubin nor Sologdin, understands.

In order to sustain this duality between individuality and community, Nerzhin must posit a more fundamental one between good and evil in the human heart. He perceives that his prison years have "both blessed and degraded" him (p. 370). He and his fellow zeks have experienced in full force the outworkings of man's miserable evil; the twentieth century has not been short in demonstrating that commodity. What Nerzhin must affirm, to reestablish the proper balance, is "the genuine grandeur" of human beings (p. 370), which is especially meaningful to him through friendships in prison. Recognition that good and evil are real and that they vie with each other in every human heart is enough to negate the deterministic notion of collectivism that "circumstances determine consciousness" (p. 297).

The human heart's impulse toward good is what fosters idealism, and Nerzhin learns much about idealism from the old painter Kondrashev-Ivanov, a fellow zek. This character explains, "A human being . . . possesses from his birth a certain essence, the nucleus, as it were, of this human being. His 'I' " (p. 297). Thus, this "ageless idealist" paints a picture of Parsifal, on horseback, looking across a deep gorge at "the unearthly perfection" of the castle of the Holy Grail. One must always keep his eye on the goal and never be distracted by the dangers set round about: this is what Nerzhin learns from the painter.

Nerzhin shows how far he has developed as a human being when he confronts and passes the two tests which tripped up Sologdin. Nerzhin is offered a specific assignment on the voice coder project, but his success would so obviously entail entrapment of innocents that he spurns the offer. To accept would mean to corrupt his true self and inevitably to impede his search for the true meaning of life. The choice to remain a docile scientist doing the masters' bidding would be safer, Gleb knows. "But why live a whole life? Just to be living? Just to keep the body going? Precious comfort! What do we need it for if there is nothing else? And good sense said, 'Yes,' but the heart said, 'Get thee behind me, Satan!' " (p. 49). Gleb so steels himself that when his moment of truth arrives and a guard proposes a possible tradeoff of successful work for forgiveness, Nerzhin replies with impudence: "You're beginning at the wrong end. Let them admit first that it's not right to put people in prison for their way of thinking, and then _we_ will decide whether we will forgive _them_" (p. 50). His decision marks him for transportation from the sharashka to the nether reaches of Campland; his departure scene will climax the novel.

As he grows, Gleb develops a "single great passion," and "there is no room in us for two passions" (p. 236). He has made "an inviolable decision . . . to learn and understand" (p. 236). He feels deeply the "spiritual inheritance" from great Russian writers like Pushkin and Tolstoy. He has known the kind of skepticism which causes one of the zeks to tell him, "History is so monotonous it's repulsive to read. . . . All history is one continuous pestilence. There is no truth and there is no illusion. There is nowhere to appeal and nowhere to go" (pp. 77-78). But Gleb, who even as a youth sensed the distortions perpetrated by Stalin, has outgrown his skeptical stage:

> No matter how clever and absolute the systems of skepticism or agnosticism or pessimism, you must understand that by their very nature they doom us to a loss of will. . . . I personally believe that people seriously need skepticism. It's needed to split the rockheads. To choke fanatical voices. But skepticism can never provide firm ground under a man's feet. And perhaps, after all, we need firm ground. (p. 78)

Gleb's call to move beyond skepticism and to pledge oneself to something, to love something, elicits from his conversationalist the response that he will choose to love "not history and not theory, but a woman!" (p. 79). This response is at least life-affirming. Gleb himself had said, "A zek has to believe that there are still real, live, adorable women in the world and that they give themselves to fellows with luck" (p. 34). The desire to see man-woman love flourish is part of a desire to see justice prevail in the world.

So Gleb's second temptation, to illicit love, is a difficult one. Love itself is good. But illicit love violates the high moral code which Gleb has adopted. He has been faithful to his world-view in big things; now he must be faithful in small things. Like all zeks, Gleb is starved for love. Though his wife lives right in Moscow, "she might as well have been on Mars" (p. 67). Simochka, a civilian worker in the sharashka, intuits that Gleb is married before he tells her, but she makes herself available to him anyway. She is a kind person with genuine sympathy for Gleb. She is also love-starved herself, and she can see only mutual benefit resulting from a liaison between them. Actually, Gleb would risk little: ten days in a punishment cell; she would risk much: her very freedom.

Gleb's moral will is strengthened by an unexpected brief meeting with his wife. Although he knows that there is no real hope of their eventual reunion, the visit has helped him to apply his moral criteria to his relationship with Simochka. He tries to explain to her that whereas he does not consider himself a particularly good man, "if you know when you die that you haven't been a complete bastard, that's at least some satisfaction" (p. 600). Good and evil are in combat in each human heart. Considering his refusal of Simochka to be a yielding to good impulses, Gleb muses: "Nine out of ten men would have ridiculed Nerzhin for his renunciation—after so many years of deprivation.... But he was happy he had acted as he had" (p. 603). Even a peccadillo is on the side of evil, and it therefore would hinder his personal development as a human being.

As a polyphonic novel, *The First Circle* presents a cross section of Soviet society, starting at the top with Stalin and descending to the menial peasant-janitor, Spiridon. However, the judgments of characters are never along economic or sociological lines. Always, the question is how they fare as inhabitants of a moral universe. How far to one side or the other, and in what particulars, have they pushed the line dividing good and evil which runs through every human heart?

One character who receives extensive treatment is Joseph

Stalin himself. Sociologically, he is at the top of the heap. Spiritually, he is at the bottom circle of hell, as was Satan in Dante's scheme. He is, in Moody's apt phrase, "imprisoned in solitary confinement of the spirit."[13]

Solzhenitsyn's portrait of Stalin is devastating. The author drips irony as he recites the titles which Stalin has taken to himself: Leader of All Progressive Humanity, Best Friend of Counter-Intelligence Operatives, Most Brilliant Strategist of All Times and Peoples, Little Father, The Nearest and Dearest, Greatest Genius of Geniuses, the Omnipotent, The Immortal— some ludicrous, some downright blasphemous. Yet Stalin finds in these grandiloquent titles "not the least contradiction here with the idea of world Communism" (p. 130).

By contrast, Solzhenitsyn portrays Stalin as "only a little old man with a desiccated double chin which was never shown in his portraits, a mouth permeated with the smell of Turkish leaf tobacco, and fat fingers which left their traces on books" (p. 99). Rejecting Stalin's self-importance, Solzhenitsyn writes boldly, "Just as King Midas turned everything to gold, Stalin turned everything to mediocrity" (p. 123). Stalin wills to live to ninety and "suffer another twenty years for the sake of humanity" (p. 101), since "there is no one to replace him" (p. 130). But he worries—about his nausea, lapses of memory, inability to enjoy good food.

The personal quality Stalin values most highly is his inflexible, iron will. He remembers having to correct "the rash and too easily trusting Lenin" (p. 101). He revels in the memory of those "glorious" years of 1936-37 leading up to the Great Purge. He thinks fondly of the revisions he has interjected into the collected works of Lenin and the other Founders: "Everyone was long since asleep who had disagreed . . ." (p. 106). But now he finds himself left in glorious isolation: ". . . there was no one to ask advice from; he alone on earth was a true philosopher" (p. 112). What should he do, for instance, about the troublesome Tito? That case typifies the general problem: ". . . half the universe was enclosed in his own breast, and that half was harmonious and clear. It was only the second half—objective reality—which cowered in global mist" (p. 113).

Whether consciously or not, Solzhenitsyn paints Stalin in terms akin to those of the Grand Inquisitor in Dostoevsky's *The Brothers Karamazov*.[14] Stalin had convinced himself that only he "knew the path by which to lead humanity to happiness, how to shove its face into happiness like a blind puppy's into a bowl of milk—'There, drink up!' " (p. 130). He imagines that there is no one in whose care he can leave humanity: "They'd make a mess of everything" (p. 131). The people never quite responded to his fatherly care as they should have: "You could try to teach them democracy, you could even chew things up for them so that all they had to do was swallow—and they would turn their heads away" (p. 114).

Through long years of habit, Stalin had become so suspicious of everyone that "mistrust was his world view" (p. 122). Whenever he interviewed a loyal henchman, "his first thought always was: how far can this person be trusted? And his second: has not the moment come for this person to be liquidated?" (p. 121). In all his life he had trusted only one man: Adolf Hitler. And that experience had almost "cost him his neck" (p. 122). So never again.

As Stalin enters his dotage, memories from childhood well up in him with renewed strength. Until nineteen he had been weaned on the Bible, church history, and the liturgies which he knew as a choirboy. Even now he could sing Strokin's "Now You Are Forgiven" "without missing a note" (p. 131). He now found himself drawn to icons and saying *brethren* instead of *comrades*. This man, who for forty years had been bent on destroying that world from which he had come, finds "one unresolved question" (p. 131): the possibility that God exists. This Satan-like ruler of an atheistic state can find no surer conclusion than this: "It had been proved that it was impossible to prove that Christ had existed" (p. 131).

Since, in the moral order, actions carry within them their inevitable consequences, the view of Stalin in old age is crucial. He had done "everything possible . . . to assure his immortality," and still it seemed to him that his contemporaries "did not admire him as much as he deserved, that their raptures were superficial, that they did not yet understand the profundity of his genius" (p. 110). His towering loneliness closes in on him "like a paralysis" (p. 134). Animal imagery, which is frequently used for those who have suffered at Stalin's hands, now turns out to be apt for him: "Growing old like a dog. An old age without friends. An old age without love. An old age without faith. An old age without desire. . . . Death had already made its nest in him, and he refused to believe it" (p. 134).

Some critics have disapproved of Solzhenitsyn's depiction of Stalin because of its supposed unrelieved blackness. The criticism is unwarranted. First, the portrait is not unrelievedly black; even in old age Stalin wrestles, if fleetingly, with questions the right answers to which could still open him to the motions of grace. But, more important, a soul in which the line dividing good and evil has been pushed so far over to one side that evil overwhelmingly predominates must be painted in very dark colors if the depiction is to be accurate.

Stalin's world-view of mistrust filters down through his underlings. Some of their portraits are quite revealing; one of the most interesting is that of Anton Nikolayevich Yakonov, Colonel of Engineers assigned to the Mavrino sharashka. The two chapters devoted to him give before-and-after glimpses into his person. In the first, this conscience-torn former zek has just visited Abakumov, one of Stalin's highest officials, and he fears that the conversation has not gone well enough to keep him from being hurled into "the pit." He is utterly miserable.

In the second chapter, his mind runs back to his "moment of truth" twenty-two years earlier. He has returned to the Church of St. John the Baptist, where he had had a decisive conversation with his then-financée, Agniya. She had warned then "that Moscow is disappearing" (p. 144), and now he finds only ruins of the church. A futuristic skyscraper is soon to be constructed on the vacant site. On that long-ago occasion he had cynically, and rhetorically, questioned, "Was our country ever Christian in its *soul*?" (p. 146). In that day he had defended the Bolsheviks for their "great respect for world culture" and their commitment to "universal, complete, absolute equality" (p. 146).

Yakonov had been miffed at his stubborn, religious fiancée's resistance to his utopian mouthings. But now, when he is in such despair that he wishes not to live any longer, he ponders anew her challenge to him. Back then, he had charged that she was attracted to the church "because it encourages your indifference to life" (p. 148). When Yakonov had signed an article written for him denouncing the West, which was "not the complete truth, but . . . not exactly a lie either," Agniya had sent him back his engagement ring, tied to a paper on which she had scrawled, in mockery, "For Metropolitan Cyril" (p. 149), a priest who had collaborated with the ancient Tatar oppressors. She had refused to sell her soul, along with Yakonov, to the new Soviet state which was in the process of eradicating her beloved old Russia.

These two brief chapters in the midst of a sprawling novel are typical of Solzhenitsyn's technique. They offer in miniature a glimpse into the central preoccupations of the novel. They even show that some loyal Communists are torn, that they remain human beings who must be judged according to moral criteria. In terms of technique, they also illustrate Solzhenitsyn's principle of polyphony.

Solzhenitsyn features other loyalists, both officers and zeks. But they are almost always less interesting than those prisoners who do not toe the party line. One zek went so far—further than Solzhenitsyn would go—as to speculate that "only a zek is certain to have an immortal soul: free people are often denied one because of the vain lives they lead" (p. 197).[15] So it is not surprising that many of the memorable characters in *The First Circle* are zeks. Some appear only briefly; yet Solzhenitsyn seems to like to place some of his favorite lines in the mouths of minor characters.

Prisoner Bobynin, an engineer, is one such. When confronted by him, Colonel Yakonov catches himself feeling a "craven desire to play up to this zek, to avoid irritating him" (p. 61).

The inner quality of Bobynin elicits from the author this comment: "One can build the Empire State Building, discipline the Prussian Army, elevate the state hierarchy above the throne of the Almighty, but one cannot get past the unaccountable spiritual superiority of certain people" (p. 61).

Bobynin's demonstration of spiritual superiority comes when he is called on the carpet by Abakumov. When Abakumov calls in Bobynin to press for faster work on the vocoder, Bobynin is uncowed:

> I have nothing, you understand—not a thing! . . . You took my freedom away long ago, and you don't have the power to return it because you don't have it yourself. I am forty-two years old, and you've dished me out a twenty-five-year term. I've already been at hard labor, gone around with a number on, in handcuffs, with police dogs, and in a strict-regime work brigade. What else is there you can threaten me with? What can you deprive me of? My work as an engineer? You'll lose more than I will. I'm going to have a smoke. (pp. 95-96)

Bobynin is not finished. This invisible zek, an "insect" according to official view, shouts at the still uncomprehending Abakumov, "Just understand one thing and pass it along to anyone at the top who still doesn't know that you are strong only as long as you don't deprive people of *everything*. For a person you've taken *everything* from is no longer in your power. He's free all over again" (p. 96).

Another minor character who seems to speak favorite lines of the author is Gerasimovich. When offered early release if he will make a tiny camera to be installed in a door frame to record all who pass through, he is so sure that the device will be put to evil use that he flatly rejects the offer. He could, he knows, have bluffed, have rejected the assignment, or even remained silent. Instead, he bellows, "Putting people in prison is not my field! I don't set traps for human beings! It's bad enough that they put *us* in prison . . ." (p. 583).

Khorobrov was so nauseated by the injustices he observed that he scrawled crude curses against Stalin on his ballot form in the first post-war elections. Of course, he was arrested; but

"he went off to camp with a simple-hearted feeling of gladness—
at least there he could speak out as he pleased" (p. 62). He had
never celebrated Christmas or Easter, but "out of contrariness
he had begun to observe them in prison" (p. 189). In protest
against Marxist ideology, he instinctively reaches for something
religious.

Another interesting character in Solzhenitsyn's gallery is
Spiridon, who belongs to the spiritual world of Matryona and
of Ivan Denisovich. It was to Spiridon that Nerzhin turned when
he explored the possibility of "going to the people" and learning
to live according to the folk wisdom of the Russian peasants.
Spiridon is totally blind in one eye and has only thirty percent
vision in the other, but he has that superior commodity of spiritual insight. Work provides a release from the burdens of the
heart, and he displays "the bright determination of a man accustomed to suffering" (p. 498). Nerzhin's view of Spiridon is
that "everything about his concept of virtue fitted together
without forcing. He did not slander anyone. He never lied about
anyone" (p. 460). The concrete center of his values was the family. "His country was—family. His religion was—family. Socialism was—family" (p. 461).

Nerzhin asks Spiridon an abstract question: ". . . what
standards are we to use in trying to understand life? For example, are there really people on earth who consciously want
to do evil?" (p. 465). Spiridon does not deal in abstractions. He
answers with the concreteness of a proverb: ". . . the wolfhound
is right and the cannibal is wrong!" (p. 466). While this reply
baffles Nerzhin, Spiridon seems to be expressing a close-to-the-
earth philosophy of living in harmony with nature. The
wolfhound, even when rapacious, never violates the order of
nature, while the cannibal, who preys on his own kind, does. In
so speaking, Spiridon takes his place in a long and honorable
tradition, which includes even Shakespeare: "Blow, blow, thou
winter wind. / Thou art not so unkind / As man's ingratitude."[16]

Nerzhin concludes, finally, that he cannot simply adopt
a peasant outlook on life, that peasants have no inherent moral
superiority. But the portrait of Spiridon remains, if not an ideal

to be imitated, yet a very sympathetic characterization. He embodies the old Russian peasantry at its best.

While pictures of zeks dominate Solzhenitsyn's gallery, the novel also includes depictions of characters on the outside. One of the most flattering is that of Gleb Nerzhin's wife, Nadya.[17] The wife of another zek advises her to be unfaithful, lest her husband, when released, think that no one had wanted her and therefore value her the less. But so loyal is she that when Nerzhin himself advises her to forget him and to marry someone else, she can only conclude, "That means you've stopped loving me!" (p. 233). Still, out of pity for her deprived husband she urges him to be "unfaithful to me, see other women. After all, you will be returning to me, won't you?" (p. 242).

One of the most heinous results of the Soviet system of "justice" is its interference with such an elemental human matter as love. Nerzhin reflects, "You lived for years without the one thing men were put on earth for" (p. 291). When he learns that Nadya will soon be allowed to pay him an unexpected visit, he suddenly realizes "that Stalin had robbed him and Nadya of their children" (p. 231). Prison may provide the opportunity for growth through suffering, but the disfigurement of human lives is an inescapable part of its effect:

> You are left whatever intelligence you might have had, your convictions if you were mature enough to possess any, and, above all, your readiness for sacrifice and your concern for public welfare. You would appear to be an Athenian citizen, humanity's ideal.
>
> But there is no core to it.
>
> The love of a woman, of which you are deprived, seems worth more than anything in the world. (pp. 291-92)

And if perchance a couple is reunited after many years of separation? One cannot step into the same river twice: things will not be the same.

> Nadya had written in her letter: "When you return. . . ." But that was the whole horror: that there would be no *return*. One could not go *back*. After fourteen years at the front line and

in prison there would probably not be a single cell of his body left from the past. They could only come together all over again. A new, unfamiliar person would walk in bearing the name of her husband, and she would see that man, her beloved, for whom she had shut herself up to wait for fourteen years, no longer existed, had evaporated, molecule by molecule. (p. 232)

Indeed, Nadya notices that Gleb is not the same, though she decides that the changes are for the good: "On the visits it was impossible to recognize him. As with all self-assertive people, misfortune had a good effect on him. He softened . . ." (p. 241).

One reason why Gleb and Nadya cannot visit regularly is that he has refused to give the authorities her address; she is a student, and knowledge that she was married to a zek would be used to force her out of school. So the information that she has somehow arranged a visit quite surprises him. The visit is one of the memorable scenes of the novel. Much of its high emotion is conveyed through the couple's simply looking at each other.

Under Gleb's first searching, embracing look, "Nadya stirred . . . and seemed to rise to meet him" (p. 252). Gleb observes with pathos "the breasts which had lost their firmness in the course of the years" (p. 252). By a glance she asks him if she is homely, and by a replying glance he indicates that she is *"just as wonderful as ever"* (p. 252). A new and profoundly provoking rule is that visiting husband and wife may not hold hands or kiss, and a guard stands by to deprive the couple of the simplest intimacy. The "conversation" proceeds through communicative eyes. His look asks if she is still his, and her look replies affirmatively. When she ventures the subject of a divorce so that she can continue her studies, he approves "in a voice of firm conviction" (p. 255). But she does not want that answer at all; she pleads that he not take her hopes away: "Her upper lip trembled, her face was distorted, her eyes expressed loyalty, only loyalty" (p. 256).

As their unexpected visit is unexpectedly cut short, he responds to a question of hers by saying, "Only God knows"

(p. 258). Gleb's reply troubles his Soviet wife: "Don't tell me you've started believing in God?" (p. 258). He responds enigmatically, "Pascal, Newton, Einstein" (p. 258), thereby echoing inchoately a lesson learned from a professor-friend who had explained that all the great scientists believed in God. (The obtuse guard, hearing Gleb's answer, tells him that the rules forbid mentioning names!) Breaking the rules, Gleb gives Nadya a kiss and a hug and tells her to "do what is best for you" (p. 258). As she leaves, she waves good-bye "with the fingers of her ringless hand" (p. 258). The visit ends. Gleb goes back to replay the visit in his mind. He imagines that her last wave of the ringless hand "was how people say good-bye to one another forever" and that "once divorced she would not even notice anything strange when she remarried" (p. 292).

In polyphonic fashion, the visit between Gleb and Nadya is set off by the visit, in the following chapter, between Gerasimovich and his wife. She has not borne up well under her burden: "One might imagine that she was the one who had been in prison" (p. 261). She has lost her attractiveness and, just recently, her job. Now she is struggling with the decision of whether to disavow her husband and, so, shed her burden. That is the self-pitying, unsupportive word she has for her suffering husband. Some, inexplicably, grow through suffering; others, understandably enough, collapse under the pressure.

After the visit with Gleb, Nadya returns to the apartment which she shares with other female students. Amidst the hubbub she tries to meditate on Gleb. Apart from him, "there was no one, no one at all, who could understand her" (p. 327). Yet, as she reflects upon the visit, she thinks that he, too, may not understand. "He had failed to tell her anything—what to do, how she should live. He had only said there would be no end to his term" (p. 327). In that case, he no longer needs her, and she is left utterly alone in the world. Also, Gleb's apparent new religiosity confuses her. "And hadn't he said something about God—some phrase or other? Prison was crippling his spirit, leading him off into idealism, mysticism, teaching him submissiveness. He was changing; when he came back, she wouldn't know him any more" (p. 318). She is correct, of course, in seeing the change in him, but her Soviet-formed outlook keeps her from evaluating it positively.

In order to continue her studies, Nadya has kept her marriage a secret, even from a gentleman, Shchagov, she allows to call on her. "Oh, she just wanted to have the illusion, for one evening, of somebody taking her somewhere" (p. 330). Shchagov recognizes that Nadya is less interested in him than he is in her, and his affections have drifted elsewhere; he has come this evening to tell her that he is engaged to another.

This second visit for Nadya in one day is another of the novel's truly moving passages. When Shchagov tells her of his engagement, she finally, after five years, confesses that she has a husband who is alive—and, further, that she saw him today at the prison. She feels a loss here: "She stood like someone crucified on the black cross of the window. There had been one tiny little warm spot in her life, and it was gone" (p. 337). But she feels also a compensating gain: "She was her husband's wife again" (p. 337). When Shchagov bolts from the room, Nadya is sure that she has offended him. But he has gone to fetch wine and glasses, and he returns to propose a toast: "Well, soldier's wife . . . don't lose heart! . . . If you've got a good head on your shoulders, there'll be happiness yet. Let's drink—*to the resurrection of the dead*!" (p. 337). The biblical imagery is hardly casual.

The link between the telephone call by Innokenty Volodin in the novel's opening chapter and the vocoder project at Mavrino is the narrative device which allows Solzhenitsyn to bring in the characters from outside the sharashka who make up the Makarygin family, into which Innokenty has married. A sister of Innokenty's wife is a civilian worker in the sharashka. The daughter of prosecutor Makarygin, Clara has been warned about the dangerous criminals who inhabit the sharashka. But when she meets a rascally young zek named Ruska Doronin, she finds herself attracted. She is stirred by his story of being arrested simply for fishing with Americans from the U.S. Embassy. Clara's independent attitude disturbs her father. She scoffs at the literature of socialist realism which she must study; it deals "with everything on earth except what one could see with one's own eyes" (p. 275).[18] Innokenty is the only family member with whom she can speak freely.

Clara tries to talk with Alexei Lansky, a young member of the Union of Soviet Writers who "did not so much write himself as reject other writers" (p. 284). Her efforts prove unsatisfactory. Lansky is a thoroughly indoctrinated Marxist and explains in the language of collectivist, progressive ideology:

> ... it's time to get used to the fact that there is a law of big numbers. The bigger the scope of an historical event, the greater the probability of individual errors. ... We grasp the process only in its basic, determining forms, and the essential thing is to be convinced that this process is inevitable and necessary. Yes, sometimes someone suffers. Not always deservedly. ... Wisdom lies in accepting the process as it develops, with its inevitable increment of victims. (pp. 284-85)

Clara, having met persons of worth who are incarcerated in the sharashka, can only splutter, "The law of big numbers should be tried out on you!" (p. 285). Even those reared under Communism can slip the traces, for they share a common humanity with Communism's victims.

Ruska is more than ordinarily mischievous. He thinks up a scheme in which he will turn ostensible informer so that he can find out for his fellow zeks who are the real informers. He is temporarily successful in this feat of bravado, thanks to the human solidarity the zeks exhibit: although almost half of the prison population is let in on the secret of his double-agent role, no one turns him in. Many consider him foolhardy, but all admire and protect him. "Much has been written to prove that people on the whole are ungrateful and disloyal. But the opposite turns out to be the case, too" (p. 558). Human nature is a mixed thing; nobility and baseness coinhabit the human breast.

Although he appears seldom in *The First Circle*, Innokenty Volodin is an important figure. His early and late appearances structurally enclose the novel. The few days which the novel covers catch him at a crucial moment of personal growth.

This privileged and comfortably situated young official, at thirty years of age, cannot achieve real maturity in just a few days, but he shows himself to be on the way as he starts down the path of suffering so familiar to veteran zeks.

Innokenty and his wife Dotnara, another daughter of prosecutor Makarygin, had seemed perfectly happy and well matched when they were married six years earlier. His phone call to Dr. Dobroumov, which opens the novel, is the culmination of his growing dissatisfaction with the self-indulgent life to which he had become accustomed. Epicurus, on whom Karl Marx himself had written a dissertation, had once seemed the embodiment of earthly wisdom. However, after Innokenty's arrest and interrogation—reminiscent of the generalized accounts of those experiences in the early chapters of *Gulag Archipelago*—epicureanism comes to sound like "the philosophy of a savage": ". . . the wisdom of the ancient philosopher seemed like the babbling of a child" (p. 643). Somewhat earlier, Innokenty had arrived at the view that "a great writer is, so to speak, a second government. That's why no regime anywhere has ever loved its great writers, only its minor ones" (p. 415). Not surprisingly, many commentators have applied this sentiment to Solzhenitsyn himself. But, more important, the innocent Innokenty has "acquired a new understanding of life" (p. 624). As he contrasts his old comfortable ways with his new straitened circumstances, he concludes: "He had had money, good clothes, esteem, women, wine, travel, but at this moment he would have hurled all those pleasures into the nether world for justice and truth . . . and nothing more" (p. 630). One's devotion to spiritual values grows as his commitment to material values declines.

The polyphonic structure of *The First Circle* allows Solzhenitsyn to reach out and create two scenes which feature Western observers of the Soviet reality—in both cases, well-meaning secular humanists who embody those Enlightenment-derived ideals which Solzhenitsyn has repeatedly castigated in his later lectures, most overtly in his commencement speech at Harvard. Given the strong reaction of Western commentators to some of the later speeches, it is surprising how little criticism has been evoked by the devastating depictions of Western liberals in *The First Circle*.

"Buddha's Smile" is a story told by Nerzhin and another zek, Potapov, to their fellow zeks. It concerns a visit by Mrs. R—— and "two venerable Quaker matrons" to "America's brilliant Ally" to see if U.S. aid to the Soviet Union was being spent as intended and also "to see whether freedom of conscience was being violated in the Soviet Union" (pp. 386-87). Mrs. R—— , widow of a famous American statesman, is a very thinly veiled protrait of Eleanor Roosevelt. In fact, the visit to Cell 72 is based on an actual visit in 1945 to Butyrskaya Prison. The officials stage-manage the whole tour, as everyone but the gullible visitors knows. The zeks are allowed good soap for baths, good haircuts, even incipient beards and sideburns. They are given edible potatoes. (At this point, the zeks being regaled with the story by Nerzhin and Potapov complain that it is not true to life!) Plank beds and the bedbugs are removed, and in their place are put good bunks with feather-stuffed comforters, blankets, sheets, and feather pillows. Good clothing is laid out. The dark olive walls are pointed an off-white. And on and on. In a corner are placed an icon of the Virgin Mary with Child and a large icon lamp. Bookshelves are put in place; they contain the Bible, the Koran, and the Talmud—even a copy of the magazine *Amerika*.

As the zeks finally learn why their cell has been transformed, Mrs. R—— and friends enter this Potemkin-village-like cell. "Mrs. R—— was very pleased that the cell which had been chosen at random . . . was so amazingly clean and free of flies, and that an icon lamp was burning in the right-hand corner even though it was a weekday" (p. 387). Many surprises await Mrs. R—— . A prisoner is reading *Amerika*, "very hurriedly, for some reason" (p. 387). She is informed that one prisoner was "an active Hitlerite who burned a Russian village, and if you'll forgive my speaking of such things, raped three Russian peasant girls. The number of children he killed will probably never be known." When Mrs. R—— asks if he has been sentenced to

death, she hears, "No, we hope he will reform. He has been
sentenced to ten years of honest labor" (pp. 387-88). The prisoner wishes to protest but chooses not to interrupt his reading
of *Amerika*. Next, a Russian Orthodox priest enters, shoves a
pocket gospel at one startled zek, and says to another, "My son,
last time you asked me to tell you about the sufferings of our
Lord, Jesus Christ" (p. 388). When a row breaks out among some
zeks who are trying to cadge some Kazbek cigarettes, put out
for show only, Mrs. R—— inquires. She receives this "free"
translation of their "genuine indignation": "They unanimously
protest against the serious predicament of Negroes in America
and demand that the Negro question be submitted to the United
Nations" (p. 388). Pretty, young waitresses then serve chicken
noodle soup, and the "canine stance" of the zeks as each seeks
his share shocks the lady guests; but the interpreter explains
that their behavior is "a Russian national custom" (p. 389).

"Having convinced herself of the falsity of the innuen-
does spread by hostile people in the West," Mrs. R—— prepares
to leave. The visit has shaken her only slightly: "But how crude
their manners are! And how low the developmental level of
these unfortunates! One must hope, however, that in the course
of ten years here they will become accustomed to culture. You
have a magnificent prison!" (p. 389).

As soon as the American guests leave, life returns to normal
in Cell 72. There is a body search. The Sermon on the Mount, torn
out of a pocket gospel, is found inside a zek's cheek; he is forthwith
beaten first on one cheek and then on the other, a clever playing
upon the biblical reference about turning the other cheek. The
nice hair styles are promptly destroyed by shaving. Only an over-
looked Buddha, smiling enigmatically in a corner, remains as a
reminder of the just-concluded charade.

Malcolm Muggeridge, a devoted admirer of Solzhenitsyn,
has commented on this section:

> ... sentimentally virtuous people like Lord Halifax and Mrs.
> Roosevelt do far more harm in the world than recognisable
> villains. Solzhenitsyn has provided the perfect parable on this
> theme. ... The estimable lady, who spawned the moral plat-

itudes of the contemporary liberal wisdom as effortlessly and plenteously as the most prolific salmon, was easily persuaded that the camp in question was a humanely conducted institution for curing the criminally inclined. A truly wicked woman would have been ashamed to be so callous and so gullible.[19]

The author shows a similar pained derision toward Western liberals in the final chapter of the novel. It is entitled "Meat," another reference to dehumanization. Some zeks, including Gleb Nerzhin, are to be transported from the relative comfort of Mavrino to the lower circles of the hell that is the Gulag Archipelago. As they prepare to depart, Solzhenitsyn says *in propria persona*, "May they rest in peace, O Lord, those who did not arrive!" (p. 649). As Nerzhin now destroys his notes on history, Solzhenitsyn offers a sobering thought, in a work which, against great odds, has become published:

> The great library at Alexandria burned. In the monasteries they did not surrender but burned the chronicles. And the soot of the Lubyanka chimneys—soot from burned papers and more and more burned papers—fell upon the zeks led out to stroll in the boxlike area of the prison roof.
>
> Perhaps more great thoughts have been burned than have been published. (p. 655)

There is no doubt that the prisoners about to be transported are going back to an inhumane setting. When the blustering Khorobrov seeks consolation for leaving the sharaskha, Nerzhin, ever the steady-eyed observer, clarifies, in words echoing the novel's opening pages, "We are returning to hell. The sharashka is the highest, the best, the first circle of hell. It was almost a paradise" (p. 673). All of the zeks who are about to be transported know that Nerzhin speaks the truth, even Khorobrov. Further, they have achieved the peace of fearlessness: "They were filled with the fearlessness of those who have lost *everything*, the fearlessness which is not easy to come by but which endures" (p. 673).

Alas, there is, however, the view of a secular Westerner

of this system which alters precious human lives. A correspondent of the French newspaper *Liberation*, driving a shiny maroon automobile, sees vans with *Meat* printed on their sides in four languages. They are carrying zeks. Without doing the minimal investigation—and presumably following his ideological predilections—he serenely sends off his report for back-home consumption: "On the streets of Moscow one often sees vans filled with foodstuffs, very neat and hygienically impeccable. One can only conclude that the provisioning of the capital is excellent" (p. 674).

And so the novel ends. A representative of well-meaning secularism is unable to imagine the great evil which other heirs of the Enlightenment have visited upon their fellow human beings. But some zeks have, with spiritual main force, appropriated for themselves that moral energy which inheres in the Great Tradition and its view of what it means to be human. Only in such spiritual and moral terms can *The First Circle* ultimately be understood aright.

7

THE MYSTERY OF SUFFERING:

Cancer Ward

Solzhenitsyn began writing *Cancer Ward* after finishing *One Day* but while still working on *First Circle*. He completed *Cancer Ward* in 1967. Like these other two novels, it is rooted in autobiographical experience. Like *First Circle*, it was never published in the Soviet Union.

Cancer Ward and *First Circle* are in some ways companion pieces, as their overlapping times of composition might suggest. There are, of course, differences. Gleb Nerzhin is a more thoroughly autobiographical character than Oleg Kostoglotov. Oleg is intellectually somewhere between the peasant Ivan Denisovich and the professional Gleb Nerzhin, and his biographical data are always a bit askew from his author's: born in 1920 instead of Solzhenitsyn's (and Gleb's) 1918, contracting cancer in 1955 instead of 1953, single instead of married. *Cancer Ward* spans four months, compared with *First Circle*'s four days. *Cancer Ward* is symbolically and metaphorically richer, less politically argumentative. The sufferings recorded in it are not a direct result of a corrupt social situation.

But the similarities between these two novels are more

significant than the differences. Both are long, polyphonic novels. Both emphasize characterization. Both focus on human suffering. Both depict a wide range of the Soviet citizenry. Both are set, generally, in the post-war Soviet Union and, specifically, in places of confinement. Most important, both embody Solzhenitsyn's moral and religious point of view.

The story of Solzhenitsyn's attempts to publish *Cancer Ward* in the Soviet Union is a fascinating one, for it marked definitively the end of his brief period of acceptability. Once again, it was Tvardovsky's *Novy Mir* which sought permission to publish. Two major meetings on the subject were convened, one quite positive, the other very negative.

At the meeting of the prose section of the Moscow writers' organization on November 17, 1966, writer after writer praised *Cancer Ward* effusively, much to Solzhenitsyn's undisguised delight. While Solzhenitsyn hotly denied that the novel was pessimistic, he responded warmly to suggestions such as that he place more distance between himself and Oleg Kostoglotov. For once, Solzhenitsyn had been able to break out of his isolation to be treated kindly by his literary colleagues; he was magnanimous and euphoric. The meeting ended with the passing of a resolution urging the prompt publication of *Cancer Ward*.

The euphoria was short-lived. A half-year passed, and nothing happened. Impatiently, Solzhenitsyn circulated an open letter, dated May 16, 1967, explaining his grievance. As he since has done often, he led with his chin: "I am of course confident that I will fulfill my duty as a writer in all circumstances—from the grave even more successfully and more irrefutably than in my lifetime. No one can bar the road to truth, and to advance its cause I am prepared to accept even death."[1]

On September 22, 1967, a second meeting was held to discuss *Cancer Ward*.[2] This time hard-liners dominated; they were hostile and acrimonious, and Solzhenitsyn responded pugnaciously. One critic asked how, given the presence of nuclear weapons in the United States, Soviet writers could choose other than to be soldiers, and he challenged Solzhenitsyn to "do battle against the foes of our nation."[3] Another complained that *Cancer Ward* approached fundamental problems "not in philosophical terms but in political terms."[4] This insistence on politicizing his fiction has been the bane of Solzhenitsyn's career and the primary distortion of his significance, both in the East and in the West. The same critic observed: ". . . the works of Solzhenitsyn are more dangerous to us than those of Pasternak: Pasternak was a man divorced from life, while Solzhenitsyn, with his animated, militant, ideological temperament, is a man of principle."[5] Another critic called on him to renounce *Cancer Ward*; and yet another exclaimed, "I'd expel him from the Union [of Soviet Writers]"[6]—which advice was eventually taken. The editor of *Pravda* intoned, "If he writes stories which correspond to the interests of our society, then his works will be published. He will not be deprived of his bread and butter. Solzhenitsyn is a teacher of physics; let him teach."[7]

Solzhenitsyn was, naturally, indignant at this hostile reception. He denied that he was a political writer or the leader of a political opposition. While it may be easy to identify with Solzhenitsyn in this confrontation, it is necessary also to see that these doctrinaire critics were, given their presuppositions, responding correctly to Solzhenitsyn. For, although he was accurate in saying that he was not a political writer, his worldview was undeniably alien to theirs and would have an impact on the stability of the Soviet political system.

The two conferences about *Cancer Ward* were crucially significant in the story of Solzhenitsyn. The first showed how close he came to parlaying that fluke success of the publication of *One Day* into standard acceptance as an author to be published. The second definitively placed him outside the bounds of acceptability and into his role as a dissident writer. Of all of the crises in Solzhenitsyn's life, only his prior conversion from Marxism to Christianity seems more profound than this one. It outweighs even the trauma of his exile in 1974.

The story of these two meetings is also critically important for discerning how to read Solzhenitsyn's fiction. It must be remembered that always he was hoping for publication in the Soviet Union. While this concern in no way caused him to write things which he did not believe, surely he always had one eye out for the censors. His delicate task was to express himself honestly, yet without running afoul of the authorities. Knowledge of this history should heighten the awareness of readers of everything that Solzhenitsyn has written up through *Cancer Ward*. In retrospect, it may have been a relief to Solzhenitsyn, possibly even a boon to his art, to have had the matter decided clearly, even if unfavorably. From now on, he could write what he thought—let the censors be damned.

The central theme of *Cancer Ward* is as broad as that of *The First Circle*. It is, as stated by a collection of Tolstoy stories to which Solzhenitsyn alludes, What do men live by? The author places his characters *in extremis*, in a cancer ward, where they cannot avoid facing their own possibly impending and certainly inevitable deaths. Each character must, like Alex in *Candle in the Wind*, seek a philosophy of life which allows him to cope with death. Souls in disarray will, of course, fail this test. The contemporary Soviet setting is simply what Solzhenitsyn knows firsthand, and it should not obscure the basic fact that life and death come to everyone and that this novel explicates the "universal law: everyone who *acts* breeds both good and evil. With some it's more good, with others more evil."[8]

Cancer, like rain, falls on the just and the unjust alike, and Solzhenitsyn carefully avoids having "bad" characters die and "good" characters recover. For instance, the cowardly, self-deceiving bureaucrat, Rusanov, leaves the hospital in passable health, even though his self-congratulation for courage shows that he has not grown through his suffering.

As has been observed, *Cancer Ward*, like *The First Circle*, is a polyphonic novel. So, although Solzhenitsyn seems again to have a favorite character—Oleg Kostoglotov, whose life story is in some respects similar to that of the author (war, prison, cancer)—this character does not receive significantly more space than several other characters. And, again, the gallery of characters is large. There are patients, doctors and nurses, and friends and relatives outside the place of confinement—all quite parallel to characters as ordered in *The First Circle*.

Although Oleg Kostoglotov lacks the trained intellect of Gleb Nerzhin, he is every bit the humanist. His highest accolade for another is, "He was a good man. A human being" (p. 31). This rough-hewn, uneducated man has an urbane manner and a taste for life. He prefers living in a mud hut to living in "a five-story cage" in the city (p. 36). He is not an unreflective peasant; he thinks and questions. Knowing that no matter how much he learns he will still die a fool, he likes his grandfather's motto: "A fool loves to teach, but a clever man loves to learn" (p. 116). This life-affirming figure still knows that one part of the human process is death, and he scorns those materialists whose outlook deprives man of his innate dignity: "After all, what does our philosophy of life boil down to? 'Oh, life is so good! . . . Life, I love you. Life is for happiness!' What profound sentiments. Any animal can say as much without our help, any hen, cat, or dog" (p. 137). So he talks openly about death, including his own. He is not morbid. He hopes that he can gain enough health to "make use of it a little and live" (p. 51). He is no simple clinger to life; this young man of thirty-five would settle for six months which could be lived to the full.

Oleg's balance between loving to live and being prepared to die undergirds his conversations with the doctors. He rejects the "logical deduction" of one doctor that he came to her "to be saved *at any price!*" (p. 75). He insists on "my right to dispose of my own life" (p. 74). He says that his prison camp experience has helped him to see through the notion that one "should cling to life at any cost" (p. 295). Specifically, he would choose to die rather than to undergo treatments which would emasculate him. His sense of responsibility for himself is offended by even the best-intentioned doctors' Grand-Inquisitor-like paternalism: "No sooner does a patient come to you than you begin to do all his thinking for him. . . . And once again I become a grain of sand, just as I was in the camp. Once again nothing *depends* on me" (p. 74). Doctors are generally treated sympathetically in this novel, as engineers and doctors generally are treated by Solzhenitsyn. But, if it is a choice between *his* impotency and *his* death, then Oleg should be the one who decides, not some doctor.

The reason why Oleg can take such a position is that he has learned the hard lesson of human finitude. As he says, "A certain philosopher once said, if a man never became ill he would never get to know his own limitations" (p. 148). So he sets limited goals for himself: ". . . to live just a little while without guards and without pain, simultaneously without one or the other" (pp. 294-95).

This lesson of human finitude entails an acceptance of death, and this acceptance leads Solzhenitsyn directly to religious thoughts, even if in the mouth of one who is not overtly religious. Oleg reminisces:

> This autumn I learned from experience that a man can cross the threshold of death even when his body is still not dead. Your blood still circulates and your stomach digests, while you yourself have gone through the whole psychological preparation for death—and lived through death itself. Everything around you, you see as if from the grave. And although you've never counted yourself a Christian, indeed the very opposite sometimes, all of a sudden you find you've forgiven all those who trespassed against you and bear no ill-will toward those who persecuted you. (p. 31)

Similarly, as Kostoglotov imagines the possibility of leaving the hospital, Solzhenitsyn puts into his mind the biblical phrasing, "Take up thy bed and walk!" (p. 260).

Like Gleb Nerzhin of *The First Circle*, Oleg Kostoglotov learns to value human solidarity. He muses, ". . . what did they have to quarrel over? They all had the same enemy, death. What can divide human beings on earth once they are all faced with death?" (p. 144). In prison an old professor of classics enjoyed giving Oleg Latin lessons because "for a brief time, they made him [the professor] feel like a human being" (p. 116). A sense of community validates individual worth and is vital to one's sense of humanity.

The patient who is Kostoglotov's primary antagonist is Pavel Nikolayevich Rusanov, a Soviet bureaucrat. Although he believes wholeheartedly in the state's egalitarian doctrine, once in the cancer ward he looks with disdain on "the eight abject beings who were now his 'equals' " (p. 9) and is upset that he is treated "just like anyone else" (p. 1). The ideology he and his family profess turns out not to be congruent with genuine human solidarity:

> The Rusanovs loved the People, their great People. They served the People and were ready to give their lives for the People.
> But as the years went by they found themselves less and less able to tolerate actual human beings, those obstinate creatures who were always resistant, refusing to do what they were told and, besides, demanding something for themselves. (p. 193)

Rusanov is successful in Stalin's mediocrity-breeding society, but he has not developed the inner resources to cope with adversity. In his moment of crisis, he resorts to whining self-pity and even to denying reality: "I have no cancer whatsoever" (p. 8). He is a pusillanimous man who scoffs at Kostoglotov's speculation about self-induced healing through the powers of the mind, calling the notion "sheer religious rubbish" (p. 135), then a few pages later entertaining the irrational hope that as a true son of Russia he might be cured by some simple Russian folk remedy.

The characterization of Rusanov demonstrates the moral bankruptcy of collectivist ideology. The ideology subordinates individual consciousness to identification with the group. Yet, as Kostoglotov wryly notes, "When the time comes for . . . [a man] to die, we release him from the collective. He may be a member, but he has to die alone. It's only he who is saddled with the tumor, not the whole collective" (p. 137). Rusanov has always defined himself in terms of the collective unit. His illness makes manifest the inadequacy of that self-definition: "He was no longer a vital cog in a large, important mechanism. In fact, he felt he had lost all power and significance" (p. 396). In a novel examining what men live by, he who cannot die well has not lived well. Rusanov fails the test.

Not only is collectivist ideology detrimental to the development of individual dignity, but it does not even encourage a benevolent sense of human solidarity. Rusanov, who remembers the Great Purge of 1937-38 as "that excellent and honorable time" (p. 188), has informed on many, including a man who shared his apartment. Now he hears with dismay that persons who have served their prison terms are being allowed to reenter society. "They'd grown used to being where they were, they were resigned to it—why let them come back here and upset people's lives?" (pp. 194-95). Rusanov's real fear is that his old apartment-mate will return and wreak physical revenge on him. In a departure from his usual métier of surface realism, Solzhenitsyn then describes Rusanov's delirious dream. This dream, recounted in the chapter entitled "Absurdities," effectively shows Rusanov's suppressed sense of guilt about denouncing others, his fear that new purges may touch him, and his moral deficiency in general.

The characterization of Rusanov is sharpened by his reactions to his two children. The father approves fully when daughter Aviette declares, "After all, one's whole life is bound up with the collective, not with isolated personalities" (p. 282). By contrast, Rusanov is puzzled and angered by son Yuri, a lawyer, who explains that he has tried to deal informally and unofficially with a petty infraction in order to save the offender a harsh sentence; Rusanov considers the action stupid, not compassionate. He senses that Aviette will get along in the system and that Yuri will not.

The character of Rusanov has caused a stir among Soviet critics, starting with that friendly first meeting about *Cancer Ward*. When some expressed the opinion that the depiction was unrelievedly negative and thus not accurate, Solzhenitsyn expressed willingness to revise and to add moral shadings. Both Solzhenitsyn and the critics seemed to be acknowledgeing implicitly that Rusanov is not an isolated case but one representative of a class of bureaucrats. Actually, the depiction is not one of unrelieved evil. There are humane impulses in him. He is a conscientious father and husband. He seeks to do good, by

his lights. As the dream sequence shows, he has enough glim-
merings of moral sensibility to feel some twinges of guilt. He
feels some sorrow for his fellow patients. And, while he does
not handle his illness well, most readers will feel some pity for
him in his suffering. He may be the least likeable figure in the
novel, but his is the evil of weakness, not of strength. His moral
development has been severely stunted by the ideology which
has been forced upon him throughout his lifetime. His deficiency is marked by his succumbing to the pressures of an inhumane state, but that is a widespread deficiency. The real
villain is not Rusanov but the false world-view in which his life
has been enveloped. He is not thereby absolved of responsibility,
but Solzhenitsyn does include in the portrait those mitigating
circumstances which have contributed to make him who he
now is.

If Rusanov in his moral debility is an indictment of Soviet
ideology, an even more damning indictment comes with the
portrayal of Vadim, an idealistic young Communist. In Rusanov
we see moral warping in consummation; in Vadim we see it in
process. Vadim's case is all the more poignant for the genuineness of his passion to expend his life nobly.

As Vadim begins his stay in the cancer ward, he sounds
almost like Kostoglotov: "But living longer doesn't mean having
more life. The real question is, what will I have time to achieve?
. . . If they give me three years, I won't ask more than that"
(p. 199). He wants to devote his remaining days to understanding the world and doing good for others. He is quite ready to
"burn himself out in one great heroic deed for the benefit of the
people and all mankind" (p. 253).

However, Vadim's idealism is distorted by an interlarded
dose of egotism. He considers himself a man of talent, and with
that opinion in mind he speculates, "By dying young, a man
stays young forever in people's memory. If he burns brightly
before he dies, his light shines for all time" (p. 249). Vadim is
also self-deluded. His mind is occupied more with his own
imagined heroism than with the good of mankind. But when

the prospect of imminent death becomes real to Vadim, his reaction is not appreciably better than Rusanov's.

One proof of Vadim's ultimate moral inadequacy is seen
when he hears about the death of a wardmate but feels "no
sympathy for him" because he "had not been a valuable member
of society" (p. 257). Vadim's announced belief in individual worth
is superficial; he means only his own worth. And, as with Rusanov, Vadim's collectivist ideology does not issue in a genuine
sense of human community. There are hints in Vadim of the
philosophy of Sologdin in *The First Circle*, even though Vadim
has not freed himself from the constraints of Marxist ideology.

Vadim is set in contrast with another young cancer victim, Dyomka. Kostoglotov takes a liking to Dyomka, considers
him quite grown up for his age, and values what he considers
Dyomka's love for truth. It is his desire for truth which drives
Dyomka, in his adversity, to seek out his devout old Aunt Styofa
in spite of himself.

> Ever since he had been in the first class, before he could read
> or write, Dyomka had been taught, knew for certain and fully
> understood that religion is a drug, a three-time reactionary
> dogma, of benefit only to swindlers. . . . And Aunt Styofa with
> her funny calendar, with the word "God" always on her lips
> . . . was obviously a reactionary figure. (pp. 122-23)

Dyomka wants to think that a man's well-being in life depends
on himself, but the facts seem otherwise. Aunt Styofa, not given
to subtleties of thought, cannot unravel such puzzles. She can
only answer simply, "It depends on God. . . . God sees everything. You should submit to him, Dyomushka" (p. 121).

This answer does not satisfy Dyomka's need to explain
the mystery of suffering. "If he can see everything, why does he
load it all on one person? I think he ought to try to spread it
about a bit" (p. 122). Still, he sees no choice but to submit—if
not to God, then to the inevitable. Dyomka's attitude shares
much with that of Ivan Denisovich. Neither can accept the
religious consolation offered, though respectful of the source.
Yet neither is guilty of hubris, and both submit to the inevitable
rhythms of life, comprehensible or not.

Aunt Styofa is similar to Aunt Christine of *Candle in the Wind*. Both accept with faith the mysteries which enfold human life. Their outlooks are in keeping with the mystical emphasis of Russian Orthodoxy. In *Cancer Ward*, where the mystery of suffering is of paramount importance, Solzhenitsyn shows how different individuals react to it, but he does not try to offer some sort of rationally palatable disquisition on it.

Whereas Vadim finds the taste for pretty girls frivolous, Solzhenitsyn seems to suggest that Dyomka's liking of them is a life-affirming trait. It is similar to the fact that one sign of Oleg's return to life is his desire for contact with women. On the other hand, there is a kind of preoccupation with the body which is not truly life-affirming, because it magnifies one aspect, the physical, to the diminution of another, the spiritual.

Asya, a delicate, blonde, sexy young girl, exemplifies this imbalance. As she and Dyomka become friends, she speaks more freely than a proper young girl should. When Dyomka broaches the subject of the novel's central question, what people live for, she answers, "For love, of course. . . . What is there in life except love?" (p. 130). When she hears that he might have to have a leg amputated, she exclaims, "Don't let them do it. It's better to die than live without a leg. What sort of life is it for a cripple, do you think? Life is for happiness" (p. 128).

Ironically, her cancer is of the breast. When Asya learns the location of her cancer, she comes crying to Dyomka: "What have I got to live for? . . . Who in the world will w-w-want me n-n-now?" (p. 393). She tosses aside Dyomka's offer to marry her at any time, and instead seizes on one last little pleasure before her mastectomy: "You're the last one who can see and kiss it! . . . Dyomka, *you* at least must kiss it, if nobody else!" (p. 394). And so "he did what her future child would never be able to do. No one came in, and so he kissed and kissed the marvel hanging over him. Today it was a marvel. Tomorrow it would be in the trash bin" (p. 395).

Yefrem Podduyev is the character who, because of his recent reading, most explicitly brings into focus the novel's main theme of what men live by. All his life Podduyev had been a generally unpleasant man who lied, swore, and told dirty stories in profusion; now, fittingly enough, he has cancer of the tongue. He had used so many women that he had lost count. He is one of those "clingers to life" whom Kostoglotov disdains. "The whole of his life had prepared Podduyev for living, not for dying" (p. 94).

It is only in extremity that Podduyev will stop to think about the quality of his life. The prospect of dying terrifies him, but he recalls the dignified equanimity with which old folks back home faced death: "They didn't puff themselves up or fight against it or brag that they weren't going to die—they took death calmly. . . . And they departed easily, as if they were just moving into a new house. None of them would be scared by cancer" (p. 97).

With time now weighing heavily on him, Podduyev, or-dinarily a nonreader, starts fingering idly a book which he finds in the ward. It is Leo Tolstoy's collection of stories *What Men Live By*. Podduyev is shaken by what he reads. Whereas he had never felt guilt over his mistreatment of women because he had never regarded them as full-fledged human beings, ". . . accord-ing to this curious book it turned out that Yefrem was the one to blame for everything" (p. 101).

The book so fascinates him that he asks wardmates what they think men live by. One suggests rations. Another says, ". . . In the first place, air. Then—water. Then—food" (p. 102). Yefrem knows that he would have given a similarly mundane answer. "The only thing he might have added was booze" (p. 102). But now he senses that "this was not at all what the book was getting at" (p. 102). Other responses are equally shallow: one's pay, one's professional skill, one's homeland. Rusanov pontifi-cates that "people live by their ideological principles and by the interests of their society" (p. 103). Podduyev finds Tolstoy's an-swer preferable: ". . . people live not by worrying only about their own problems but by love of others" (p. 104). The ideo-logue Rusanov may scoff. But Podduyev has had a revelation. This rascal cannot achieve moral maturity overnight, but his eyes have been opened to a reality higher than physical gratification. Even an unlikely candidate can experience some growth through suffering.

Chaly, a newcomer to the ward, offers another way of facing life and death. He has a flippant optimism which, while disconcerting to some sufferers, pleases Rusanov, who, in the name of his ideology of optimism, can overlook Chaly's violation of rules about bribes and vodka. But the bluff and blustering Chaly, with his card playing and his macabre jokes about his cancer, is just an escapist who fails the moral test as surely as Rusanov, his admirer. He is all surface and no depth.

Shulubin is another newcomer to the hospital, but he receives much more space than Chaly because he has much more to contribute to the question of how one should live. Shulubin, a librarian, is an educated, cultured man who has thought deeply on the questions of individuality and community. Suffering from cancer of the rectum and facing a colostomy, this aloof figure is trying to prepare himself for that dreaded future in which his humiliating, offensive debility will cut him off from human fellowship. Although much of what he says coincides with Solzhenitsyn's own views, it is a mistake to see him, as some critics have done, as the authorial spokesman in this novel. Shulubin's opinions surface in conversation with Kostoglotov, who is the only wardmate whom Shulubin respects enough to take into his confidence. It is crucial to see those many points on which Shulubin and Solzhenitsyn agree and those relatively few, but vital, points on which they disagree.

Shulubin was an old Bolshevik who had fought in the Civil War. Whenever a so-called enemy of the people was put on public display, he dutifully joined the horde of condemners. Having come to recognize himself as a mere time server, he realizes the suppression of individuality involved. Consequently, he explains to Oleg: "Do you remember what they used to write in the papers? 'As one man the whole Soviet nation arose in indignation on hearing of the unprecedented, heinous crimes of. . . .' Do you know what 'as one man' meant for us? We were individual human beings, and then suddenly we were 'as one man'!" (pp. 432-33). Shulubin can no longer believe that those mass vilifications in which he participated were sincere: "I just cannot believe that our whole people suddenly became weak in the head" (p. 434). It was just that even intelligent people wanted most of all to survive. He declares that persons such as he should have stood outside and against that artificial and false sense of community. But he knows that most do not have the inner strength to resist that "more refined form of the herd instinct, the fear of remaining alone, *outside the community*" (p. 435). Even he had "bowed low and kept silent" (p. 436). The degeneration of his physical condition, the death of his wife, and the callousness of his grown children have combined to free Shulubin from his craven submissiveness before an illicit state authority. He had once "agreed to become a little man" (p. 438); he will do so no longer.

Yet Shulubin's rejection of a false community leads not to isolated individualism but to true community, that of universal human solidarity. He says to Oleg, "Sometimes I feel quite distinctly that what is inside me is not all of me. There's something else, sublime, quite indestructible, some tiny fragment of the universal spirit. Don't you feel that?" (p. 483). Both truth and happiness must be understood in terms of human solidarity. On the subject of truth, Shulubin affirms what Solzhenitsyn asserts in his *Nobel Lecture* and demonstrates in *August 1914*: "If decade after decade no one can tell the true story, each person's mind goes its own separate way. One's fellow countrymen become harder to understand than Martians" (p. 458). And, as for happiness, the effort to find it in isolation from others is "a mirage"; what is needed is "mutual affection": "A beast gnawing at its prey can be happy too, but only human beings can feel affection for each other, and this is the highest achievement they can aspire to" (p. 443). Shulubin's declaration that "one should never direct people toward happiness" (p. 443) is flatly at odds with the utopian collectivism of Stalin in *The First Circle*. The happiness which accompanies human communion will never come at the expense of individual dignity but will always enhance it. It is on the subject of human solidarity that Shulubin articulates ideas dear to Solzhenitsyn.

Shulubin is also on Solzhenitsyn's side when he elevates ethical values over material values. In a brief exchange between Shulubin and Vadim, the idealistic young Communist says that he finds science the most interesting of subjects. The cranky old librarian does not sneer at science per se, but he denies that by itself it can create anything that is ethically good. Vadim counters that the task of science is not to create ethical values but material values, then proceeds to ask what Shulubin means by ethical values. The answer is, "Values directed toward the mutual illumination of human souls" (p. 379). But, because there is no room in young Vadim's received world-view for the concept of soul, he can make no sense of Shulubin's response.

In some respects, Shulubin is similar to Lev Rubin of *The First Circle*. Both are old-line Bolsheviks who have grown through suffering. Yet Rubin, against all empirical evidence, remains loyal to the theory of Marxism, whereas Shulubin makes a substantial break with that ideology. But even Shulubin's break is not complete.

When Shulubin seeks to develop a social theory of his own, he labels it ethical socialism. Critics have been unaccountably quick to ascribe Shulubin's view directly to Solzhenitsyn. Such an ascription is a mistake. Several years after writing *Cancer Ward*, Solzhenitsyn commented on this matter of Shulubin's position of ethical socialism:

> In no socialist doctrine ... are moral demands seen as the essence of socialism—there is merely a promise that morality will fall like manna from heaven after the the socialization of property. Accordingly, nowhere on earth have we been shown ethical socialism in being (and indeed the juxtaposition of these two words, tentatively questioned by me in one of my books, has been severely condemned by responsible orators). In any case, how can we speak of ethical socialism, when we do not know whether what we are shown under that name is in fact socialism at all?[9]

We may conclude that if Solzhenitsyn was attracted to Shulubin's viewpoint, the attraction was both tentative and brief; the character can in no way be understood as the spokesman for the author's long considered and firmly held position. Furthermore, all of the evidence from the nonfiction pronouncements of the 1970's argues against viewing Solzhenitsyn as a socialist of any stripe. He never calls himself one. If he does not insist that he is an inveterate foe of any and all forms of socialism, the lesson to be learned—and a main theme of this whole study—is that he is not a political writer. Indeed, as we have seen in the chapter on the *Nobel Lecture*, he has explicitly disavowed that the writer's task is "to defend or criticize one or another mode of distributing the social product, or to defend or criticize one or another form of government organization."[10]

In addition to evidence external to *Cancer Ward* that Shulubin's ethical socialism is not to be ascribed directly to Solzhenitsyn, evidence from within the novel adds extra weight. Shulubin's insistence that "man is a biological type" (p. 440) sounds quite alien to Solzhenitsyn's emphasis on things spiritual. When, after hearing Shulubin out, Oleg asks if what the old Bolshevik is describing might not be called "Christian socialism," Shulubin recoils: "It's going too far to call it 'Christian' " (p. 441). He wants an ethical base for society but not one rooted in a religious view of life. Again, he sounds different from Solzhenitsyn. Finally, political and economic considerations loom large for Shulubin. He warns Oleg against making a major mistake: "Don't ever blame socialism for the sufferings and the cruel years you've lived through. However you think about it, history has rejected capitalism once and for all!" (p. 440). Shulubin adds, "Capitalism was doomed ethically before it was doomed economically, a long time ago" (p. 440). Once more, this sounds more like the old Bolshevik who Shulubin is than like Solzhenitsyn. Nowhere has Solzhenitsyn made the point, and the whole tenor of his railings against ideology in *Letter to the Soviet Leaders* and *From Under the Rubble* speaks to the opposite effect. It is the character, not the author, who cannot part with an economic analysis of society.

Nevertheless, if some distance must be set between Shulubin and Solzhenitsyn, it is certainly true that Shulubin has grown much and is to be admired. He has freed himself from the most confining of the shackles within which he has grown up and lived for all his life, and that is no mean feat. It is precisely because Shulubin exalts the ethical over the material that Oleg can ask if he is espousing a Christian socialism. Indeed, it may well be that in the very formulating of that question, Oleg is intuiting correctly the logical end of the matter before old Bolshevik Shulubin is ready to concede it. Solzhenitsyn would appreciate Shulubin's citation of the religious writer Vladimir Soloviev for his view of "ethics first and economics afterwards" (p. 442). Shulubin may be limited by his prior experience; but he has made much headway against great odds, and that is enough to make Solzhenitsyn's portrait of him a deeply appreciative one.

Cancer Ward is not only about patients but also about doctors and nurses, whom Solzhenitsyn depicts, on the whole, quite sympathetically. He has made himself surprisingly knowledgeable about medicine.

Two medical women are especially important in the novel as they impinge on the story of Oleg Kostoglotov: Vera, a doctor, and Zoya, a nurse. Both of them are attracted to this unusual man. The two represent different qualities which appeal to Oleg, and their names are symbolic. Vera stands for truth; Zoya, for life. But both transcend their symbolic values and become developed characters in their own right.

While Solzhenitsyn has never been timid about drawing female characters and describing male-female relationships, such relationships are more prominent in _Cancer Ward_ than in the other works, presumably because the hospital setting brings many men and many women into daily contact. Solzhenitsyn values human sexuality. One index of Oleg's state of health is his responsiveness to women.

On the other hand, it is always possible to abuse a good thing, including sexuality. In a chat with Vera, Oleg mentions the Soviet sex manuals available to them in their youth, and he expresses disdain at their strictly physiological view of life. He denies that "physiology is the sole cause of incompatibility" in marriage and asserts that "such consistent, logical, irrefutable materialism" misses the real point of married life (pp. 334-35). Solzhenitsyn always avoids a dualism of body and soul; sexuality is not inherently a foe of spirituality. Though Vera does not reply, she agrees exactly with Oleg. His blunt talk about sexual matters cheers her, even if she cannot find the right words to thank him.

Vera, we learn, is a young widow. She reflects now that she and her husband were not much more than children when they were married. He soon went off to the war and was killed. Now a grown woman in her prime, she cherishes the memory of her ever young lover and has remained faithful to that memory. She muses, "There is great satisfaction in remaining faithful; perhaps it is the greatest satisfaction of all. Even if no one knows about your faithfulness, even if no one values it" (p. 346). Yet she grieves, much like Nadya in *The First Circle*, that now "there was no one at all to advise her what to do or how to live" (p. 346).

As Vera becomes acquainted with Oleg, a new joy stirs within her. As he confides in her, she finds herself opening up and telling him things she had kept private for years. For instance, he is the only one who learns of the nickname her husband gave her: Vega—a combination of the first two letters of her first name, Vera, and the first two letters of her last, Gangart. From then on, Oleg calls her Vega. The mutual human sympathy and respect which these two establish overcomes even his disapproval of her insistence that he undergo treatments which might save his life but rob him of his libido.

Zoya's appeal for Oleg is different from Vega's. Vega is the older of the two women, and she represents stability and order for Oleg in his dislocation. She converses on a more intellectual plane than does Zoya. A vivacious and strikingly beautiful woman, Zoya has been intimate with more than one young man. "Still, it was never the real thing. It all lacked that stable, deliberate continuity which gives stability to life, indeed gives life itself" (p. 155). She finds in Oleg that steadiness in life which Oleg finds in Vega. "His stability and strength after all that he had endured were what Zoya sensed in him most keenly. His strength had been put to the test. It was something she had never met before in the boys she went with" (p. 168).

Zoya, too, begins to talk freely with Oleg. It is to him that she says that her name means *life*—and he does notice that "there was a certain force about Zoya" (p. 170). Solzhenitsyn gives us the scene of the first stolen kiss between Oleg and Zoya. Her affection for him causes her to tell him that the injections which he is to receive will, as a side effect, suppress his sexual potency. The desire remains but the ability departs; later, even the desire goes. Although she knows that the injections are a vital part of his treatment, she does not want him to have them.

Late in the novel, when Oleg is about to be released from the hospital, both Vega and Zoya offer Oleg overnight lodging at their apartments—and longer, if necessary—before he heads back to his own location in exile. The offers astonish him, and he feels that he does not understand women. What he may not be understanding is his own worth as seen by two people with similar aspirations toward true humanity. For both offers are made out of genuine compassion, not sexual calculation. Oleg had done them much good, and both seek to reciprocate. But the dehumanization of Gulag keeps its grip on its victims long after they depart: ". . . the icy world that had shaped Oleg's soul had not room for 'unpremeditated kindness.' He had simply forgotten that such a thing existed. Simple kindness seemed the most unlikely explanation of their having invited him" (p. 474).

The archetypal doctor in this novel is Ludmila Afanasyevna Dontsova, the superior of Vera Gangart. Solzhenitsyn implies approval of Dr. Dontsova's decision to remain a generalist rather than to become a narrow specialist. She forgoes personal gain and prestige in order to remain close to the elemental issues of life and death which are a doctor's reason for being.

It is this dedicated but shrewd doctor who finally argues Oleg into submitting to the treatments which might cost him his potency. "She was there to save life, no more and no less. . . . Ludmila Afanasyevna was unshakably convinced that any damage to the body was justified if it saved life" (p. 85). Dr. Dontsova's whole life is involved in making ethical decisions in that gray area where right and wrong are often unclear. If she and Oleg clash, both are life affirmers, and both are to be praised. And both give the lie to those fatuous strictures that *Cancer Ward* is a pessimistic, negative book.[11]

Ironically, Dr. Dontsova neglects her own health. When she feels stomach pains which she knows could be caused by overexposure to x-rays, she dallies, with what Solzhenitsyn calls "typical Russian temporizing" (p. 86). Cancer does not discriminate, and she is stricken by the very disease which she has given her life to fighting.

When Dr. Dontsova finally decides to tell someone about her stomach pains, she goes to her aging mentor, Dr. Oreshchenkov, whose advice and example had caused her to reject specialization. He had long ago turned aside from the self-gratifying prospect of becoming one of those "Honored Scientists" who "went about with a suite of followers, like some new Christ with his Apostles" (p. 416). The very nature of the human being was what kept him from becoming a specialized professor: ". . . the patient's organism isn't aware that our knowledge is divided into separate branches. You see, the organism isn't divided. . . . If you wanted to understand the patient as a single subject, there'd be no room left in you for any other passion. . . . The doctor should be a single subject as well. The doctor ought to be an all-rounder" (p. 425). In the same spirit, he rejects socialized medicine, misleadingly labeled free universal health service, because in practice it "isn't free treatment, it's depersonalized treatment" (p. 423).

The loss of his wife causes this seventy-five-year-old doctor to ponder deeply, and "an image of the whole meaning of existence" comes to his mind:

> The image he saw did not seem to be embodied in the work or activity which occupied them [family members and acquaintances], which they believed was central to their lives, and by which they were known to others. The meaning of

> existence was to preserve unspoiled, undisturbed and undistorted the image of eternity with which each person is born. Like a silver moon in a calm, still pond. (p. 428)

A person is not to be defined according to his function in life. Rather, each person is created in the image of God and is to find his basic self-definition in that source.

Solzhenitsyn's high regard for medical personnel extends to the admirable orderly, Elizaveta Anatolyevna, a "free, proud human being" (p. 479). She, too, feels a mystical bond with Oleg. Something in his bearing causes her to respond to him "with all the dignity of a lady of a certain age receiving a welcome guest under her own roof. Agreeably and without hurry they regarded one another. The look meant that they were always ready to give one another help" (p. 475). Her husband is in prison, and she finds in Oleg someone of whom she can ask advice. How much should she tell her eight-year-old son? Oleg quickly advises, "Burden him with the truth!" (p. 478). She bewails, "Where can people read about us? *Us*? Only in a hundred years' time?" (p. 479). It is this kind of heart's cry which caused Solzhenitsyn to write *The Gulag Archipelago*. Oleg, too, feels the bond tied by common suffering. One of his feelings is shame at what his nation has done to people. But the overriding feeling is one of healing peace in the reassurance of human solidarity: "Another person's misery had rolled over him and washed his own away" (p. 480).

Whereas the novel is set in the cancer ward and the town which harbors it, two of the truly appealing characters surface in Oleg's remembrance of his years in exile in desolate Ush-Terek. These two are the Kadmins, a happy old couple with whom Oleg had lived. Like Oleg, this highly literate pair lives in internal exile, but they have found happiness in a hovel. Compared with before, they now have "less money but more peace of mind" (p. 265): "It is not our level of prosperity that makes for happiness but the kinship of heart to heart and the way we look at the world" (p. 266). She is grateful to her mother, who "combined sternness toward her family with general Christian principles" (p. 266).

The husband, son of a communications engineer, likes the saying "Order in affairs maintains peace of mind" (p. 268). His favorite proverb is "Things know their place," and he explains, "Things know themselves where they belong, and we shouldn't get in their way" (p. 268). Victims of the disorder imposed by the Soviet rulers upon private lives, the Kadmins have the inner powers to create their own order. They cheer themselves and Oleg by saying, "Things have been worse" (p. 297). Oleg cheers himself by writing to them, ". . . and may your light shine" (p. 298). Their caring for pets is another of the Kadmins' humanizing traits: ". . . if we stop loving animals, aren't we bound to stop loving humans too?" (p. 269).

The example of the Kadmins causes Oleg to conclude, "The wise man is content with little" (p. 272). This is a sentiment Solzhenitsyn voiced in *Candle in the Wind*, as well as in a grand peroration in *The Gulag Archipelago*:

> What about the main thing in life, all its riddles? If you want, I'll spell it out for you right now. Do not pursue what is illusory—property and position: all that is gained at the expense of your nerves decade after decade, and is confiscated in one fell night. Live with a steady superiority over life—don't be afraid of misfortune, and do not yearn after happiness; it is, after all, all the same: the bitter doesn't last forever, and the sweet never fills the cup to overflowing. It is enough if you don't freeze in the cold and if thirst and hunger don't claw at your insides. If your back isn't broken, if your feet can walk, if both arms can bend, if both eyes see, and if both ears hear, then whom should you envy? And why? Our envy of others devours us most of all. Rub your eyes and purify your heart—and prize above all else in the world those who love you and wish you well. Do not hurt them or scold them, and never part from any of them in anger; after all, you simply do not know: it might be your last act before your arrest, and that will be how you are imprinted on their memory.[12]

No characters in Solzhenitsyn's fiction embody more fully than the Kadmins this creed for life.

Solzhenitsyn has a knack for concluding a novel with a memorable *tour de force* passage. The final two chapters follow Oleg out of the hospital, through the city, to the zoo, and finally to the train which will return him to Ush-Terek and the Kadmins. The chapter titles—"The First Day of Creation . . ." and ". . . and the Last Day"—suggest the cosmic context within which the whole novel, with its themes of the mystery of suffering and the meaning of life, is to be understood. The penultimate chapter emphasizes the sheer joy of being alive; the woman who leaps to Oleg's mind is Zoya. The final chapter emphasizes the need to temper this exhilaration with the awareness of the presence of evil in the midst of the good of the created order; the woman who keeps coming to mind is Vega. Life and truth are Oleg's twin desiderata. There is more on Vega than on Zoya. For the sake of truth, Solzhenitsyn has said that he would lay down his very life. These two chapters contain the most lyrical use of symbolism in Solzhenitsyn's fiction.

As Oleg leaves the hospital, it is a beautiful spring morning. To him, "It was the morning of creation. The world had been created anew for one reason only, to be given back to Oleg. 'Go out and live!' it seemed to say" (p. 485). He savors everything. He especially hopes to see a flowering apricot tree, and finally he does. The "pink miracle," with "buds like candles," is "his present to himself—his creation-day present" (pp. 489-90). He also enjoys watching people pass by. "He could find nothing in this newly made world of his that was uninteresting, unpleasant, or ugly. Whole months, years of life could not compare with today, this one supreme day" (p. 493). Quality of life is what counts, not quantity. Briefly, he imagines visiting Zoya, though his thoughts soon shift to Vega.

It is when Oleg enters a department store that the first cloud darkens his day. As he overhears a man ask not only for a certain shirt size but also a specific collar size, he thinks of fellow zeks even now rotting in trenches and being thrown into mass graves, and the incongruity overwhelms him. The store seems a "cursed temple," and he concludes that "the dense complexity of this world [is] too much for him" (p. 501). And to think that Vega is at home in this world. He begins to feel removed from her, and he is afraid.

Leaving the store, the symbol of that materialism which perverts true humanity, Oleg heads for the zoo. He is in search of the pristine integrity of nature; besides, his young friend, Dyomka, had asked him to visit the zoo. Oleg finds himself feeling more at home among the animals than among the townspeople: ". . . the animal world was more understandable anyway, more on his own level" (p. 502).

As Oleg observes the animals and thinks of the various characteristics they represent, Solzhenitsyn transmutes his musings into symbolic comments on the types which constitute Soviet society. The first animal which captures Oleg's attention is a spiral-horned goat standing on top of a rock. "Oleg stood there for five minutes and departed in admiration. The goat had not even stirred. That was the sort of character a man needed to get through life" (p. 503). By contrast, a squirrel runs on a treadmill seemingly endlessly; his only release will be through death. Oleg sees in the goat and the squirrel "two equally possible modes of existence" (p. 504). He moves on. White-headed vultures are caged in and are "in torment, spreading their wings and beating them although there was nowhere to fly" (p. 504). He feels better about the badgers; a sign says, "The badger lives in deep, complicated burrows" (p. 504). The ex-zek thinks, "Aha—just like us! Good for you, badger, how else can one live?" (p. 504). The zoo brings Oleg no real joy; for he realizes that, even if he could do so, he would not set the captive animals free. "This was because, deprived of their home surroundings, they had lost the idea of rational freedom. It would only make things harder for them, suddenly to set them free" (p. 505). And what, one thinks, of the people under Soviet rule?

Oleg's worst experience at the zoo, one which he cannot shake, is his trip to the monkey cages. There he sees a hastily scrawled sign: "The little monkey that used to live here was blinded because of the senseless cruelty of one of the visitors. An evil man threw tobacco into the Macaque Rhesus's eyes" (p. 506). Oleg is dumbfounded at this motiveless malignancy.

Also, he is struck by the sign's moral explanation, as opposed to those ideological ones usually forthcoming in Communist propaganda: "This unknown man, who had already made a safe getaway, was not described as 'anti-humanist' or 'an agent of American imperialism'; all it said was that he was evil. This was what was so striking: how could this man be simply 'evil'?" (p. 506). And Oleg gives a mental warning: "Children, do not grow up to be evil! Children, do not destroy defenseless creatures!" (p. 506).

When a hostile critic asked Solzhenitsyn about the significance of the man who threw the tobacco in the monkey's eyes, the author responded that the man was "meant to represent Stalin specifically."[13] Actually, it is not clear from the text itself that the symbolic applicability of this vignette must be restricted to such a limited referent. But, in any case, the judgment being passed is a moral one: the man is evil. If the author is referring to Stalin, he is using the same moral categories which he used in drawing the portrait of Stalin in *The First Circle*.

Oleg then moves on to another animal which could readily be interpreted as a symbol of Stalin: a tiger. Oleg first notices its whiskers and then thinks, ". . . yes, it was the whiskers that were most expressive of his rapacious nature" (p. 507). The bushy mustache was a prominent facial feature of Stalin's. But it is when Oleg notices the tiger's yellow eyes that ". . . strange thoughts came to Oleg's mind. He stood there looking at the tiger with hatred" (p. 507). Why so? Could he be thinking of Stalin? Perhaps *The First Circle* provides a clue: Stalin is described there as having "yellow tiger eyes," eyes which "burned with a tiger-like gleam."[14]

The last animal Oleg views is a bewitching Nilgai antelope, "a miracle of spirituality" (p. 507). It reminds him of Vega and her invitation. He thinks that he might still find her at home.

The final chapter opens with Oleg's ambivalent thoughts about going to Vega. On the one hand, ". . . it would be an uncontainable joy being with her" (p. 509). On the other hand, "he would probably blunder, say the wrong things. After all he was no longer used to living among the human race" (p. 509). He gathers enough courage to pick up some violets and go to her place. But she is not home. He gives the flowers to two Uzbek schoolgirls and leaves.

He is cheered briefly when he checks in with the N.K.V.D. *komendant* who is in charge of exile locally and finds him kind and sympathetic: ". . . a few humane men behind these vile desks and life became completely different" (p. 518). It is high time, he thinks, that some police officials become humane: "How could it be otherwise? A man dies from a tumor, so how can a country survive with growths like labor camps and exiles?" (p. 520). Although Solzhenitsyn has insisted that he is writing about literal cancer and that the medical subject is not to be interpreted as a symbol for a social attack on the Soviet Union[15]—and, overall, that is a fair disclaimer—this particular passage clearly links cancer and the state of Soviet society. Nor is it incidental that Solzhenitsyn uses cancer imagery in *The Gulag Archipelago* to describe the effect of Soviet prison camps on the body politic.[16]

Once again, Oleg contemplates going to Vega. But on a trolley something happens which dissuades him. Pressed between two pretty girls, he can feel the body of the blonde from chin to knee. And the warning which he had received becomes real to him: "The libido remains, the libido but nothing else . . ." (p. 521). In such a state, he cannot impose himself upon Vega. Though she would be the first to understand and though "they had come to a high-minded agreement that spiritual communion was more valuable than anything else" (p. 522), he simply cannot ask more of her than he requires of himself, and hence he decides not to go to her.

Oleg goes instead to the railway station to get a ticket home. When he encounters there a typical bureaucratic bungle, he almost creates a row in order to get "his bit of justice, a tiny, miserable bit but nevertheless justice" (p. 524). But he submits quietly. As he thinks of his momentous day, he remembers the faith and hope with which it had begun. He contrasts his initial idealism with the sordid reality he has encountered.

Before boarding the train, Oleg writes a few notes to friends whom he is leaving forever. He tells young Dyomka about the zoo, especially about the Macaque Rhesus monkey, and encourages him to "live up to your ideals" (p. 527). He also sends greetings to Shulubin. Only these two wardmates does he deem worthy of his correspondence. Also, he sends a brief, touching note to Zoya, explaining that he prefers to remember her as he knew her rather than risking ruining things by coming to her house. He declares, "I'm so grateful for you for allowing my lips to get a taste of genuine life. Without those few evenings I should have felt absolutely, yes absolutely, robbed" (p. 528).

His very moving letter to Vega opens with a burst of bravura: "Darling Vega." He tells her that he tried her place and that it was probably good that she was not home, given his apparent impotency. While he predicts that she "will come to bless this day, the day you did not commit yourself to share my life" (p. 529), he concludes with ingratiating sentimentality: ". . . I still wanted all the time, _all the time_, to pick you up and kiss you on the lips. So try to work that out. And now, without your permission, I kiss them" (p. 529).

As Oleg is about to board the train, a "maniac" tries to cut in the front of the line. Oleg, recognizing the type, a self-styled camp hoodlum, approaches him and in measured tones says, "The place where ninety-nine weep but one laughs" (p. 531). The "maniac" knows the famous camp line and, having met his moral match, defers and waits his turn, much to the amazement of the unknowing people in line. Oleg continues his struggle for justice in an unjust world.

On the final page of the novel, Oleg, now on board the train, reflects on his experiences: "The others hadn't survived. But he had. He hadn't even died of cancer. And now his exile was cracking like an eggshell" (p. 532). Yet the awareness of evil in the world, which can never again be absent, engenders anguish. He thinks of the blinded monkey. "An evil man threw

tobacco in the Macaque Rhesus's eyes. Just like that . . ."
(p. 532).[17] And the novel ends.

Oleg Kostoglotov is unable to comprehend motiveless
evil-doing. He finds no pattern in human behavior. Good men
and bad alike contract cancer; good men and bad alike succumb
or survive. This world seems marked by caprice rather than
fairness. Yet, in the face of this incomprehensible puzzle, the
noble thing is to continue to try to unravel it and to find meaning in life.

What should men live by? The novel gives no pat answers. In proper polyphonic fashion, it depicts various options
which persons practice in fact. It shows the hard path which
persons seeking the meaning of life must follow. It also shows
failures in that pursuit. The novel does not sentimentalize. The
grimness of life is presented in stark and memorable detail.
There is no easy explanation for the mystery of suffering. Yet
there are the overcomers, most notably Oleg Kostoglotov. They
do not give in; against great odds they hold out. They do not
thereby gain an intellectual comprehension of the meaning of
life, but they do live well as developing human beings. When
they are called upon to die, they will also be able to die well.

8

HISTORY RECOVERED:

August 1914 and *Lenin in Zurich*

For a variety of reasons, *August 1914* is the most problematic of all of Solzhenitsyn's novels. First and foremost, it is just one installment of what is to be a much larger, unified work; so, despite some demurrers to the contrary, it cannot be fairly evaluated until it is possible to see how this piece fits into the whole of the enterprise. Second, it is set in a bygone era which hardly any current readers can remember personally. Whereas the autobiographically based novels and even *The Gulag Archipelago* have, like *August 1914*, a rooting in historical events, almost all of that writing, unlike *August 1914*, strikes the current reader as belonging to his own lifetime and the contemporary world experience. Then, *August 1914* draws on information which, at least for almost all Western readers, is arcane and unknown material about the long ago and the far away; and the novel makes no concessions to the uninitiated. Furthermore, Solzhenitsyn's polyphonic structure and deemphasis of plot are uncongenial to most readers of modern fiction. Finally, the extensive technical knowledge of military matters demonstrated in this novel is imposing for most general readers, who lack military training.

Yet Solzhenitsyn offers this novel as the first part of his *magnum opus*; he has called this work-in-progress "the chief artistic design of my life."[1] It was in 1936, when Solzhenitsyn was still a high school student, that he developed the plan to become a writer whose great life work would be to chronicle the history of Russia during the 1910's. As time passed, the decision must have seemed positively providential, for Solzhenitsyn grew to the firm conviction that because of the global impact of the Bolshevik Revolution, the events which led up to it were the most important series of events in modern world history, not just for Russia but for mankind as a whole.

Nevertheless, the events of Solzhenitsyn's life kept interfering with his plans. War and prison made any writing close to impossible. Also, they provided very fascinating material of their own for writing. This new material was so rich and important that it would take years to treat. Furthermore, it had an urgency about it that caused the author to delay his historical research and writing; he could not let fade the memory and passion of his personal experience and firsthand knowledge.

Solzhenitsyn's original intention, which he apparently has not abandoned, was to write a series of three novels, each to focus on pivotal events. After *August 1914* were to come *October 1916* and *March 1917*. It seems that Solzhenitsyn is now well along in composing these sequels but that he wants to put them in highly polished form before sending them forth into the world. There have been hints that he will continue the series through and even beyond the 1917 Revolution. Time will tell. He has been quite secretive about his plans for future writing. He is no longer young, and we know of other earlier works which have not yet appeared in print and which must also lay claim on his time and attention. Then, he is so unhappy with many hasty translations of his published works that working with translators to improve them may place additional demands on his time. On the other hand, he is a prodigious and intense worker, and he has a well-refined vision of his authorial mission in life. We can expect him to flesh out his idea of a well-rounded lifework for himself. At the very least, we can count on seeing *October 1916, March 1917*, and a screenplay, entitled *The Tanks Know the Truth*, on a prison rebellion of the kind chronicled in the third volume of *The Gulag Archipelago*.

Solzhenitsyn's term for *August 1914* is a "knot," or a juncture, a pivotal moment in an unfolding story of major moment. Taken together, these "knots" will show progression, but single knots are not devoted to such purpose: the whole will reveal a pattern not discernible in the separate fascicles. On the other hand, Solzhenitsyn would not have published *August 1914*, his first fascicle, separately had he not believed that it could bear critical scrutiny standing alone, despite the contextual enrichment which future installments would add to it. So this volume must be approached with the twin understanding that it is a novel in its own right and that it is also one piece of an uncompleted work. Interpretive judgments of *August 1914* can be ventured, but they must be tentative and subject to modification as further "knots" appear.

The relationship in Solzhenitsyn's writing between literature and history is an intricate matter. With very few exceptions, this relationship appears in everything that Solzhenitsyn writes; yet the nature of this relationship varies from work to work. Perhaps the most helpful way to view this subject is to see all of his major works as literary, with the two poles of his literary field being *fiction* and *history*. We readily accord serious fiction the status of literature; we need only to think of Thucydides, Gibbon, and the like to realize that the writing of history can also rise to the level of the literary. Solzhenitsyn seeks to be a serious practitioner of the novelist's craft; at the same time, he feels himself under a compulsion, as a member of his people, to recover the truth of history, both in its concrete facticity and in the interpretation of its overall meaning and design.

Solzhenitsyn's works can be placed on a continuum from the more fictional and less historical to the less fictional and more historical. At one end is *Candle in the Wind*; at the other is *The Gulag Archipelago*. The massive *Gulag* is totally devoted to recovering history and is in no sense fiction; yet, as its sub-title states and the following chapter tries to show, it is a literary endeavor. By contrast, *Candle*, with its imprecise setting, has no intrinsic element of the historical. Next to *Candle* stands *Cancer Ward*. In its focus on issues of living and dying, it is the most readily universalized of the autobiographical works; and it has the fewest obviously political and historical implications; indeed *One Day* was allowed to be published precisely because it was seen as a comment on the historical realities of the Stalin era. After these comes *The First Circle*. In its scope, in its pre-sentation of real zeks some of whom have even gone on to publish their memoirs, and especially in its portrayal of such prominent Soviet personages as Stalin and Abakumov, it adds an increment of historical interest beyond that of the immedi-ately preceding twin works.

The interaction between fiction and history which is most difficult to explicate is that of *August 1914*, standing between the autobiographically based works and *Gulag*. It shares with *Candle in the Wind* the distinction of not being rooted in the author's personal experience, but in terms of the continuum that is its only similarity. It has both historical and fictional characters. Here Solzhenitsyn leaves behind his personal remi-niscences and moves to a time setting which antedates his own birth. To write this novel (and its sequels), he read history books, even traveling to distant libraries to find them—for instance, visiting California's Hoover Institution twice. In *August 1914* the telling of true history becomes an end in itself to a degree which outstrips anything in the autobiographically based works. Some reviewers reacted as if the book were not a novel at all but history only; that reaction is mistaken. Solzhenitsyn here is trying to do an unusual thing, though not one without prec-edent. He is seeking to be loyal equally to the nature of fiction and the nature of historical writing.

August 1914 is the only one of Solzhenitsyn's major works to receive preponderantly negative reviews in the West. It was being written in the late sixties and early seventies, and the awarding of the Nobel Prize for Literature, in 1970, came midway in the process of composition. One thing this timing suggests is that *August 1914*, more surely than any other work by Solzhenitsyn, was written with the *Nobel Lecture*'s religiously grounded theory of art clearly in mind.

The general disfavor of reviewers is worthy of note. A common tack was to compare Solzhenitsyn unfavorably with Tolstoy, since both were writing historical fiction.[2] One critic found Solzhenitsyn "a monotonous writer."[3] Another found *August 1914* "lumbering," "dulling" and assigned it to the level of those historical reconstructions by Margaret Mitchell and Taylor Caldwell.[4] Yet another complained of the novel's "pedantic and highly moralistic tone."[5] And one accused Solzhenitsyn of political bad manners for being "rude and unfair" to the liberals and "advanced circles" of 1914; she added, "He has it in for those people, just as he would have it in for you and me, if he could overhear us talking."[6]

This last remark seems to get close to the heart of the matter. Although, as this study shows, Solzhenitsyn's writing career is marked by a striking consistency of vision, his literary reputation in the West underwent a precipitous decline between 1972 and 1974. Sometimes the very critic who had praised Solzhenitsyn before damned him afterwards.

Jeri Laber is one such critic. In 1968 she lauded both *The First Circle* and its author, calling him "the symbol and the embodiment of an undaunted creative spirit" and declaring that "he is not a polemicist."[7] But by 1974 she has come to consider him "an authentic reactionary." She elaborates: "Reactionary, authoritarian, chauvinistic—hardly adjectives that sit comfortably with the typical image of a freedom-fighter and Nobel Prize winner."[8] But, she tells us, this vision of Solzhenitsyn should not have surprised us. It was obvious all along! She now speaks of "the inflated praise he has received from Western reviewers, whose admiration for Solzhenitsyn's courage is often mistakenly expressed as esteem for his works. . . ."[9] She is undoubtedly correct in this statement, and it fits her as well as anyone. The Laber of 1974 characterizes his work as didactic, dull, ponderous, heavy-handed, humorless, monotonous; his characters lack dimension; his "political and philosophical theories . . . are oversimplified and irritatingly presented with a repetitious self-indulgent verbosity."[10]

Readers might be befuddled by Laber's flip-flop in tone. But Laber herself guilelessly clears away any confusion. Taking note of Solzhenitsyn's "misleadingly 'liberal' image," an image which developed from commentaries like her own review of *The First Circle*, she explains, ". . . he is not the 'liberal' we would like him to be."[11]

Several events in 1972 and 1973 contributed to the radical alteration of Solzhenitsyn's literary reputation. In 1972 he was baptized into the Russian Orthodox Church; he circulated his public prayer; he protested the servility of the Russian Orthodox Church before the atheistic Soviet state; and he published *August 1914*. In 1973 he published his *Letter to the Soviet Leaders*. Even those who earlier had not had ears to hear what he was saying could no longer miss it. The implicit had become explicit. It was not that errors in understanding Solzhenitsyn ceased; in fact, they increased. But now the errors were of a different kind. And not infrequently they were tinged with the animus of political ideology.

There was now no question about two important matters. First, Solzhenitsyn showed himself to be infused with the spirit and history of Mother Russia; for all his global consciousness, as in the *Nobel Lecture*, he was neither a socialist ideologue nor a deracinated intellectual. Also, he showed himself to be an old-fashioned, ardent believer in the Christian faith of his fathers. Clearly, neither of these positions is readily accessible to the current generation of Western secular critics. So it is not surprising that *August 1914*, which among Solzhenitsyn's novels is the most thoroughly Russian *and* the most thoroughly Christian, was greeted with a general chorus of disapproval. This novel is the least comprehensible and pleasing of Solzhenitsyn's works to a Western reader with secular presuppositions.

August 1914 offers this problem for readers of Solzhenitsyn: it is a creation of a new fictive "world" for the author. All of his other fiction belonged to the same fictive world, so that before the appearance of *August 1914* we could have spoken of "Solzhenitsyn's world" with the same clarity with which critics have referred to "Hardy's world" or "Twain's world" or "Faulkner's world." The task facing Solzhenitsyn in *August 1914* and succeeding "knots" is to appropriate as a second fictive world the historical Russia of the nineteen-teens.

Despite this difference, *August 1914* is organized according to the same general principle of polyphony which governs *The First Circle* and *Cancer Ward*. The time span is again short: about eleven days in the month of August of 1914. The number of characters is again enormous, and again they range through all the social, and in this case also military, strata: from leader Lenin to simple peasant foot soldiers. Most scenes are set at the war front in eastern Germany, but an important minority of the scenes are set behind the line in Russia; so setting in place is somewhat more diversified than in the earlier novels, though not too dissimilar from the balance of scenes inside and outside the sharashka of *The First Circle* or the scenes inside and outside the hospital of *Cancer Ward*.

At the same time, there is an important difference between *August 1914* and the earlier two polyphonic novels. In each of those two, for all the plethora of characters, one figure stands out as the closest to the outlook of the author: Gleb Nerzhin in *The First Circle* and (a bit less so) Oleg Kostoglotov in *Cancer Ward*. The situation is significantly different in *August 1914*, for here the author's lines are spoken not by one major figure but by two: General Samsonov and Colonel Vorotyntsev. Neither takes precedence of author's favor over the other. We need both in order to see Solzhenitsyn's vision of what it takes to bring old holy Russia into the twentieth century as a viable entity with a future.

To offer two characters, each of whom partially represents the authorial viewpoint, is an easy and natural extension of Solzhenitsyn's use of the polyphonic technique in fiction. The best traits of Samsonov and the best traits of Vorotyntsev combine to provide a picture of what Solzhenitsyn would like to see in that beloved Russia which the times have, without recourse, propelled into the hurly-burly of the twentieth century. Samsonov has those qualities of personal piety and national dedication which Solzhenitsyn admires deeply; he also is impractical, uncalculating, and slow-witted—hardly the ideal modern military leader. On the other hand, Vorotyntsev has unbounded energy, the wit of a natural-born leader, and a veritably Germanic sense of the importance of military strategy which old Russians like Samsonov generally lack.

While *August 1914* has, like other Solzhenitsyn novels, universal applicability, it, more than any other Solzhenitsyn novel, explores specifically the Russian soul. The nature of that soul is clarified by the collision of tradition and modernity. *August 1914* seeks to show what is good and what is bad in traditional old Russia and what of the modern world can profitably be grafted onto that old stock and what cannot. The whole novel is an effort to show, by focusing on a pivotal moment in Russian history, what is useful and what is not as old Russia moves into the contemporary era.

The great obstacle confronting Solzhenitsyn is that the Bolshevik Revolution and its aftermath have so obscured and distorted Russian history that the very truth of history must be explicated as part of the process of elucidating the Russian soul. These are the twin tasks facing Solzhenitsyn in *August 1914*. In charting the movement from the old regime of the Tsars to the new regime of the Bolsheviks, he must both straighten out the historical record and offer his explication of the underlying meaning of these events. To the extent that Innokenty Volodin, in *The First Circle*, is correct in asserting that a great writer is like a second government, Solzhenitsyn seeks in this novel to be that second government and to offer his view of history as an alternative to the official narrative offered by the Soviet regime.

The novel opens with two chapters devoted to Isaaki (Sanya) Lazhenitsyn. Both the last name and the nickname echo the author's own name. Critics widely have surmised that this character is based on the author's father, who was an artillery captain in the First World War, as his son was in the Second. Sanya appears seldom in the rest of the novel, and it is a reasonable guess that he will reappear, possibly in a major role, in the ensuing knots. In these opening pages, Sanya expresses what becomes the controlling mood of the author: "I feel sorry for Russia."[12] In this sorrow is a mingling of the disgust felt by Sanya's fellow young intellectuals and the deeply rooted affection and loyalty which most of his fellow citizens feel. Although Sanya articulates his ambivalence poorly, the reader feels that his love of Mother Russia is much stronger than his disdain for tsardom and misplaced patriotism.

The opening paragraphs contrast "petty human creation" (p. 1) with the grandeur of God's creation as they describe the setting of Sanya's home placed at the feet of the mountains of the Caucasus. All of the human actions of the novel are to be seen against the backdrop of the divine order of the universe; men are not autonomous, even when they think they are. Solzhenitsyn himself, having in mind the divinely ordered cosmos and modern human perversions of it, points out a ludicrous irony: Soviet officials directed that if this novel were to be published, *God* would have to be written without the capital letter, although of course *KGB* would be in all capitals. To write *god* instead of *God* would be "historically false" for 1914; it is also "the cheapest kind of atheistic pettiness."[13]

A favorite device of Solzhenitsyn is to express certain of his own thoughts quite directly through minor characters; he has done so elsewhere, and in *August 1914* he uses several characters for that purpose. One such, Professor Andozerskaya, a woman who teaches medieval history, declares, "The stuff of history is not *opinions* but *sources*. And your conclusions are determined by the source materials, even if they contradict your preconceived views" (p. 630). Since *August 1914* is both historical and fictional, Solzhenitsyn includes both real and fictional characters. In either case, the issues with which they wrestle are the actual ones of the time. The author's first interest is a regard for surface facts, a concern for truth at its most basic level. These facts will illuminate and foster proper interpretation. And interpretation in this novel will center on who, or what, is the real Russia.

Solzhenitsyn's method for answering this central question of the novel is to embody various aspects of the Russian character in different characters, some drawn from the historical record, others drawn from his imagination, all of them having fictive credibility. The Russian character, on a smaller scale like humanity itself, is too rich and diverse to be embodied in one ideal personage.

Schematically, this characterizing of Russia may be summarized as follows. Samsonov represents that aspect of old Russia which the author values and wishes to see preserved. Vorotyntsev represents that aspect of modern life which the author sees as a necessary addition to old Russia if it is to be viable in the twentieth century. On the negative side, the inept, cowardly, time-serving generals in the Tsarist army represent that defective aspect of the traditional Russian order which Solzhenitsyn sees as only harmful in its ongoing effect. Then, there are those young intellectuals who are pretentiously revolutionary and who can only impose the corrosive influence of post-Enlightenment ideologies on the sturdy Russian soul. Tradition has its good and its bad; modernity has its good and its bad. A good future for Russia lies in the linkage of the two goods, but the likelihood of history is all against this conjunction; only thus far does *August 1914* progress. It seems unlikely that a healthy Russia can survive in the inhumane forest of the twentieth century.

Solzhenitsyn has shown his love of old Russia through characterizations in many of his works: Matryona, Ivan Denisovich, Spiridon. But these are peasants who demonstrate immunity to the new Soviet influence. With the change in time setting of *August 1914*, Solzhenitsyn can now show his love of Mother Russia in a character who is not from the cultural backwaters but who, as commander of the Russian Second Army, plays a prominent role in the history of his nation. General Samsonov is Solzhenitsyn's greatest evocation of the old Russian spirit. Samsonov is a mixture of strengths and weaknesses, and in both he is prototypically old Russian.

Samsonov appears in only nine of the novel's sixty-four chapters, but no character is more important than he. He represents "submissive, long-suffering Russia" (p. 622). He has a bear-like appearance; he is "corpulent, with a protruding stomach" (p. 105). He offers a toast which expresses his values: "Gentlemen: I give you the Russian soldier, the soldier of Holy Russia, to whom endurance and suffering are second nature!" (p. 191). He is a religious man who counts the days according to the spiritual significations of the ecclesiastical calendar. When he is in trouble, he prays: ". . . he was praying for the success of his troops not in order to save his own reputation but to serve the might of Russia . . ." (pp. 364-65). His selfless patriotism receives only praise from Solzhenitsyn.

Nevertheless, Samsonov is ineffectual. He is described as "the ponderous, baffled Samsonov" (p. 134). Almost the first thing we learn of him is that he is "unable to cope . . ." (p. 87). He is also described as a man with a "badly confused mind" (p. 183). There is "a look of sad resignation in his big eyes" (p. 190). He is the general whose troops suffer a defeat which is a turning point in the entire war effort. While he has been betrayed by the ineptness and pigheadedness of those above him in command, he is not absolved of guilt in the debacle. He did his best, but it was not good enough. "Samsonov sensed that he was doing something wrong, or rather, that he was failing to do something essential, but he was unable to grasp what it was, because he could not penetrate the veil that dimmed his inner eye" (p. 334). He is described as having "a helpless look about his great forehead: a white target above a defenseless face" (p. 409). He is called "a sacrificial lamb" with "the look of pre-ordained doom" (p. 496). In all this, "the knowledge that he, General Samsonov, had served his sovereign and his country so lamentably was a terrible, painful burden for him to bear" (p. 532).

Although he is not clever enough to avert disaster, he is wise enough to understand the momentous implications of the events and his own share of responsibility for them.

> He had wanted only to do good, yet what he had achieved was an unmitigated evil. If such disasters could result from decisions taken with the best intentions, what might be the outcome of actions whose motivation was base and selfish? And if there were more defeats, might not rebellion rear its head again in Russia, as had happened after the Japanese war? (p. 532)

Samsonov's ineffectuality is highlighted poignantly in an important scene when his troops begin to flee in panic and he is unable to marshall the sentiments or words to rally them. Shortly thereafter, we read, he "had lost all sense of his proper function" (p. 492). He allows his decisions to be made by his staff, a group which he knows better than to respect or trust. He joins in the retreat with them, until finally, as an indication of the ultimate ineffectuality, his own body fails him, and he must be carried by the troops.

Yet, even in ignominious military defeat, Samsonov is not stripped of all dignity; Solzhenitsyn especially resonates with Samsonov's religious approach to life. Although Samsonov sees the cowardice of his superior, General Zhilinsky, and even foresees, accurately, that Zhilinsky will unfairly lay full blame for the defeat on him, in true Christian fashion Samsonov accords forgiveness rather than blame. In his hour of dark night of the soul, Samsonov muses, "It was as though Christ and the Virgin Mary had rejected Russia" (p. 490). He receives news of impending disaster as "nothing less than a sign of divine retribution. Why had his judgment been so clouded that he had abandoned his army? The finger of God was pointed at him" (p. 534).

Samsonov's religious interpretations include more than a sense of divine retribution, however. Through his tribulation he grows spiritually. That authorial spokesman, Professor Andozerskaya, who praised the medieval age for its "intense spiritual life" which was "predominant over material existence" (p. 630), announced, "There is, too, the spiritual life of the *individual*, and therefore each individual has, perhaps in spite of his environment, a *personal* responsibility—for what he does and for what other people around him do" (p. 631). Similarly, another authorial mouthpiece, Varsonofiev, asserts: ". . . we should develop our *soul*. There is nothing more precious than the development of a man's own soul; it is more important than the well-being of countless future generations" (p. 473). Samsonov does just this: he develops his soul. Even in defeat he achieves a "melancholy calm and new-won understanding" (p. 493).

Samsonov demonstrates that a man can fail in his social function yet succeed as a human being. Before he dies, his defeat having been sealed, he is

> . . . no longer surrounded by an earthly foe, no longer threatened; he had risen above all such perils. The cloud which darkened the army commander's brow was not, after all, one of guilt but one of ineffable greatness: perhaps outwardly he had done things which were wrong by the petty canons of strategy and tactics, but from his point of view, what he had done had been profoundly right. (p. 498)

In this scene he meets Colonel Vorotyntsev for the last time, but does not recognize his erstwhile colleague in arms. Samsonov is beyond the concerns of this world now. Again Solzhenitsyn is not censorious; on the contrary, he depicts him as having moral grandeur.

Following the final meeting of the novel's two primary figures, Samsonov goes into the forest and kills himself. Yet once more, Solzhenitsyn passes no negative judgment. For the suicide, far from being motivated by cowardice, is a resigned bowing to the inevitable, an acceptance of an appointed fate. Samsonov's death is simply the inevitable consequence of his previous actions, and his suicide is an offering up of himself as a sacrifice to God. "There was nothing hostile about this forest: it was not a German or a Russian forest but simply God's forest which gave refuge to all manner of creatures" (p. 541).

Since Samsonov is a believer, death by his own hand produces internal conflict; suicide, after all, is a sin. But he can see no other acceptable response to his situation; defeat has robbed him of his very purpose of living. He will do what he must do. His final words are, appropriately, a prayer: "O Lord, if Thou canst, forgive me and receive me. Thou seest—I could do no other, and can do no other now" (p. 541). To the end Samsonov is a man of faith. "What had happened was evidently part of God's purpose, and that was something which was beyond the comprehension of the men of our time" (p. 530).

General Samsonov is the only truly tragic figure in all of Solzhenitsyn's fiction. Of the others only Lev Rubin comes close, but his ideological cravenness keeps him from such stature. Samsonov is heroic but also flawed, and his flaw is a major contributor to his demise. Only a nondeterministic understanding of life can leave space for genuine tragedy, as distinguished from calamity; and Solzhenitsyn is thinking of Samsonov when he comments, *"Fate does not seek its victim—the victim seeks his own fate"* (p. 373). In a tragic view, fate is never altogether distinct from responsibility. Yet, at the same time, tragedy always entails mystery. Some men bow to incomprehensible fate and curse. Others bow to the same incomprehensible fate and retain faith that a Superior Being understands the meaning which eludes them. Samsonov is of the latter type.

Nevertheless, there was that defeat, and it does a country little good to retain spiritual virtue if it cannot survive in the actual world. The goal must be to combine virtue and viability. For survival the practicality of Colonel Vorotyntsev, the novel's other leading figure, is needed to augment Samsonov's religiosity.

It is significant that Colonel Vorotyntsev is younger (around forty) than General Samsonov (fifty-five). Samsonov appears first, Vorotyntsev appearing soon after. It is also significant that when these two meet, they have immediate rapport. On the one hand, ". . . it dawned on Samsonov that in this man God had sent him the very person he lacked on his staff—someone he could talk to" (p. 105), an "efficient and fast-thinking" man (p. 116). On the other hand, Vorotyntsev had "a liking for Samsonov, because he had not lied or tried to embellish the facts" (p. 114).

Yet, theirs is a case of opposites attracting. Samsonov is overweight and plodding; Vorotyntsev is "robustly built, but straight-backed and light on his feet," with "bright, mobile eyes" (pp. 105, 106). Vorotyntsev embodies intelligence and energy; he is efficient and modern, as Samsonov most definitely is not. Vorotyntsev has an "obsession," like a good engineer, "to solve a _riddle_" (p. 115). Samsonov is a Russian longsufferer; ". . . patience was not one of Vorotyntsev's virtues" (p. 261). The colonel epitomizes certain Western traits, even though he is emphatically not a Westernizer in personal outlook. He demonstrates no openness to revolutionary ideology or socialism or even liberalism. Yet his efficiency is a trait which Russians have usually perceived to be distinctly Germanic. Vorotyntsev himself employs those very terms as he nurses "the proud conviction that there were some Russians like himself who had a Germanic sense of efficiency and the Germans' power of steady application, characteristics which gave him an edge over well-meaning but impetuous and erratic men like Krymov" (p. 181).

It is his Germanic intelligence and energy which causes Vorotyntsev to despise the Tsar, ". . . who headed a system of which he felt ashamed" (p. 443). Its corruption, its army's unyielding seniority system, its refusal to face the realities of the modern world—all these Vorotyntsev finds inexcusable. It is these same traits which cause him to be impatient with General Samsonov when he makes false moves during the crucial encounter at Tannenberg.

Nevertheless, Vorotyntsev is no less a patriot than Samsonov. In the colonel's view, "The only emotions truly worthy of a man were civic duty, patriotism, a concern for all mankind" (p. 142). Furthermore, "Ever since his youth, Vorotyntsev had been obsessed by one profound desire: to be a good influence on the history of his country . . ." (p. 267). His praise for the Russian common man sounds much like Samsonov's. He speaks of "the immeasurable strength latent in the Russian people" (p. 304) and thinks that "Russia was inexhaustibly strong, even if she was governed by a pack of fools" (p. 128). Whereas the common soldiers of the Russian army were "ridiculed by liberal writers," to Vorotyntsev ". . . they represented, in purified and concentrated form, the vitality and courage of the whole nation" (p. 412).

Not only is Vorotyntsev a patriot, he is also a humanist—
not of Samsonov's religious stripe, but a humanist nevertheless.
In one of the best scenes of the novel, he attempts successfully
to rally a fleeing regiment to the probably suicidal task of cov-
ering the retreat of other Russian troops in the area. Standing
before them, he considers alternate possibilities. He could in-
voke the concept of honor or their obligation to Russia's allies,
but such abstractions ill suit their desperate straits. He could
ask them to die for the Tsar, but he despises the Tsar and the
corrupt system over which he presides. He could appeal to the
name of God. But why should God prefer a Russian victory to
a German? He could appeal to the fatherland, but he knows the
concept means less to them than it does to him. Finally, he
says, simply, "Brothers! . . . Isn't it selfish to save ourselves at
the expense of others? We haven't far to go from here to reach
Russian territory, we could easily make it—but if we did, other
regiments would simply be cut to pieces" (p. 415). And, though
without enthusiasm, they do respond to the call to help their
brothers in need. If there is one separator of sheep from goats
in this novel, it is just this: Who will help his brothers? Those
who do not are the villains; those who do are the heroes. Vorotyntsev's speech is the kind of which Samsonov would have
been proud. It is also the kind which Samsonov himself could
not deliver in similar straits.

Vorotyntsev's pragmatic orientation is seen in both the
content and the imagery of his observation that the world

> . . . was moving invisibly, inaudibly, and imperceptibly into
> a new era; that the entire atmosphere of the planet—its oxy-
> gen content, its rate of combustion, the mainspring pressure
> in all its clocks—had somehow changed. All Russia, from the
> imperial family down to the revolutionaries, naively thought
> that they were still breathing the same old air and living on
> familiar ground; only a handful of engineers and officers were
> gifted with the perception to sense that the stars themselves
> had moved into new conjunctions. (p. 130)

This opinion is significant for understanding several fac-
ets of the outlook of both the author and his character. While

Vorotyntsev represents that portion of the Western outlook which Solzhenitsyn accepts, it is precisely that part which alienates the author more than ever from the mainstream of the literary and intellectual elite of the West. He praises certain army officers (like Vorotyntsev) and engineers. It is worth recalling that Solzhenitsyn himself was trained in physics and mathematics, not in the humanities or social sciences. While he is unquestionably a great humanist, he does not succumb to a two-cultures view, but holds in tension the sciences and the humanities, as does the colonel. Solzhenitsyn's implicit comment here about the ostensibly forward-looking revolutionary visionaries is that they are fighting old battles which emerge from outdated assumptions about the world and society.

Vorotyntsev's combination of practicality, patriotism, and humanity is highlighted in the final scene of the novel. The military brass have gathered to explain to the Grand Duke the Russian defeat at Tannenberg, and the guilty and cowardly officers are trying to place the total blame for the debacle on the dead Samsonov. At this point Vorotyntsev demonstrates his solidarity with Samsonov and with the cause of truth. As the lowest-ranking officer in this important meeting and knowing that the men assembled are guiltier than Samsonov, Vorotyntsev determines "to speak out once and for all and say what [he] really thinks—it's more than a pleasure, it's a sacred duty! One ought to get it all off one's chest and then die afterward if necessary" (p. 690). One is reminded of Solzhenitsyn's own statement: "No one can bar the road to truth, and to advance its cause I am prepared to accept even death."[14]

Svechin, a friend of Vorotyntsev, tries to dissuade him from his hopeless bravery by reminding him that "the people who get things done around here are not the rebels but the doers. They go about it discreetly and they don't make a lot of fuss, but they get things done. . . . It's senseless to try to fight the authorities; the way to deal with them is to steer them discreetly in the right direction" (p. 691). As a matter of fact, it turns out that Vorotyntsev's forthright honesty does not accomplish his goal of advancing justice, clearing Samsonov's name, and bringing retribution on the corrupt generals. Yet he is noble for trying, even if he does not succeed. Since elsewhere the author praises Vorotyntsev precisely for the qualities Svechin encourages, he must be saying that bearers of both qualities, rebels (truth-tellers) and doers (some engineers and officers), are needed and that in fact it is those two characteristics which form the parameters of Vorotyntsev's human stature.

Another of Solzhenitsyn's doers, an engineer named Obodovsky, extends the pattern of the minor character as authorial spokesman. This former anarchist, who is contemptuous of the new breed of youthful revolutionaries, has changed his mission in life from destroying to creating. He explains, "As for industry, anyone who has created something with his own hands knows that production is neither capitalist nor socialist but *one* thing only: it is what creates national wealth, the common material basis without which no country can exist" (p. 664). It takes courage for Solzhenitsyn to say this in the Soviet Union, and it is said in praise of the doers.

Since Vorotyntsev combines Samsonov's compassionate humanity with the practical effectiveness which Samsonov lacks, it is tempting to read the novel as bestowing the laurel wreath of heroism on Vorotyntsev, as showing him to be the consummation in himself of the virtues needed in modern Russia. The problem with this view is that it leaves entirely out of account why Solzhenitsyn is so unstinting in his praise of the person of Samsonov. There must be something of value embodied in him which does not characterize Vorotyntsev. This trait, I have argued, is Samsonov's perception of the religious significance of all human events. As Solzhenitsyn portrays his two main characters, it is precisely Samsonov's religious vision which allows him to achieve a moral grandeur which is not ascribed to Vorotyntsev. Vorotyntsev is noble but earthbound, and Solzhenitsyn's ideal man must include that transcendence represented by Samsonov.

But as the sun's rays cast not only light but also shadows, so Solzhenitsyn shows us not only the beneficent elements in old Russia and the modern world, but also the malevolent elements in each. The dark element in old Russia he embodies in that numerous collection of corrupt generals who dot the pages of the novel. Solzhenitsyn's high praise for soldiers dispels immediately any thought of considering him anti-military. It is the incompetence of the leadership which he attacks: ". . . from the first battle on, a Russian general's badges of rank come to be seen as symbols of incompetence; and the further up the hierarchy, the more bungling the generals seem, until there is scarcely one from whom an author can derive any comfort" (p. 441). Solzhenitsyn blames the seniority system for this sad state of affairs. We are shown the extent of the incompetence by viewing the situation through Vorotyntsev's eyes; he recognizes that

> . . . every headquarters (and the higher the headquarters the more marked the phenomenon) was staffed by people who were selfish, rank-conscious, hidebound, and slack, whose only concern was to eat and drink their fill. They regarded the army as a convenient, highly polished, and well-carpeted staircase, upon whose steps medals and badges of rank were handed out. . . . The staircase was so arranged as to encourage the ascent of slow-witted men who did what they were told, rather than those with brains and independence of mind. . . . But woe to you if you once diverged from the letter [of regulations and directives], if you ever thought for yourself or acted on your own initiative; then you would not even be forgiven your successes, and if you failed, you would be eaten alive. (pp. 123-24)

Representative of the useless generals is Zhilinsky, who "understood nothing" (p. 90) but who also "made it clear that he knew best about everything and had no intention of consulting his subordinates" (p. 92). Zhilinsky and another general, Rennenkampf, have close personal connections with the Tsarist court, and they therefore serve as vehicles to show that the corruption of old Russia reaches right into the highest levels of government—in fact, begins there and filters down. Those with close ties to the Tsar's family and inner circle receive promotions in the army, regardless of their ability. Grand Duke Nikolai Nikolaevich, who is commander-in-chief of the army,

knows that his top generals are mostly incompetents; he recognizes the value of Vorotyntsev as soon as he meets him. But
he is caught in the web of the corrupt court, at the center of
which is the Tsar himself. The Tsar forces certain incompetents
upon him, and their cronyism with the Tsar protects them from
any retribution from the Grand Duke.

The debility of old Russia reaches its nadir in the Tsar
himself, whose facile invocation of the will of God stands in
marked contrast to both the authentic praying of Samsonov and
the hardheaded skepticism of Vorotyntsev. After the defeat he
says, "But we must submit to the will of God. He who endures
to the end shall be saved" (p. 687). A fine sentiment—in some
other context and spoken by a different kind of person. Solzhenitsyn's acid comment on this self-justifying attitude is presented in the epigram "Praying kneads no dough" (p. 688).

But while Solzhenitsyn opposes the Tsar for his decadence, he also opposes equally firmly the Tsar's most vocal critics, the revolutionary intellectuals. He must admire that
intelligent energy represented by Vorotyntsev, but he criticizes
that modern ideology which seeks to remake the Russian man
according to some utopian model. His repeated rejection of this
line of thought is presented most straightforwardly through his
spokesman Varsonofiev, whose words appear as part of a conversation with two young radical students:

> Who is conceited enough to imagine that he can actually *de-
> vise* ideal institutions? The only people who think they can
> are those who believe that nothing significant was ever done
> before their own time, that their generation will be the first
> to achieve anything worthwhile, people who are convinced
> that only they and their current idols possess the truth, and
> that anyone who doesn't agree with them is a fool or a knave.
> . . . Do not be so arrogant as to imagine that you can invent
> an ideal social order, because with that invention you may
> destroy your beloved "people." (pp. 472, 474)

In his insistence on the irrationality of history, Varsonofiev (and
through him Solzhenitsyn) echoes Dostoevsky: "History . . . is
not governed by reason. . . . History grows like a living tree. And

as far as that tree is concerned, reason is an ax . . ." (p. 474). Far
from trying to invent a new individual and society, we should
recognize that "there is a justice which existed before us, without us and for its own sake. And our task is to _divine_ what it
is!" (p. 476).

The vices of ideology are embodied primarily in Sasha
Lenartovich, a radical student who is drafted into the army and
serves most reluctantly—and poorly. Solzhenitsyn pictures him
as one who, in the name of the people, actually despises the
people and considers himself superior to them. The contrast
between Arsenii Blagodaryov, the young peasant who is clever,
teachable, cooperative, versatile, and courageous and in whom
Vorotyntsev finds an ideal aide-de-camp, and the effete, spoiled,
selfish Sasha is striking. Sasha supposes that his life will have
great significance as he devotes it to the cause of the revolution.
He also supposes himself to be selflessly dedicated: "For the
great, bright cause of revolution Sasha was prepared to lay down
his life at any moment" (p. 382). The problem he sees confronting him during the war is that "he might all too easily die a
pointless death for the _wrong_ cause. Nothing could possibly be
worse than to die at the age of twenty-four defending autocracy"
(p. 382). When the battle turns against the Russian army and he
finds his life endangered, Sasha can find only one rational response: surrender himself to the Germans. "Surrender was a
sensible and practical step: the important things—his life, his
educated mind, and his political views—would be preserved.
There was nothing reprehensible in that; later he would devote
those talents to the workers" (p. 501). A series of comical bun-
glings ensues in his attempt to surrender, until the realization
dawns that "surrendering had proven to be even more dangerous
than fighting" (p. 529).

Placing this ideologue under the stress of battle makes
it apparent that his ostensible humanity is sham. When helping
wounded colleagues to escape might endanger the lives of others, Sasha favors leaving the wounded to their fate. Ideology is
not exactly life-affirming. Further, ideology is contradicted by
the experience even of the ideologue. For one thing, he is forced

to admit grudgingly that Vorotyntsev, who insists on helping his wounded colleagues, is "an extremely rare type of officer: a genuinely intelligent and educated man" (p. 561). For another, when the troops he is with score a victory, he feels the natural human emotion of elation, though it violates his ideological presupposition of "the worse, the better." At the same time, the thought flits through his consciousness that perhaps the love of a woman is the most real thing, even more important than ideology and political action. His commitments may force him to consider this a base, unworthy thought, but he cannot escape it. Here, as he often does, Solzhenitsyn accents the value of the concrete in contrast to the grand abstractions of the ideologue.

In this most overtly Christian of his novels, Solzhenitsyn highlights the conflict—especially for the Russian soul but also, by extension, for humanity at large—between tradition and modernity. At all times and in all places, fallen humanity will besmirch ideals. Yet the ideals remain and are in large part embodied. As Solzhenitsyn's earliest novel, *One Day in the Life of Ivan Denisovich*, embodies admirable human action in Ivan and an explanatory Christian context for it in Alyosha, so *August 1914* presents a roughly similar arrangement in Vorotyntsev and Samsonov. Time and place are different, but the eternal and universal questions of the human heart remain constant. And the outlines of Solzhenitsyn's depiction of it and the religious context within which he does his drawing become clearer and clearer.

Readers who might not on first contact sense the momentousness of *August 1914* will immediately realize that something crucial is at stake in *Lenin in Zurich*. Lenin, after all, is better known than the Battle of Tannenberg. Solzhenitsyn is here trying to draw the character of perhaps the most influential man of the century.

Lenin in Zurich is an oddity among Solzhenitsyn's publications—in a real way a non-book. It is composed of a series of chapters about Lenin gathered from the three novels which were to constitute the author's intended masterpiece, the last

two of which are not yet published—and will not be, Solzhenitsyn says, "in the very near future."[15] There are eleven chapters: one from *August 1914*, seven from *October 1916*, and three
from *March 1917*.[16]

When *August 1914* was published, its single chapter on
Lenin was omitted. Now we can understand why: Solzhenitsyn
envisioned a unified portrait of Lenin and did not want the first
small part of it presented alone. The chapter might have seemed
tendentious and unconnected to the rest of the novel. In addition, the author's decision suggests something of the unified
design of the three novels as a whole, of which the publication
of *Lenin in Zurich* gives us our first concrete suggestion. As we
see the character of Lenin carried over from *August 1914* into
the succeeding volumes, we wonder what lies ahead for such
characters as Colonel Vorotyntsev, Sasha Lenartovich, Isaaki
Lazhenitsyn, and others. For instance, in *March 1917* Lenin is
at center stage in only the opening three chapters. Which characters will be at center stage as that novel unfolds, dealing as
it must with the crucial period of the overthrow of the Tsar?
Incidentally, those three chapters from *March 1917* are fast-
paced, almost breathless, much different from the slow-moving
opening chapters of *August 1914*. So, without knowing in what
ways, we can be sure that when the whole trilogy appears our
interpretation of the aesthetic worth of *August 1914* will be
affected, for we shall then be able to read that fascicle in context.
Finally, we can be confident, from the publication of *Lenin in
Zurich*, that the overall design of the trilogy is quite clear in the
mind of the author and that he is far along in the writing of it.

Whereas *Lenin in Zurich* is not quite a book, it is at the
same time unified, since all of its chapters investigate the character of Lenin. Nevertheless, one may still ask why Solzhenitsyn rushed them into print well before he was ready to send
forth the whole trilogy. Here we can only speculate. The answer
may have to do with political maneuvering; it undoubtedly is
a matter of timing.

The publication came rather shortly after Solzhenitsyn's
forced exile in 1974 and shortly after the appearance of the first

two thirds of *The Gulag Archipelago*. One of the most significant pieces of the massive reconstruction of history in *Gulag* was Solzhenitsyn's powerful—and original—case that Lenin, not Stalin, fathered the system of Soviet prison camps. The crime against humanity which is Gulag is so massive that one cannot but wonder about the mind of the person who set it in motion. It is the psyche which is explored in this volume. *Lenin in Zurich* presents vital evidence for Solzhenitsyn's case against Lenin. Solzhenitsyn must have known that many readers would find it difficult to believe his revelations in *Gulag*, and it was obviously important to him that they be accepted as beyond refutation. A psychological exploration of the mastermind behind the Gulag, he must have thought, could only lend additional credibility to his historical reconstruction of it.

Perhaps Solzhenitsyn also thought that, whereas the whole trilogy was intended primarily to serve the long-term purpose of restoring to the Russian people the truth of a crucial "moment" in their history, the chapters in it about Lenin could meet an urgent and more immediate need, namely, the demythologizing of Lenin. As is by now well known, Solzhenitsyn fears for the immediate future of the world, a future over which Lenin casts a long shadow. Soviet hagiographers have enshrined him, and he is revered through wide parts of the world. Lenin lives. Any reconsideration of his character and beliefs would lead naturally to a reconsideration of beliefs about the nature of the social realities of the modern world. It is quite possible, then, that Solzhenitsyn had a polemical purpose in mind in publishing *Lenin in Zurich*.

Critical judgments of *Lenin in Zurich* have differed widely. Simon Karlinsky vouches for the scholarly accuracy of the depiction of Lenin.[17] Thomas Molnar asserts, "Solzhenitsyn's Lenin is one of the richest creations of historical *and* fictional literature."[18] Robert Conquest has a similarly high view: Lenin's "personality has been grasped with subtle skill. . . ."[19] After affirming the authenticity of Solzhenitsyn's handling of the history involved, he declares, "From apparently unpromising materials Solzhenitsyn has once again shown that history may be vividly subsumed into literature."[20] In terms which comport well with general themes of this current study as a whole, he concludes,

> The richness, the variety, the unpredictability, of the real world is available to Solzhenitsyn as it is not to the schematists of revolution. It has taken a giant human being to come to grips with this giant alien, and to demonstrate without unfairness or tendentiousness that humanity is superior. Solzhenitsyn can understand and include Lenin: Leninism cannot understand or include Solzhenitsyn.[21]

By contrast, George Feifer finds that _Lenin in Zurich_ "rarely grips the senses."[22] The fault, he thinks, is that "it is simply not well enough written."[23] Feifer even goes so far as to suggest the possibility that "parts of _Lenin in Zurich_ are a self-portrait by the author," in that both Solzhenitsyn and Lenin shared the "distinctly un-Russian" traits of orderliness, ascetic tendencies, and compulsive working habits and that both were provincial Russians "with messianism in place of cosmopolitan tolerance and an urge to criticize _everyone_ about _everything._ . . ."[24]

Actually, such sharp differences of opinion have marked all recent comment on Solzhenitsyn. Leaving aside questions about the effect of the ideological predilections of the commentators on their commentaries, we may safely say that one of the crucial issues to be resolved by future critics of Solzhenitsyn's writing is how successful he is in giving literary expression to historical material.

Solzhenitsyn has said that he has spent forty years, all of his adult life, thinking about the character of Lenin.[25] Stalin also was a major figure in the twentieth century, and Solzhenitsyn drew his portrait in _The First Circle_. In both cases, the approach is the same: to try to get inside the mind and show us, largely by means of interior monologue, the essence of the man. Stalin, however, receives four brief chapters, or a total of some thirty-six pages; Lenin receives eleven long chapters, or a total of some three hundred pages. Also, Stalin is seen during one evening, while Lenin is seen in process over a period of some three years.

As with his depiction of Stalin, so in his depiction of Lenin, Solzhenitsyn bent every effort to be accurate—not to paint a picture of unrelieved evil but to shade in the nuances of moral being. "In a curious way," says Conquest on this point, "Stalin appeared the more human of the two. His faults of character, frightful though they were, were those of a really bloody human being. Lenin, on the contrary, seemed an alien monster centered on a single cold obsessive drive."[26] Nevertheless, Solzhenitsyn has sought to show him as a human being, even if perhaps less human than Stalin, and to show him as a monster only to the extent that he really was one.

The portraits of Lenin and Stalin underline an important principle in Solzhenitsyn's view of history: the primacy of the individual. Whereas Tolstoy saw the motive power of history in terms of huge, impersonal forces which drive men, Solzhenitsyn always emphasizes that it is individuals who make history what it is. That is, he emphasizes personal responsibility for one's deeds and for their consequences. What happened to his beloved nation after the success of the Bolshevik Revolution grows, in large part, directly out of Lenin's soul and acts. The quest to fathom Lenin's soul is an effort to go back to the roots of Soviet reality. That is not to say that Lenin always knew what his decisions would lead to; indeed, the inability to imagine what would be the long-range outcomes of a given course of action is an important ingredient in the story of Lenin and his comrades. But actions carry within themselves the seeds of their inevitable consequences; and, since actions grow out of the soul, it is the soul which must be understood.

Solzhenitsyn's Lenin does, as Conquest notes, have many of the marks of the monster—and other marks which, while not monstrous, are hardly endearing. He is willing to do anything for the cause, to commit any crime: fraud, robbery, counterfeiting, extortion. He thrills to violence. Like Stalin after him, he considers himself the only "infallible interpreter" (p. 19) of revolutionary principles. We read that "all opposition exasperated him—especially on theoretical questions where it implied a claim to leadership" (p. 94). In a passage which echoes one on Stalin's megalomania, Lenin muses on "all his incomparable abilities (appreciated now by everyone in the party, but he set a truer and still higher value on them) ..." (p. 108). And as Stalin trusted Hitler, only to be betrayed, so Lenin felt that Plekhanov had betrayed him, and he vowed therefore that "he would never believe anyone again ..." (p. 77). Even among his co-conspirators, "he never forgave a mistake. No matter who made it, he would remember as long as he lived" (p. 24). His view of leadership is monolithic: "Split, split, and split again! ... Go on splitting until you find yourselves a tiny clique—but nonetheless the Central Committee. Those left in it may be the most mediocre, the most insignificant people, but if they are united in a common obedience you can achieve anything!" (p. 55). His view of others is thoroughly impersonal and utilitarian: "All the men and women Lenin had ever met in his life he valued only if, and as long as, they were useful to the cause" (p. 80). In him the hater and the ideologue combine: "In every country, stir up hatred of your own government! That is the only work worthy of a socialist" (p. 43). Without an iota of regard for the suffering that war inflicts on human beings, he cheers the outbreak of the Great War: "Such a war is a gift from history!" (p. 37). Even Parvus, a fellow revolutionary who values Lenin highly, thinks, "All that Lenin lacked was breadth"; he saw in Lenin "the savage, intolerant narrowness of the natural schismatic" (p. 143).

If these characteristics were all we knew of Solzhenitsyn's Lenin, we could properly view him as sharing very little in our common humanity. But the author takes great pains to show that Lenin is "one of us." He, too, is a morally responsible agent, though that line running through the heart dividing good and evil can be pushed very far toward one side.

The most noteworthy example of his humanity is his love for Inessa. Whereas usually "a single hour wasted made Lenin ill" (p. 69), this engine of revolution would drop his work for long stretches of time just to be with her. When she is away, he is jealous, afraid that she is practicing what he preaches about free love. Still, marriage to her is out of the question. She would distract him from his mission, and her five children would slow him down. He chooses to stay with his wife, Nadya. "Living with her made no excessive demands on his nerves" (p. 84), and her loyalty, which extends even to accepting Inessa's frequent presence, has its uses.

Dostoevsky has taught us that every human being is a mass of contradictions. Lenin is no exception, though here again on an extraordinary, gargantuan scale. Examples abound. This intense, single-minded man, who "generated energy almost without eating" (p. 100), was also "ultra-cautious" (p. 114), even irresolute; when in March 1917 the Tsar abdicated and a Provisional Government was established in Russia, Lenin could not decide when or even whether to return to his homeland. While always calling men to action, he had "never set his hand to anything *practical*" (p. 163). Of this theorist of revolution, we read, "There was only one thing he was incapable of—*action*. The one thing he could not do was—blow up a battleship" (p. 181). What, instead, was he, and what did he do? "Lenin was—a writer of articles. And pamphlets. He gave lectures. He made speeches" (p. 180). He thinks, "One good leaflet and all Europe would rise in revolt. What about that?!" (p. 199). So Solzhenitsyn calls him "a typical armchair philosopher, a dreamer" (p. 155), a bookish man like Marx.

Evident too is the disparity between Lenin's ideology and his personal style. While many who are egalitarian in principle are dictatorial in practice, the conflict in Lenin's case is extreme. He never shared authority, preferring the blind discipleship of those he condescendingly labeled mediocre to fraternity with fellow ideologues of personal strength and integrity. In the name of democracy he established centralism. This ardent advocate of collectivism was himself an isolated, highly eccentric individual. Pursuing revolution in the name of the masses, he considered peasants "ignorant rabble" (p. 13).

Most surprising, perhaps, is the contradiction between Lenin's supreme self-confidence in interpreting the course of history and his repeated misunderstanding. The leader of the most prodigious of modern revolutions is shown to be obtuse, miscalculating, bungling. The onset of the war in Europe took him completely by surprise. After war did come, he again misjudged: ". . . Germany was not winning . . ." (p. 100). Also, he never anticipated the momentous events in Russia in March 1917; quite the opposite. "You could know your Marxism inside out and still not find an answer when a real crisis burst upon you . . ." (p. 44).

Nevertheless, the miscalculations of the ideologue did not deflect him from his dream. "What mattered was not who was to blame [for the war] but how to turn the war to the best advantage" (p. 22). If the war caught him off guard, he still chose to see it as "the event you have lived to interpret and complete!" (p. 32).

If it seems to us now that Lenin was prescient here, since the chaos brought about by the war did culminate in the Bolshevik Revolution, such is not exactly the case. For his goal was world revolution, not the Russian Revolution. Following Marx, he expected revolution to come first in advanced, industrialized countries. So, with the myopia of locality, he challenges his "numbskull" cohorts: "Don't you realize that Switzerland is the most revolutionary country in the world??!" (p. 58). As late as October 1916, he insists: ". . . SWITZERLAND IS THE CENTER OF WORLD REVOLUTION TODAY!!!" (p. 61). Further—partly because Switzerland is made up of three language groups but probably partly just because he is located there—". . . from Switzerland the flame of revolution will be kindled throughout Europe" (p. 185). Yet, in a moment of despair, he speaks of moving to America after the war. Then, with but the slightest encouragement, he decides that he will "bring about revolution not in Switzerland but in Sweden," will "begin it all from there!" (p. 200). His might be called an *ad hoc* approach to revolution.

Lenin's contradictoriness is also seen in his attitude toward Russia itself. And here we must recall that Solzhenitsyn is writing to Russians about Russia. He wants them to understand what their now sainted hero really thought of them. Far from loving his homeland, Lenin was a deracinated intellectual who flatly called himself an anti-patriot. We would expect that he would find the Russian peasants "corrupted and emasculated by Orthodoxy" (pp. 101-102). But would we expect him to lament that "he had been born in accursed Russia" (p. 108)? His sense of alienation from Russianness was profound:

> Why had he been born in that uncouth country? Just because a quarter of his blood was Russian, fate had hitched him to the ramshackle Russian rattletrap. A quarter of his blood, but nothing in his character, his will, his inclinations made him kin to that slovenly, slapdash, eternally drunken country. . . . He was tied, you say, to Russia by twenty years as a practicing revolutionary? Yes, but by nothing else. (pp. 103-104)

And so perhaps his hatred for Russia bore on his wanting the Germans to win the war. He was delighted by Russian casualties: "The bigger the figures, the happier they made him. . . . But at the same time these figures drove him to despair: no people on earth were so long-suffering and so devoid of sense as the Russians. Their patience knew no bounds" (p. 101). Of course, his fervor for revolution was also a factor: "On the simple calculation that my worst enemy's worst enemy is my friend, the Kaiser's government was the best ally in the world" (p. 157).

For all that, when the newspaper accounts of March 1917 reach Lenin, his thoughts zigzag once again. With thorough inconsistency, he burbles to himself, "It is *only natural* that revolution has broken out in Russia first. That was to be expected. We did expect it. Our proletariat is the most revolutionary in the world . . ." (p. 235).

Lenin is, for Solzhenitsyn, the classic case of the ideologue's self-imposed dehumanization. For all of his energy, for all of his gifts, he has torn himself loose from humanity's social fabric. Lenin, we read, has concluded that "there can be no such relationship between human beings as simple friendship transcending political, class, and material ties" (p. 19). Here lies the difference between a genuine humanism and an analysis of human beings merely as members of a class. Lenin is not without humanity, but it is a humanity stunted and deformed under the pressure of ideology.

9

A NATION OF MARTYRS:

The Gulag Archipelago

With *The Gulag Archipelago* Solzhenitsyn has introduced into the global vocabulary a word with enormous symbolic meaning. The massive outcry against Hitler's bestiality has made of *Holocaust* a paradigmatic symbol of man's inhumanity against man in the twentieth century. At one stroke, a lone man introduced with *Gulag* a second symbol for the same.

Solzhenitsyn's attitude toward the Soviet regime is one of unrelieved hostility. He states boldly and without qualification

> that nowhere on the planet, nowhere in history, was there a regime more vicious, more bloodthirsty, and at the same time more cunning and ingenious than the Bolshevik, the self-styled Soviet regime. That no other regime on earth could compare with it either in the number of those it had done to death, in hardiness, in the range of its ambitions, in its thoroughgoing and unmitigated totalitarianism—no, not even the regime of its pupil Hitler, which at that time blinded Western eyes to all else.[1]

In like mood, Solzhenitsyn writes: "Hitler was a mere disciple, but he had all the luck: his murder camps have made him famous, whereas no one has any interest in ours at all" (vol. III, p. 359).

The horror of the Hitler regime is now gone except in bitter memory. The Archipelago of the Gulag, as readers of Solzhenitsyn know, is still very much with us. This new symbol now colors even the tergiversations of diplomacy between today's super-states. It seems safe to say that no other work in the annals of world literature has had such a profound immediate effect as *The Gulag Archipelago*.

It is deeply ironic, then, that this work was forced toward publication by that very regime against which it is directed. Events approached a head in September 1973, when the KGB detained Elizaveta Voronyanskaya, the woman who had typed the manuscript for Solzhenitsyn and with whom he had left one copy for safekeeping. After five sleepless days and nights of continuous interrogation, she broke and told the secret police where her copy was kept. They confiscated it, and she went home and committed suicide.

With even members of the Central Committee of the Soviet Communist Party now reading his history of the labor camps, Solzhenitsyn concluded that he had no choice but to release his entire text for publication in the West, piece by piece. His fear was that the KGB would publish parts of it pulled out of context to make him appear a Nazi sympathizer. He had given fair warning that he had written works which would appear immediately if he were imprisoned or killed, works which would serve as his literary last will and testament.[2] He decided that the time to publish had come; it was time to make his move.

Solzhenitsyn's original plan had been different. He began *The Gulag Archipelago* only a few years after his release from the tentacles of the Soviet detention system. He worked on it for the next decade, on and off, even while writing on other works, which he hoped might be published in the Soviet Union. By working extremely long hours, he squeezed in time for bits and pieces of *Gulag*, then carefully hiding those fragments. Through most of the sixties, he was still struggling to have his fiction published in the Soviet Union. He was still hoping to speak, even if in slightly muted terms, to his countrymen. *The Gulag Archipelago* was to be released posthumously. He did not want his searing indictment of the prison camps to interfere with the possibility of his publishing his novels. More importantly, he wanted to avoid possible recriminations against those who had served as informants for his *Gulag*.

But, finally, the KGB forced his hand, and Solzhenitsyn played out the first parts of his magisterial manuscript, with the promise of more to come. In December of 1973 he published the first two of the seven parts of *Gulag* in Russian, and by the next month various translations appeared. When he received covert death threats, he called a news conference and publicized the threats widely.

The Soviet authorities were placed in a quandary. If they killed him, the writings of this once unknown schoolteacher, who now, thanks to them, had a worldwide reputation, would be enhanced by the halo of martyrdom. Something similar would happen if they put him in prison or in a psychiatric hospital. In the end, they decided to send him into exile from his homeland.

Perhaps they had some sense of the dread in this thoroughly Russian writer of being banished from Russian soil and Russian compatriots. He himself had described exile abroad as a punishment equivalent, for a Russian writer, to execution by shooting.[3] At any rate, on February 12, 1974, the police took him away, despite his obstinacy, to the Lefortovo Prison in Moscow. The charge: "the systematic commission of acts incompatible with Soviet citizenship and damaging to the Union of Soviet Socialist Republics."[4] The next day, he was flown to Frankfurt, West Germany. To his relief, his family soon followed, with various manuscripts in tow. The KGB must have assumed, doubtless correctly, that he had already secreted copies in the West. He went to Zurich, then finally to rural Vermont, where he lives today. Little new has appeared in print since the exile, and the question remains how well this writer can function in an alien environment. Time will tell if this author, who has been cut off from his cultural roots, will maintain the spiritual equilibrium needed to fulfill his mission. Given the discipline he has developed in overcoming hardships in the past, the odds are on his side.

Reaction to Solzhenitsyn's exile was swift and prolific. Many deracinated Western intellectuals congratulated the Soviets for their humane action. Reactions of Russian dissidents generally differed. Andrei Sakharov saw Solzhenitsyn's banishment as a vengeful act, asserting, "The conscience of humanity must cry out against what has happened."[5] For the most part, Western voices gave Solzhenitsyn a hero's welcome and denounced the USSR for expelling him. References to the book which was the immediate cause of expulsion were abundant and overwhelmingly sympathetic.

Despite its notoriety, *The Gulag Archipelago* is more known about than known. It is a highly unusual, even idiosyncratic book. It is probably the worst of Solzhenitsyn's work for a Westerner to read first. Its length, approaching two thousand pages, is imposing. Its commingling of historical research, personal reminiscence, and literary method is unique. Its language, even in translation, is eccentric and highly individual. Its abrupt shifts in tone, from factual to sarcastic to meditative, can be baffling. Its subject is sensational and, to Western readers, distant. Its organization is kaleidoscopic and unpredictable. Its primary audience is Russian, not Western.

To understand Solzhenitsyn's method of composing *The Gulag Archipelago* is to understand something of the work's heterogeneity. Solzhenitsyn began writing it in 1958 and did not finish it until about 1967. Thus, he was composing this huge nonfiction work all during the time he was creating the autobiographically based literary works, which means that this work serves as an essential gloss on those stories, plays, and novels. The authorial perspective which shaped *Gulag*, which book Solzhenitsyn knew would be forbidden, is consonant with the perspective which shaped those works for which he was seeking publication. In order to work on *Gulag* undetected, Solzheni-

tsyn set himself a herculean work schedule which would make
it seem that his known writing projects would be enough to
occupy all of his waking hours. As soon as he finished chunks
of *Gulag*, he would carefully hide them, then return to composing further chunks. Throughout the whole arduous process
of clandestine composition, he never once had in front of him
the entire work. To avoid repetition and to maintain organization, he had only his memory on which to rely.[6]

The truth of history has always been a major concern of
Solzhenitsyn. His deep belief is that the heirs of the Bolshevik
Revolution have tried to hide or to distort Russian history. In
Gulag he tries to recover the historical truth of the Soviet prison
camps, from 1918 to 1956. He claims for this work that "it all
took place just as it is here described."[7] He operates with the
meticulousness of a careful historian, seeking corroboration of
eyewitness accounts, admitting the lack of corroboration when
it was unavailable, appealing to future readers for corrections.

"Gulag" (more accurately, GULag) is the acronym for the
Chief Administration of Corrective Labor Camps. Solzhenitsyn
asserts that its reign is the first occasion in human history when
the systematic torture of millions was undertaken. Solzhenitsyn
had set several works in the camps operated by the Gulag. Now
he set out to capture some sense of the whole, of the immense
range of the sufferings he had experienced and heard of, recounted from one individual's closeup view. Horrors dominate
the work, though especially the third volume presents heroic
episodes of rebellion by the hapless zeks.

Solzhenitsyn's primary reason for writing *Gulag* was not
to condemn the Soviet Union in the eyes of the world or even
of the Russian people. His main intention was to commemorate
those brothers and sisters of his who together formed what he
called the zek nation, a nation with only oral traditions and
without a written history. From the very moment of his arrest,
he tells us, a plan to write the history of this unknown nation
of many millions began to take shape in his mind. Only when
he had finished his commemorative tome could he say, "I have

fulfilled my duty to those who perished and this gives me relief and peace of mind."[8]

The work is long because there is much to tell. Solzhenitsyn accepts the calculations by an émigré professor of demographic statistics that between 1918 and 1959 sixty-six million zeks died in the camps (vol. I, p. 10).[9] Later, Solzhenitsyn offers an updated estimate of seventy million.[10] This is roughly eleven times the number who perished in Hitler's camps. If Nazi terror has given modern man a benchmark for measuring the enormity of human evil and has even revised modern views of the very nature of man, how much more do Solzhenitsyn's revelations heighten our awareness of the barbarity of our century. The brutality of the well-nigh universally maligned Russian Tsars of the nineteenth century appears paltry when compared with that of the Bolsheviks. Yet, as one American editorialist noted, "You would have to travel from coast to coast . . . to discover ten educated Americans who would tell you that the oppression of the czars was milder than the oppressions of the czars' Soviet successors. But only look at the hard data."[11]

Because Solzhenitsyn had limited firsthand information on the extent of the operations of the Gulag, he sought material from other sources. He read whatever he could locate. He also interviewed 227 witnesses. It is with the whole zek nation in mind that he asks, in the dedication, for forgiveness "for not having seen it all / nor remembered it all, / for not having divined all of it." He hopes that other accounts will yet appear, which process is already underway. At the end of his whole laborious endeavor, he encourages the other survivors of the camps to correct and add, as necessary. "Only then will the book be definitive. God bless the work!" (vol. III, p. 527). For all the massiveness of his testimony, much remains untold. As he is furtively working away, he thinks of the publication of *One Day* and muses, "If the first tiny droplet of truth has exploded like a psychological bomb, what then will happen in our country when whole waterfalls of Truth burst forth? And they will burst forth. It has to happen" (vol. I, p. 298).

The greatest problem Solzhenitsyn faced in writing this

massive tribute was that the atrocities to be catalogued were so
monstrous as to defy credence: "Just as oxcart drivers of Gogol's
time could not have imagined the speed of a jet plane, those
who have never gone through the receiving-line meat grinder of
Gulag cannot grasp the true possibilities of interrogation" (vol. I,
p. 133). The typical reader has no point of reference in his or her
experience by which to fathom the magnitude of the horror of
Gulag. Solzhenitsyn must make the unimaginable imaginable
when the zeks themselves could not believe what was happening to them.

> Thus many were shot—thousands at first, then hundreds of
> thousands. We divide, we multiply, we sigh, we curse. But still
> and all, these are just numbers. They overwhelm the mind and
> then are easily forgotten. And if some day the relatives of those
> who had been shot were to send one publisher photographs of
> their executed kin, and an album of those photographs were
> to be published in several volumes, then just by leafing through
> them and looking into the extinguished eyes we would learn
> much that would be valuable for the rest of our lives. Such
> reading, almost without words, would leave a deep mark on
> our hearts for all eternity. (vol. I, p. 442)

A closely related problem is that the cumulative impact
of one story of suffering after another can overload and numb
the mind. Many readers who at first find the work chilling
later consider it monotonous. Solzhenitsyn often acknowledges
the problem: "It is not I who am repeating myself, but Gulag"
(vol. I, p. 577). Later, he elaborates, "But here I note that I am
beginning to repeat myself. And this will be boring to write, and
boring to read, because the reader already knows everything that
is going to happen ahead of time . . ." (vol. I, pp. 582-83). He
cannot escape this problem, and much later in the work he is
still saying, "The tedium of it all! Nothing but the same thing
over and over again" (vol. III, p. 400).

Still, for all his attention in *Gulag* to the integrity of the
historian's craft, Solzhenitsyn always considers himself first and
foremost a literary writer. Not for nothing is the work subtitled
"A Literary Investigation." And in the face of the insuperable

difficulties forced on him by his historical material, Solzhenitsyn resorts to a wide variety of devices to maintain reader interest. The uniqueness of the work lies in the fusion of the focus on historical accuracy and the use of any literary elements which do not detract from that focus.

The title itself illustrates what the subtitle asserts. The factual material to be investigated is that prison system governed by the Gulag. But the separate camps may be seen in a literary image to constitute islands, an archipelago—in this case, scattered over a vast expanse of land rather than water. Together, they make up a veritable nation (of zeks), another recurring image; yet each camp is an isolated island cut off from help from elsewhere. "Gulag" is Solzhenitsyn's monolithic historical given; "archipelago" is his invented addition to show the camps' unity and separateness simultaneously. Also, the title carries a rhyme which translation does not retain; it is the Arkhipe*lag* Gu*lag*.

Among the plethora of literary elements, five are worthy of special note: organization, point of view, tone (especially irony and sarcasm), language, and imagery. Combined, they make *Gulag* quite different from most works of historical research.

Gulag lacks simple, straightforward organization. Most history books are organized chronologically. While Solzhenitsyn inserts through his volumes chapters which, taken together, give some sense of the development of the camp system from its beginnings in 1918 to the end of his own stay in 1956, he does not gather these chapters together. Rather, he intersperses among them many chapters devoted to other purposes. There are generalized accounts of typical zek experiences—arrest, interrogation, and the rest—which loosely suggest the progressive stages of prison life. There are chapters on separate groups: guards, thieves, women, children, religious believers. There are sections of judiciary transcriptions, autobiography, authorial speculation. There is much, much more. The material is highly heterogeneous. When a pattern for a series of chapters emerges, it is usually thematic: for example, the chapters in volume three on attempted escapes. But for the most part Solzhenitsyn seems to wish to keep shifting the focus in an effort to maintain the reader's interest. The organization of *Gulag* recalls in certain respects the organization of Solzhenitsyn's polyphonic novels. What some might consider an inability to organize is probably better understood as a sensitivity to the limited attention span of most readers.

One of the most important literary techniques in *Gulag* is the manipulation of point of view. In some passages the author submerges himself into the background; but there are not many such passages, and they are seldom prolonged. Almost always the reader is aware that Solzhenitsyn is mediating the material to him. Whereas most scholarly treatises on history are marked by a studied effort at authorial distance, this work is infused with a highly personal tone. Solzhenitsyn is always intensely involved, never antiseptically detached. Even when he is most meticulous, his métier is the heat of life and death, not the coolness of note-cards. If structure seems to serve the purpose of diversity, authorial point of view constitutes the main unifying device in this massive work. Readers constantly feel themselves listening to the author as he ruminates on his country and its fate in modern times. Always, it is not just the events but the author's interpretation which readers find themselves confronting and thus judging. It is easy enough to discern the author's voice in those many passages in which he recites his own experiences; it is essential to see that these are not the only places where we, as readers, are listening to him speak *in propria persona*.

Irony and sarcasm abound in the work, as they do in Solzhenitsyn's fiction.[12] But in no other work does he drip irony and sarcasm as acidly as in *The Gulag Archipelago*; they are useful to express moral outrage. Remarking on the limited material available to him, Solzhenitsyn says wrily, "We could not broadcast pleas for more on the radio" (vol. II, p. 138). An epigraph to this blood-chilling work cites the cruel Krylenko: "In the period of dictatorship, surrounded on all sides by enemies, we sometimes manifested unnecessary leniency and unnecessary softheartedness" (vol. I, p. 1). Mordantly, Solzhenitsyn explains why people were sometimes buried alive: "Not out of brutality, no. It had been ascertained that when dragging and lifting them, it was much easier to cope with living people than with corpses" (vol. II, p. 390). Equally acid is his mock praise of the secret police: "One has to give the *Organs* their due: in an age when public speeches, the plays in our theaters, and women's fashions all seem to come off assembly lines, arrests can be of the most varied kind" (vol. I, pp. 9-10). Of the transport of zeks to the camps, Solzhenitsyn comments, "They don't heat the car, they don't protect the other prisoners from the thieves, they don't give you enough to drink, and they don't give you enough to eat—but on the other hand they don't let you sleep either" (vol. I, p. 572). Solzhenitsyn recounts in sarcastic tones the purge of 1937-38 in which the Communists rounded up, among others, other Communists: "And may my compassionate reader now have mercy on me! Until now my pen sped on untrembling, my heart didn't skip a beat, and we slipped along unconcerned, because for these fifteen years we have been firmly protected either by legal revolutionality or else by revolutionary legality. But from now on things will be painful . . ." (vol. I, p. 407). Finally, in a list of examples which could go on and on, Solzhenitsyn puts irony to the use of his characteristic device of understatement. A chapter on "The Peasant Plague" opens thus: "This chapter will deal with a small matter. Fifteen million souls. Fifteen million lives" (vol. III, p. 350). It is a small matter in that, whereas much honor was heaped upon the war dead, virtually no official notice was ever taken of the huge attrition among mere peasants. Solzhenitsyn wants posterity to remember those almost unnoticed human beings, too.

If Solzhenitsyn's frequently sardonic tone is unusual for a work of serious historical research, so is the language he employs. Even in translation, some of this linguistic novelty comes through. The basic diction of *Gulag* is brisk and energetic; it eschews the usual idiom of scholarship. It is filled with parentheses and dashes, with authorial asides; at times, it is elliptical in the extreme. The language is a fascinating fusion of camp slang, unknown to the general Russian citizenry, and old Russian, for which a nineteenth-century dictionary is a necessary aid. What Solzhenitsyn omits, except to ridicule occasionally, is that stilted idiom of Marxist ideology, which he believes has perverted the language of press, school, and even literature. The conclusion is inescapable that Solzhenitsyn wishes to have the profound effect on his native tongue that many great writers have had on theirs: Dante, Luther, Shakespeare.

The imagery in *Gulag* enhances our sense of immediacy; it also conveys value judgments. The second chapter, devoted to an historical overview, is entitled "The History of Our Sewage Disposal System." Once Solzhenitsyn has invented this unexpected but powerful image, he can elaborate on it in many ways. For example:

> Through the sewer pipes the flow pulsed. Sometimes the pressure was higher than had been projected, sometimes lower. But the prison sewers were never empty. The blood, the sweat, and the urine into which we were pulped pulsed through them continuously. The history of this sewage system is an endless swallow and flow; flood alternating with ebb and ebb again with flood; waves pouring in, some big, some small; brooks and rivulets flowing in from all sides; trickles oozing in through gutters; and then just plain individually scooped-up droplets. (vol. I, p. 25)

Elsewhere, prisoners are likened to the major rivers of Russia: the Volga, the Ob, the Yenisei. The larger the stream of prisoners, the larger the river chosen as image.

One of the most pervasive strains of imagery in *Gulag*, and in the novels as well, is animal metaphor: the lamb, the goat, the beaver, the dog, the worm. Like sewage, these images convey dehumanization. Appearing most often is the rabbit, illustrating the meekness with which most zeks accepted their lot. Of such "rabbits," Solzhenitsyn comments, "All these people had forgotten beyond recall ... that each of them was a man, that he carried the divine spark within him, that he was capable of higher things ..." (vol. III, p. 70). The insect is also frequently used—borrowed from Lenin, no less!

Another recurring strain of metaphor is cancer. One chapter is entitled "The Archipelago Metastasizes." The camps are a cancer in the body politic. Just as the terror of cancer is that it can spread throughout the body, so "in this same way our whole country was infected by the poisons of the Archipelago. And whether it will ever be able to get rid of them someday, only God knows" (vol. II, p. 632).

Because Solzhenitsyn insists upon the literary, as well as the historical, character of *Gulag*, literary critics will inevitably look for generic models. The author's description of it as "this home-grown, homemade book" (vol. II, p. 80) puts the matter in some doubt. Nevertheless, the search for a genre can be illuminating, even with all due caution against the vice of oversimplifying by pigeon-holing. So Lionel Abel says something useful when he describes *Gulag* as "investigative poetry."[13]

Several interesting parallels exist between *Gulag* and the epic. Certainly, the size of the work and the scope of the subject are epical, as has been noted by some commentators and by the author himself. A whole people, the nation of zeks, is celebrated. There are even glimpses of Homer—for example, of the rosy-fingered dawn. Still, there is no sustained effort to follow the conventions of this convention-bound genre. So any description of *The Gulag Archipelago* as an epic must remain loose and no more than suggestive of certain of its traits.

At the same time, there is a genre of writing which, while not a strict literary genre, is useful for opening up the very essence of *Gulag*. It is the genre of the martyrology.[14] Many difficulties in knowing how to read *Gulag* can be lessened, if not resolved, if the work is approached as a commemoration of innocents who suffered at the hands of wicked persecutors. Historically, martyrs were religious believers persecuted and killed for their faith. Although Solzhenitsyn repeatedly lauds the believers in prison, they are certainly not the exclusive subject of his work. Rather, he memorializes those ordinary men and women who try to retain some modicum of their innate humanity; the villains are the dehumanizers. The line Solzhenitsyn draws is between simple humanity and a powerful modern force aligned against it. Thus, if some of his "martyrs" are not

especially heroic, they are worthy of commemoration nevertheless.

To call *Gulag* a martyrology is not to find a single term
encompassing the whole of the work, since righting the
wrongs of a deficient and distorted account of history is an essential part of Solzhenitsyn's motivation; nor is it to provide a
label of which the author himself was fully aware. Rather, it is
simply to clarify for the reader how he or she should approach
the work.

Whatever else was in Solzhenitsyn's mind, the commemorative quality of *Gulag* is clear. Of his fellow zeks, Solzhenitsyn observes that "no one will ever engrave their forgotten
names on a marble tombstone placed over their bones" (vol. II,
p. 581). He is "writing for mute Russia" (vol. II, p. 317). In an
important sense, in fact, he is not writing the work on his own;
thinking of his 227 witnesses, he declares *Gulag* to be "our
common, collective monument to all those who were tortured
and murdered" (vol. I, p. xi). His laborious and time-consuming
work grows "solely from a sense of obligation—because too
many stories and recollections have accumulated in my hands
and I cannot allow them to perish" (vol. II, pp. 213-14). Try as
he does to be selective, he must insist that the reader's interest
take a back seat to the martyrologist's task of retelling. Every
human life is precious and worthy of a respectful memorial. If
the telling of horror story after horror story runs the risk of
monotonous reading, the author has a higher obligation than to
provide aesthetic pleasure. *Gulag* is monumental in more than
one way.

The uniqueness of *Gulag* makes it difficult to assess in
relation to the rest of Solzhenitsyn's writings. Some consider it
his greatest work. If the future confirms that judgment, however, Solzhenitsyn's initial literary ambition will not have been
fulfilled. For it is his projected series of novels on the cataclysmic events of the nineteen-teens that he intends as his masterpiece. This observation is in no way intended to denigrate the
magnificent achievement of *Gulag*. But it is worth noting the
author's own acknowledgment that, in contrast to the material

of the fictional series, the material of *Gulag* was not of his own free choosing. He wrote *Gulag* out of a sense of obligation—obligation to his present and future compatriots.

A striking parallel may be drawn between the writing careers of Solzhenitsyn and Milton. Each began his career with a clear plan of what his great work would be and made notes and outlines accordingly. Each confronted a physical ailment that made fulfillment of the original goal seem highly unlikely. Milton went blind; Solzhenitsyn has battled cancer. More to the point, each writer felt contemporary events so impinging on him that his sense of duty to his fellow countrymen forced him to let his energy be deflected for a time from his intended masterpiece. So Milton write his prose treatises on matters of church and state; he called them the writing of his left hand. So Solzhenitsyn wrote *The Gulag Archipelago* and several essays on current affairs. Each, finally, in late career, returned to work on his intended masterpiece.

Any suggestion that *Gulag* is the writing of Solzhenitsyn's "left hand" must quickly be qualified. While some of Milton's prose treatises are memorable—*Areopagitica* comes to mind at once—no single one of them nor any group of them begins to compare with *Gulag* in scope or literary craftsmanship. Very few today read Milton's prose for its own sake; many will in fact read *Gulag* for its own literary merit.

If the form of *Gulag* is unique among Solzhenitsyn's writings, the same is not to be said for its controlling vision. It is readily imaginable that this nonfiction work on Soviet reality would be even more susceptible to a political interpretation than the fictional works. Precisely to forestall this error, Solzhenitsyn early gives stern warning: "So let the reader who expects this book to be a political exposé slam its covers shut right now" (vol. I, p. 168). *Gulag*, too, is governed by a moral vision.

Indeed, as Solzhenitsyn describes a horrendous episode of the sinking of barges with hundreds of zeks aboard, he pauses to comment that the episode "belongs to the history of *morals* [his italics], which is where everything else originates as well" (vol. I, p. 435). When Solzhenitsyn does deign to speak of politics, his view of the subject is memorably low: "After all, politics is not even a science, but is an empirical area not susceptible to description by any mathematical apparatus; furthermore, it is an area subject to human egotism and blind passion" (vol. I, p. 391).

His attacks on the Soviet system are never for political, but always for moral, malfeasance. For instance, he writes,

> Should we wrap it all up and simply say that they arrested the *innocent*? But we omitted saying that the very concept of *guilt* had been repealed by the proletarian revolution and, at the beginning of the thirties, was defined as *rightist opportunism*! So we can't even discuss these out-of-date concepts, guilt and innocence. (vol. I, p. 76)

It is the Soviet officials who seek to politicize that human reality which is essentially moral; it is their view that *"the heart of the matter is not personal guilt but social danger"* (vol. I, p. 282). By contrast, Solzhenitsyn's view is that "the meaning of earthly existence lies . . . in the development of the soul" (vol. II, p. 613).

Because morality is rooted in spirituality, it is not surprising that in *Gulag* Solzhenitsyn praises persecuted religious believers frequently and generously. Also, in his authorial comments he refers to God with natural ease: "And may you be judged by God but not by people" (vol. I, p. 128). Roy Medvedev, a dissident who remains committed to Leninism, understands clearly the centrality of religious belief in Solzhenitsyn's worldview. In his perceptive and appreciative review of *Gulag*, he observes that for Solzhenitsyn ". . . no political doctrine, but only religion is capable of assuming the moral leadership of society. Only faith in God can serve as a basis for a humane morality."[15] Medvedev, with thoughts of inquisitions and theocracy in his mind, finds himself "little attracted to Solzhenitsyn's ideals."[16] "For the overwhelming majority of the Soviet people," he says, "religion no longer is and no longer can become the truth, and it is highly unlikely that young people in the 20th century will look to faith in God for their guidance."[17] But he recognizes that Solzhenitsyn has switched his allegiance from Marx to Christ, and he declares, "Any sincere change in belief merits respect and understanding. Solzhenitsyn exposed no one and betrayed no one. Today Solzhenitsyn is an opponent of Marxism and he does not hide the fact."[18] Medvedev knows how to read _The Gulag Archipelago._

Moral development begins, as Solzhenitsyn reiterates throughout his works, with the individual's awareness of his or her own worth: "Each of us is a center of the Universe ..." (vol. I, p. 3). The individual's moral development is never easy, and continuous collective efforts to dehumanize take their deadly toll. Since, however, growth comes through suffering, for the overcomers those efforts have the effect of a trainer's hand: "And thus it is that we have to keep getting banged on flank and snout again and again so as to become, in time at least, human beings, yes, human beings" (vol. I, p. 549).

As in Solzhenitsyn's other works, the individual's moral development comes not in a social vacuum but in that awareness of community which is rooted in the fixity and universality of human nature. "Human nature, if it changes at all, changes not much faster than the geological face of the earth" (vol. I, p. 562). Saints and sinners, political prisoners and common criminals—all are to be judged by a single standard, since "they have all belonged to that same ordinary, sinful, everyday humanity among which you have spent your whole life" (vol. I, p. 501). Only when zeks began to form a sense of solidarity did escapes and uprisings occur, as the third volume amply documents.

This sense of human community is, as Solzhenitsyn shows elsewhere as well, a far cry from Marxism's imposed collectivism. Solzhenitsyn refers to the pronoun _we_ as a "joyous word," and he contrasts the collectivist perversion of it and the beauty of true human communion:

> Yes, that word which you may have despised out in freedom, when they used it as a substitute for your individuality ("All of us, like one man!" Or: "We are deeply angered!" Or: "We

demand!" or: "We swear!") is now revealed to you as something sweet: you are not alone in the world! Wise, spiritual
beings—*human beings*—still exist. (vol. I, pp. 183-84)

The Gulag Archipelago is so massive and diverse that it defies
brief summary. Also, it does not lend itself to the kind of over-
arching survey used in the three preceding chapters on the long
novels. Those works were organized according to the polyphonic principle; there is no single organizing device in *Gulag*.
In order to convey some sense of the flavor of the work as a
whole, the remainder of this chapter is devoted to a scrutiny of
four important areas of concern in *Gulag*: the horrors which
were committed, the basis on which the perpetrators of atrocities are to be judged, the effort to recover the truth of history,
and the autobiographical insights which Solzhenitsyn provides.
While the selection of these four topics leaves much untreated,
it is adequate to bring the reader to an introductory appreciation
of the inner workings of *Gulag*.

It is especially the recounting of specific horror after horror that many readers find depressing, even to the point of wanting to stop reading. But what some find too painful to bear in
the reading, real people had to bear in actual experience. The
following passage is illustrative:

> But the most awful thing they can do with you is this: undress
> you from the waist down, place you on your back on the floor,
> pull your legs apart, seat assistants on them . . . who also hold
> down your arms; and then the interrogator (and women inter-
> rogators have not shrunk from this) stands between your legs
> and with the toe of his boot (or of her shoe) gradually, steadily,
> and with ever greater pressure crushes against the floor those
> organs which once made you a man. He looks into your eyes
> and repeats and repeats his questions or the betrayal he is
> urging on you. If he does not press down too quickly or just
> a shade too powerfully, you still have fifteen seconds left in
> which to scream that you will confess to everything, that you
> are ready to see arrested all twenty of those people he's been
> demanding of you, or that you will slander in the newspapers
> everything that you hold holy. (vol. I, pp. 127-28)

This passage, from the chapter on interrogation, elaborates on just one of the thirty-one tortures catalogued therein: some physical, some psychological, some a combination of the two. Here are some more: interrogation during the night, abuse by foul language, preliminary humiliation (as when a woman is locked in a box naked and male jailers peer through a peephole and laughingly appraise her attributes), tickling (usually on the inside of the nose with a feather: ". . . it feels as though someone were drilling into his brain"), having a lit cigarette placed on the skin, being jammed into a grave-like pit with no toilet facilities for days at a time, being deprived of water, being quizzed for days in a row by an assembly line of interrogators, starvation, having fingernails squeezed by a machine, and bridling ("A long piece of rough toweling inserted between the prisoner's jaws like a bridle; the ends were then pulled back over his shoulders and tied to his heels. Just try lying on your stomach like a wheel with your spine breaking—and without water and food for two days!" [vol. I, p. 117]).

Nor does torturing stop when interrogation does. For instance, when zeks were being transported in the crowded hold of a barge from one island of the Archipelago to another, "they urinated in glass jars which were passed from hand to hand and emptied through the porthole. And anything more substantial went right in their pants" (vol. I, p. 578).

Upon arrival at a camp, the zeks' torture is in no way diminished. Because rations were distributed not to individuals but to groups of ten, if one died, "the others shoved his corpse under the bunks and kept it there until it started to stink. They got the corpse's rations" (vol. I, p. 535). One episode tells that starving zeks "ate the corpse of a horse which had been lying dead for more than a week and which not only stank but was covered with flies and maggots" (vol. II, p. 126). Nor was cannibalism unknown. And a typical threat to zeks was, "I'll make you suck snot from corpses!" (vol. II, p. 33). After having been starved, beaten, deprived of sleep, incredibly overcrowded (sometimes "*three* [Solzhenitsyn's italics] persons for each square yard of floor space" [vol. I, p. 125]), zeks who did not fulfill their unrealistically high work norms faced punishment.

In winter he [the guard] ordered them to strip naked in the mine shaft, poured cold water over them, and in this state they had to run to the compound; in summer they were forced to strip naked, their hands were tied behind them to a common pole, and they were left out, tied there, under a cloud of mosquitoes. (The guard was covered by a mosquito net.) Then, finally, they were simply beaten with a rifle butt and tossed into an isolator. (vol. II, p. 127)

And when those times came, as they inevitably did, when Stalin's courts fed more victims into the Archipelago than Stalin's camp managers could handle, there would come the order: *"Reduce the number of prisoners.* (And not by releasing them, of course)" (vol. II, p. 126). Then, sick zeks would be left to die or would become targets for officers' shooting practice. When those tactics proved insufficient, there were mass murders and mass graves. For instance: "At Zolotisty they used to summon a brigade from the mine face in broad daylight and shoot the members down one after another. (And this is not a substitute for night executions; they took place too)" (vol. II, p. 129). It is no wonder that Solzhenitsyn savagely parodies Marx's famous maxim, "From each according to his ability, to each according to his need": "From us everything, to us nothing" (vol. II, p. 98).

Solzhenitsyn heightens the emotional impact of this cataloguing of brutalities by devoting chapters to the plight of women and children in the Gulag camps. Just as Solzhenitsyn pays more attention to women in his fiction than readers might have had reason to anticipate, so in *Gulag* he devotes a separate chapter to them. It was common that there would be one woman for six or seven men in a prison camp and that therefore special pressures were placed on women. Mainly, the officials sought them out for sex, though the zeks, too, were eager for womanly comfort (recall one of the primary plot lines in *The Love-Girl and the Innocent*). So the trustees would send newly arrived women prisoners down the corridor, naked, one at a time and then decide who got whom. "In the camp bath the naked women were examined like merchandise" (vol. II, p. 229). Attractiveness was a curse. The woman who refused sexual submission could expect a very difficult time. When women were rare, as in Kolyma, gang rapes occurred. So most women submitted. Young girls, with little sense of selfhood, "quickly became the most reckless of all" (vol. II, p. 231). Submission was also encouraged by the despairing sense that "there was no meaning, no purpose, left in life" (vol. II, p. 231).

It is in his chapter on women that Solzhenitsyn shows most markedly the intimate connection between the physical and the spiritual in human sexuality. Sometimes this interconnection has a negative effect: when "the vulnerable female functions" cease because "the woman arrested is spiritually wounded"; in that case, he estimates, "five weeks are enough to destroy both the woman and the human being" (vol. II, pp. 228, 237). In other cases, sexual union overcomes all of the enforced tawdriness. Solzhenitsyn describes those small victories movingly:

> Plundered of everything that fulfills female life and indeed human life in general . . . what else could the women camp inmates turn to except love? With God's blessing the love which came might also be almost not of the flesh. . . . But from its own unfleshly character, as the women remember today, the spirituality of camp love became even more profound. . . . Women who were already elderly could not sleep nights because of a chance smile. . . . So sharply did the light of love stand out against the dirty, murky camp existence! (vol. II, p. 239)

To combat their humiliation, some female prisoners sought to become pregnant: "Irreparably humiliated, the camp women were reconfirmed in their human dignity through motherhood . . ." (vol. II, pp. 244-45). And, as was invariably the case, when one of them wanted to have her child christened, "there was always a woman who could pronounce a prayer—any prayer would do—and the child was dipped in warm water and baptized, and the glowing mother invited everyone to the table" (vol. II, p. 245).

Solzhenitsyn's chapter on "The Kids" shows that the sins of the fathers are visited upon the children—and we have not yet reached the third and the fourth generations. As early as 1927, Solzhenitsyn's digging has discovered, forty-eight percent of all prisoners were between sixteen and twenty-four. His view is that of the many reprehensible aspects of the Gulag, "perhaps the most abominable of all was that maw that swallowed up *the kids*" (vol. II, p. 447). There was no minimum age for incarceration of political prisoners, and Solzhenitsyn tells the story of a six-year-old who was imprisoned for up to eight years for filching a pocketful of potatoes. If the camps perverted adults, they had an absolutely devastating effect on children, who "accepted the Archipelago with the divine impressionability of childhood. And in a few *days* children became beasts there! And the worst kind of beasts, with no ethical conceptions whatever . . ." (vol. II, p. 452). These children, with "tiny, immature hearts," who "saw the world as it is seen by quadrupeds" (vol. II, pp. 462, 452), had not lived long enough to develop a conscience: "In their consciousness there was no demarcation line between what was permissible and what was not permissible, and no concept whatever of good and evil" (vol. II, p. 457). So young boys even gang-raped women and girls—and the little girls so abused often did not react, since they had no more moral sensitivity than the boys. These kids were especially hard on old people and often ripped their rations from their hands; if an oldster pleaded that he was dying of starvation, the kids would retort, "So you're going to kick the bucket soon anyway—what's the difference?" (vol. II, p. 458). At every point, the kids followed the example of the thieves, that group of prisoners who constantly preyed on the so-called "politicals" and whom Stalin always considered "socially friendly" elements. In exasperation and outrage, Solzhenitsyn passes his judgment not on the children, but on the Soviet authorities who so dehumanized them: "Oh, you corrupters of young souls! How prosperously you are living out your lives!" (vol. III, p. 222). Sardonically he concludes, "And let any country speak up that can say it has loved its children as we have ours!" (vol. II, p. 467).

Throughout the extensive cataloguing of horrors, Solzhenitsyn consistently strives to show, by imagery and by simple narration, that the Soviet system diabolically intended to dehumanize people, stripping them of any vestiges of human dignity, reducing them to the level of animals. If the mayhem was committed in the name of some high-sounding utopian ideology, then the events themselves were a damning indictment of that ideology. But the fallaciousness is always to be seen ultimately in the actual dehumanization the ideology has spawned. Let the ideologists believe privately what they will, just as long as they do not wreak public havoc on those other private persons who seek simply to live normal human lives which are imbued with the dignity which comes from being created in the image of God.

Solzhenitsyn is at great pains to try to comprehend what motivates those members of the Soviet hierarchy, from high to low, who either ordered or committed the atrocities which fill his account. As the powerless zeks are always judged by a moral standard, so are those powerful officers of the land. As for those blue-capped secret police, "there were never any spiritual or moral barriers" (vol. I, p. 99) to keep them from being torturers. In their crazed lust for power and gain, they inevitably and irretrievably excluded themselves "by the nature of their work and by deliberate choice from the *higher* sphere of human existence . . ." (vol. I, p. 147). Early on, Solzhenitsyn says, he had "already deduced the generalized judgment that a camp keeper *could not be a decent person*" (vol. II, p. 550). The issue, for jailer and jailed, is always the quality of human being; the criterion is always the moral one.

Solzhenitsyn has consistently eschewed the simplistic categorizations of people as good or bad. Each individual, he insists, tends in both directions. Still,

> evildoing . . . [evidently] has a threshold magnitude. Yes, a human being hesitates and bobs back and forth between good and evil all his life. He slips, falls back, clambers up, repents, things begin to darken again. But just so long as the threshold of evildoing is not crossed, the possibility of returning remains, and he himself is still within reach of our hope. But when, through the density of evil actions, the result either of

their own extreme degree or of the absoluteness of his power, he suddenly crosses that threshold, he has left humanity behind, and without, perhaps, the possibility of return. (vol. I, p. 175)

It is on these elemental grounds of personal morality that Solzhenitsyn indicts those who dehumanize others, from the lowest camp guard to the privileged secret police officer to Andrei Vishinsky to Joseph Stalin himself.

At the same time, Solzhenitsyn does not fail to excoriate the ideology which has fueled the Soviet exercise in inhumanity. Any ideology which proposes itself as a substitute for the traditional Christian view of the world and man is, for Solzhenitsyn, deeply suspect; and Marxism is one such. So Solzhenitsyn explains an important principle: "To do evil a human being must first of all believe that what he's doing is good, or else that it's a well-considered act in conformity with natural law" (vol. I, p. 173). It is ideology which provides just such a rationalization. Therefore, declaims Solzhenitsyn, "Thanks to *ideology*, the twentieth century was fated to experience evildoing on a scale calculated in the millions. This cannot be denied, nor passed over, nor suppressed" (vol. I, p. 174).

But complicity in the moral evil sanctioned by ideology does not assure ease of mind; examples to the contrary abound in *The First Circle* and *Cancer Ward*. Only in an ideologically enslaved country could the following fantastic vignette be depicted. (It is one which has caught the fancy of a number of reviewers.) A district conference of the Communist Party concluded with a tribute to Comrade Stalin. Everyone at once jumped to his feet and applauded—for three whole minutes, for four, five, six, seven, eight. "They were done for! Their goose was cooked! They couldn't stop now till they collapsed with heart attacks!" Nine minutes! Ten! And "to the last man" they all had "make-believe enthusiasm on their faces." Then,

after eleven minutes, the director of the paper factory assumed a businesslike expression and sat down in his seat. And, oh, a miracle took place! Where had the universal, uninhibited, indescribable enthusiasm gone? To a man, everyone else stopped dead and sat down. They had been saved! The squirrel had been smart enough to jump off his revolving wheel. . . . That same night the factory director was arrested. (vol. I, pp. 69-70)

Throughout *Gulag*, Solzhenitsyn sets up a running contrast between "us" and "them": the persecuted zeks and the persecuting officials. Of all the many groups constituting the "us" of the zek nation, the one which receives the most lavish praise is the religious believers, be they Russian Orthodox or other. The believers were the most steadfast of all prisoners Solzhenitsyn knew in prison. Ironically, they were labeled politicals, but that was only because they were not thieves—and because the politically bound Soviets had little imagination for labels. Solzhenitsyn, who was not a believer when he entered the Gulag, immediately noticed this crucially distinctive feature of the religious zeks: "They knew very well *for what* they were serving time, and they were unwavering in their convictions!" (vol. II, p. 310). He lauds that "multitude of Christians," true martyrs, who "died unknown, casting only in their immediate vicinity a light like a candle. They were the best of Russia's Christians" (vol. II, p. 310). And, as for their being ostensible "politicals," doubtless he would agree with Mihajlo Mihajlov's comment: "Solzhenitsyn writes with complete justification that it is specifically the Christians in the USSR who are truly political, in the sense that it is they who undermine the very essence of totalitarian rule, i.e., the belief in the unlimited power of external circumstances, which supposedly direct man's inner world (i.e., his soul)."[19] Those who willfully persecuted such as these did could under no circumstances be forgiven.

Although the bulk of *The Gulag Archipelago* relates what Solzhenitsyn knew from his own experience or from that of his 227 roughly contemporary witnesses, he did what research he could do to recover the true history of the Gulag system. And despite his straitened circumstances, what he discovered was sensational in the extreme. His most spectacular discovery, which had been carefully hidden away from historical researchers, was that the prison system he memorably labeled the Gulag Archipelago was set into motion by Lenin himself less than one year after the 1917 success of the Bolshevik Revolution. When Mihajlo Mihajlov, a Yugoslav citizen of Russian birth, had charged that the Soviet concentration camps were first established in 1921, he was greeted with derision and castigation. Solzhenitsyn went Mihajlov three years better! By his assertion and its supporting documentation, he has wrought a major revision in modern history.

Lenin, then, not Stalin, must take the credit for establishing the prison system Solzhenitsyn goes on to show to be the most heinous in the history of mankind. If the three chapters pulled from Solzhenitsyn's unfinished series on the nineteen-teens which constitute *Lenin in Zurich* offer a well-developed portrait of Lenin as a revolutionary figure, we must turn to *The Gulag Archipelago* to see Solzhenitsyn's depiction of Lenin in power. It is, therefore, of more than passing interest that Roy Medvedev, a loyal Leninist, maintains in his review of *Gulag* that "Solzhenitsyn cites Lenin without distorting his words. . . ."[20]

It was Lenin, not Stalin, who asserted, "The court must not exclude terror" (vol. I, p. 353). It was Lenin's view of the intelligentsia that "in actual fact *they are not [the nation's] brains, but shit*" (vol. I, p. 328). It was Lenin who, long before Hitler, coined the term *"concentration camps"* (vol. II, p. 17). It was Lenin who, on July 23, 1918, decreed, *"Those deprived of freedom who are capable of labor must be recruited for physical work on a compulsory basis"* (vol. II, p. 14). It was Lenin who set the pace for incarcerating religious believers. It was Lenin who established the principle of arbitrariness in sending people to the Gulag, so that never was the zek nation populated primarily by common criminals. In other words, Stalin only continued the practices which Lenin began and put firmly in place. Stalin's only contribution was a quantitative one. Solzhenitsyn is unable to accept the revised history of post-Stalinist times which is designed to whitewash the reputation of Lenin and pass him down to posterity as a hero.

At the same time, Solzhenitsyn's hostility toward Stalin is, if anything, even more pronounced in *The Gulag Archipelago* than in *The First Circle*. His vehemence overflows when he thinks of the case of six peasants who were put to death for taking a few small clippings of hay from a collective farm:

> Even if Stalin had killed no others, I believe that he deserved to be drawn and quartered just for the lives of those six....
> And yet they still dare shriek at us (from Peking, from Tirana, from Tbilisi, yes, and plenty of big-bellies in the Moscow suburbs are doing it too): "How could you dare expose him?" "How could you dare disturb his great shade?" "Stalin belongs to the world Communist movement!" But in my opinion all he belongs to is the Criminal Code. (vol. I, p. 437)

Of course, Solzhenitsyn's attempt to recover the truth of history extends far beyond reciting hitherto unpublished deeds by Lenin and Stalin. Mainly, he tells true stories about Gulag inmates. He shows the connivance of the writer Maxim Gorky in the coverup of Gulag atrocities. He makes publicly available some transcriptions of court proceedings which otherwise might be lost forever. The list goes on and on. Solzhenitsyn's attention to historical detail is unremitting. Much of it strikes many Western readers as dry and boring. They have painfully little awareness of the known, much less the unknown, facts of modern Russian history. But to Russians, from this generation on, Solzhenitsyn will be known as an important historian, regardless of what time might do to his literary reputation.

Although Solzhenitsyn, who has lived one of the truly dramatic lives of the twentieth century, has not yet written an autobiography, much of his life can be pieced together from his works. News sources, reviews, and critical books tell us some things about him. Various of his fictional works, rooted as they are in autobiography to one degree or another, tell us more. But *The Gulag Archipelago* offers some invaluable insights which are available nowhere else. Not only does his voice afford the primary unifying device for *Gulag*, but he turns out to be the most interesting personage in the account. What he tells us about himself comes in bits and pieces, never in consecutive narrative and only as his life story illustrates those broader themes which inform his treatise. Still, these insights into his character are intriguing and worthy of our deliberate notice.

While Solzhenitsyn drops titillating hints, especially in the third volume, about some of the writing he did while imprisoned and exiled, the autobiographical passages most to be cherished are those which illuminate Solzhenitsyn's conversion from Marxism to Christianity, about which Solzhenitsyn has never published a direct account.

Early there are glimpses of the author as a Red Army captain and a newly arrested prisoner. Solzhenitsyn is merciless toward himself in these passages. As an officer, he ate better than the rank and file and never questioned the justice of his privileged status. When arrested, he would not deign to carry his own suitcase, and a captured German was forced to be his porter. "Pride," he says of himself, "grows in the human heart like lard on a pig" (vol. I, p. 163). He is ashamed that when arrested he did not resist but succumbed meekly, rabbit-like. Nor is he proud of his behavior during interrogation: "I might have borne myself more firmly; and in all probability I could have maneuvered more skillfully. But my first weeks were characterized by a mental blackout and a slump into depression" (vol. I, p. 134). He finds some consolation—and here he contradicts statements by his first wife—in that at least he said nothing which would cause others to be arrested (vol. I, p. 134). But, as he adds candidly, "I came close to it" (vol. I, p. 134).

Solzhenitsyn reminisces that he was invited to enter training to become a secret police officer. With a little more pressure, he concedes, he might have given in to the temptation. Even after his release from prison and exile in 1956, he was recruited to become an informer. While there was no longer a question of his possible compliance, he admits to what he considers a self-centered thought: "What about my manuscripts?" (vol. II, p. 368).

The first year in prison was a momentous time in Solzhenitsyn's life. He had come with an ideologue's smug complacency: "In my most evil moments I was convinced that I was doing good, and I was well supplied with systematic arguments" (vol. II, p. 615). It was not long before he saw himself as the "slave of my oppressed and frightened body" (vol. II, p. 268). Solzhenitsyn notes that it is generally in the first year when "the prisoner's entire future and whole prison personality are being decided" (vol. II, p. 392), and this was emphatically true in his own case: ". . . very early and very clearly, I had this consciousness that prison was not an abyss for me, but the most important turning point in my life" (vol. I, p. 187). Even when he was a mere youth, his desire was to understand the Bolshevik Revolution, and "to understand the Revolution I had long since required nothing beyond Marxism" (vol. I, p. 213). So when the arguments among the zeks raged, he sided with the Marxists. For a while. "At first I argued alongside them, taking their side. But somehow our arguments seemed to me too thin. And at that point I began to keep silent and just listen. And then I argued against them" (vol. II, p. 338). Encountering an impenetrable, imperturbable Marxist scholar of economics, Solzhenitsyn saw a set of mind which he eventually ascribed to himself: "He speaks in a language which requires no effort of the mind. And arguing with him is like walking through a desert" (vol. II, p. 341).

Solzhenitsyn met an old revolutionary, one Fastenko, who had known Lenin personally, yet "was quite cool in recalling this" (vol. I, p. 193). Discovering Solzhenitsyn's admiration for Lenin, Fastenko would speak to him only obliquely: for instance, "Thou shalt not make unto thee any graven image!" (vol. I, p. 193). Fastenko insisted, "You're a mathematician; it's a mistake for you to forget that maxim of Descartes: 'Question everything!' Question *everything*!" And Solzhenitsyn pondered, "What did this mean—'everything'? Certainly not *everything*! It seemed to me that I had questioned enough things as it was, and that was enough of that!" (vol. I, p. 193). Much later, Solzhenitsyn was to muse, ". . . no doubt, there was much that

Fastenko would have liked to explain to me that he still could not bring himself to" (vol. I, p. 193).

And so the intellectual search—and argument—went on. Solzhenitsyn was nonplussed by a conversation with an Orthodox clergyman from Europe:

> He did not confine himself to theology, but condemned Marxism, declaring that no one in Europe had taken it seriously for a long while—and I defended it, because after all I was a Marxist. And even a year ago I would have confidently demolished him with quotations; how disparagingly I would have mocked him! But my first year as a prisoner had left its mark inside me—and just when had that happened? I hadn't noticed: there had been so many new events, sights, meanings, that I could no longer say: "They don't exist! That's a bourgeois lie!" And now I had to admit: "Yes, they do exist." And right at that point my whole line of reasoning began to weaken, and so they could beat me in our arguments without half-trying. (vol. I, p. 602)

Reflecting on those early prison days, Solzhenitsyn wonders if he was a "monstrosity": "Scraps and snatches of tangled-up beliefs, false hopes, and imaginary convictions still floated about in my head, even though they were already tattered and torn. And though I was already entering on the second year of my term, I still did not understand the finger of fate, nor what it was pointing out to me . . ." (vol. II, p. 286). He was a puzzle to himself and to others. He wonders, ". . . how can one preserve one's own life and at the same time arrive at the truth? And why is it necessary to be dropped into the depths of camp in order to understand one's own squalor?" (vol. II, p. 194). An Estonian friend remembered him "as a strange mixture of Marxist and democrat." Solzhenitsyn agrees: "Yes, things were wildly mixed up inside me at that time" (vol. II, p. 213n.).

Although Solzhenitsyn's change from Marxism to Christianity was gradual, a pivotal encounter was with Boris Gammerov, a man five years his junior. Solzhenitsyn once scoffed at a published prayer by Franklin Roosevelt, bestowing on it the "self-evident evaluation" of hypocrisy. Gammerov asked, "Why do you not admit the possibility that a political leader might sincerely believe in God?" (vol. I, p. 612).

> And that is all that was said! But what a direction the attack *had* come from! To hear such words from someone born in 1923? I could have replied to him very firmly, but prison had already undermined my certainty, and the principal thing was that some kind of clean, pure feeling does live within us, existing apart from all our convictions, and right then it dawned upon me that I had not spoken out of conviction but because the idea had been implanted in me from outside. And because of this I was unable to reply to him, and I merely asked him: "Do you believe in God?"

"Of course," he answered tranquilly (vol. I, p. 612). Gammerov introduced him to the thought of Vladimir Soloviev, one of Russia's great religious philosophers, whom Solzhenitsyn had never before read.

Solzhenitsyn was also profoundly influenced by Dr. Boris Nikolayevich Kornfeld, a convert from Judaism to Christianity. Kornfeld's spiritual ardor and prophetic insights contributed powerfully to Solzhenitsyn's dawning realization that "the meaning of earthly existence lies not, as we have grown used to thinking, in prospering, but . . . in the development of the soul" (vol. II, p. 613).

In a 1976 interview, when asked about his encounter with religious faith, Solzhenitsyn responded, "I now know that I would have discovered it anyway, outside the camps or in. You could say that experience of the camps opened my eyes more quickly. Camp life strips Communism bare in a drastic way. Their ideology disappears completely. First comes the fight for survival, then the discovery of life, then God."[21] His own life has shown him "that the ways of the Lord are imponderable. That we ourselves never know what we want. And how many times in life I passionately sought what I did not need and [had] been despondent over failures which were success" (vol. II, p. 501).

To commemorate the spiritual odyssey of his life, Solzhenitsyn wrote a poem. It begins with his rearing in the church,

moves on through his desire for knowledge and rejection of re-
ligion, and concludes with his reveling in "the even glow of the
Higher Meaning / Which became apparent to me only later on."
The final stanza reads:

> And now with measuring cup returned to me,
> Scooping up the living water,
> God of the Universe! I believe again!
> Though I renounced You, You were with me!
>   (vol. II, pp. 614-15)

10

EAST AND WEST:

Polemical Writings

Solzhenitsyn is, above all else, a writer of literature, primarily fiction. Still, as the amazing events of his life catapulted him onto the stage of world affairs and, for a time, into the limelight of the news media, he could not escape making some pronouncements of a nonliterary nature. As he explained in the *Nobel Lecture*, the Russian literary tradition has never seen the proper role of the artist as one of withdrawal into a private world of imagination; rather, it has always seen the artist as involved in the cultural and civic issues of his time.

Nevertheless, in his wildest imaginings Solzhenitsyn could not have anticipated finding himself in the position of actually being listened to, by persons around the globe, as a kind of "second government." This new role brought with it its own moral imperative of new responsibilities. While he could not let those responsibilities distract him excessively from his main mission in life, neither could he let them go unheeded. So he has spoken out. And, because he followed his own advice that each person should develop his "own world-wide view,"[1] he has had much to say.

It is largely on the basis of these nonliterary utterances of the 1970's that it became fashionable to call Solzhenitsyn a prophet. *Prophet* can be used to mean someone who has extraordinary insight into the nature of contemporary reality and has the courage to tell the truth as he or she sees it, even if many find it unpalatable. It can also suggest that the bearer is not primarily an artist but something else. (Are Dostoevsky and Tolstoy prophets or artists?) Although it is not unilluminating to consider Solzhenitsyn a prophetic voice—much about him is indeed reminiscent of the style of the Old Testament prophets—it would be an egregious distortion of his life's work to use that term in order to dismiss or belittle his standing as a man of letters.

The obvious irony, then, is that it is precisely the nonliterary works which have received the lion's share of the news media's coverage of Solzhenitsyn and his writing. This phenomenon, while deplorable, is not surprising. It is in the nature of news that it focuses on the ephemeral. Offer media people a long novel explicating the universal issue of what it means to be fully human, and they will yawn. Offer them a dissenting view on the rage for détente between the USA and the USSR, and they will quiver at attention. Or give them an address at Harvard University devoted largely to tracing historically the spiritual decline of the West, and rest assured that, if in passing the speech makes illustrative references to the Vietnam war, television programming, pornography, and American politicking, these fugitive passages will be the ones featured by the media. The media's accumulated mass of discussion of these points suffices to condition the public to viewing Solzhenitsyn as a political commentator who happens to have written some novels, rather than the other way around. Then, if the media's general opinion of the writer is negative, cocktail party conversation around the nation will knowingly dismiss even those literary works which the conversationalists have not read.

It is no wonder that Solzhenitsyn does not look kindly on the actual operations of the free press in the West. He has scored it for its "hasty, immature, superficial, and misleading judgments."[2] He feels that he, though not he alone, has been victimized by it. It would be bad enough, in his view, if the press gave disproportionate treatment to his nonliterary statements; it would be worse if the treatment of those remarks were at the same time uncomprehending and incorrect.

The view of Solzhenitsyn which has filtered through the Western press and into the popular consciousness is anything but accurate. What follows is a sketch of that view, done at the risk of caricaturing the media's caricature.

Solzhenitsyn, as recreated by the press, is not a very likable man, and some of his views are downright reprehensible. From the royalties on his books, he is very wealthy. He lives opulently on a Vermont estate and exhibits an excessive concern for security there.[3] Although he has taken refuge in the United States, he imperiously and ungratefully despises this nation; he finds it morally corrupt. He attacks its permissiveness, which fosters readily available pornography. He is incredulous at American's simpleminded, passive acceptance of the pap served up by American television. He scorns the West's free press. He belittles the democratic process of free elections, seeing it as a circus staged to deceive the electorate rather than to enlighten it. He derides American diplomats for facilely abandoning staunch allies and pusillanimously caving in before the wily Soviet antagonists. He opposes détente. He charges that because it lacked civic will, America simply lost the war in Vietnam. If he could, he would resuscitate the long-gone Cold War. He hankers after authoritarianism and would like to reinstate tsardom in Russia. He has a romantic nostalgia for the simple past and prefers a primitive agrarian culture to a technologically advanced one. He is a narrow, intolerant religious zealot. All in all, he is reactionary, authoritarian, nationalistic, chauvinistic, elitist, anti-democratic, anti-liberal, anti-modern, anti-West. Obviously, only a man with very limited knowledge of the West could take the positions he takes. And only a man with grandiose visions of his own importance could be presumptuous enough to lecture the world in the stern manner he adopts. If Westerners were at first inclined to lionize a man they perceived as a bold freedom fighter, they could no longer do so in good conscience once he showed himself for what he is.

Few readers who have heard Solzhenitsyn discussed will fail to hear in this sketch some familiar echoes. Most of the charges against him are forthrightly refuted by statements out of his own mouth. Since, however, he has not deigned to answer his critics, some of the issues are left for our speculation, which can be based only on fragmentary information. First, the figures on his personal wealth are undisclosed. What we do know is that from his royalties he has poured money into a fund to aid the families of those still in Soviet concentration camps. And no one suggests that he writes to make money. Next, the charge that he prefers a reclusive living arrangement is the purest speculation. It is true that he values highly his privacy. On the other hand, it is no secret that KGB agents function even within the United States, and he has very little protection for himself and his family. Then, far from scorning the West, he has said that he and his Russian contemporaries "worshipped" the West. Those aspects of contemporary Western civilization of which he has been critical—television, pornography, electioneering, bias in news coverage, American diplomacy—have all been regular targets of criticism right within the Western press. Somehow, it is considered a breach of etiquette for this refugee to say the same things. Of course, it must be true, in the nature of things, that Solzhenitsyn does not know as much about the West as do many who have been born and bred here. But he is an exceptionally fast learner, and there is no doubt that he knows much more about America than most Americans know about Russia. The most cursory study of the man shows that he does not speak on a subject until he has achieved an impressive mastery of it. He does, of course, make mistakes. (Portugal has not become a member of the Warsaw Pact.) Some of his strictures (as that against Daniel Ellsberg) are matters for editorial comment more than for prophetic pronouncement. Nevertheless, as the following exposition of some of Solzhenitsyn's most controversial prose treatises hopes to show, his is a defensible position; it has coherence and makes sense, even if readers find it necessary to disagree with it.

It was in 1972 that Solzhenitsyn made public his commitment to the Christian faith. One of the three roughly contemporary manifestations of it—the other two being his joining the Russian Orthodox Church and the release of his public prayer (quoted earlier)—was an open letter to Patriarch Pimen, leader of the Orthodox Church in Russia. In it Solzhenitsyn dramatically interjected himself into the current affairs of the church of his childhood. If it might be expected that church officials would be delighted by a luminary's declaration of membership, such was not universally the case this time. For Solzhenitsyn's letter was pointedly critical of the ecclesiastical hierarchy.

The focus of the criticism was the church's accommodation to the state. Solzhenitsyn finds it scandalous that in a state officially dedicated to atheism, the church is regulated by a government agency, the Council for Religious Affairs: "A Church ruled dictatorially by atheists—this is a spectacle unseen in two thousand years."[4] From this unhappy political arrangement flow all elements of the execrable state of organized religion in the Soviet Union. The church fathers are left free, even encouraged, to make pronouncements about religious and political matters abroad, but they must not say things about the church within Soviet borders which will antagonize their atheistic overseers. They dare not complain, for instance, when a parent bringing his child for christening is required to show his passport, thus opening the door to harassment by the state authorities. The pressures are such that "all ties of the child with the Church usually end after baptism," and that "inimitable, purely angelic experience of the church service" (p. 551) which is uniquely available to children is lost. A similar loss afflicts the whole culture of the Russian nation: "Step by step we have lost that radiant ethical Christian atmosphere which for a thousand years shaped our mores, our way of life, our beliefs, our folklore, and the very fact that the Russian word for the people—_krest'iane_ [peasants]—was derived from 'Christians.' We

are losing the last traces and signs of a Christian people" (p. 552).
Russian Christians are so beleaguered that "in our country we
cannot even get hold of the Gospels" (p. 554) and dare not even
ask for the ringing of church bells.

Solzhenitsyn tries to show Pimen and his fellow higher-
ups the illogic of their accommodational stance:

> By what reasoning could one convince oneself that the cal-
> culated *destruction*—one directed by atheists—of the body
> and spirit of the Church is the best method of *preserving* it?
> Preservation, but *for whom*? Certainly not for Christ. Pre-
> served, but *by what means*? By *lies*? But after falsehood, with
> what hands is the Eucharist to be performed? (pp. 554-55)

And he points out to them the way out of the bondage imposed
by ecclesiastical subservience. It is the way of the early Christian church: sacrifice—even martyrdom, if necessary. Never can
the church accede to the notion "that external fetters are stronger
than our spirit" (p. 555). Some priests (Solzhenitsyn names two)
do confirm, "by their sacrifice and example, that the pure flame
of Christian faith has not been extinguished in our land" (p. 553).
It is their noble model which all church authorities should
emulate.

Solzhenitsyn's vision is always that the eternal is greater
than the temporal, the heavenly greater than the earthly, the
spiritual higher than the political, the church above the state,
God supreme over man. So Solzhenitsyn pleads, "Do not let us
suppose, do not make us think, that for the bishops of the Russian Church temporal power is higher than the heavenly one,
that earthly responsibility is more awesome than accountability
before God" (p. 555).

If Solzhenitsyn shows himself to be openly and unabashedly Christian in this letter, he is making clear beyond
confutation the beliefs about the nature of God and man—and
their relationship—which infuse all his writing.

Perhaps no work of Solzhenitsyn's has been so widely interpreted as a political tractate as his *Letter to the Soviet Leaders*,

sent on September 5, 1973, less than a half year before his exile. This long letter did more damage to Solzhenitsyn's reputation in the West than did all the rest of his writings put together. However, it in no way marked a change in his world-view; again, it demonstrated his remarkable consistency of vision.

Nowhere is Western misunderstanding of Solzhenitsyn clearer than in the reaction to his *Letter to the Soviet Leaders*. Newspaper articles about its publication ran under such headlines as "A Russian Nationalist Looks to the Past"[5] and "Solzhenitsyn 'contemptuous' of the U.S."[6] Anthony Astrachan, author of the latter article, declared that "the letter shows Solzhenitsyn to be a great Russian patriot, whose nationalism verges on chauvinism and racism though it never falls into the abyss."[7] He continued, "It reveals him as a passionate opponent of unbridled technological progress and a contemptuous critic of the West."[8] Noting that Solzhenitsyn "is no liberal," Astrachan, who had spent two years in Moscow, lectured his readers: "The letter is thus a reminder to outsiders that the courage to oppose Soviet tyranny from within does not make a dissenter a Western liberal."[9]

Jonathan Yardley found Solzhenitsyn "a fierce Russian nationalist who is contemptuous of the Western democracies and sympathetic to authoritarian rule."[10] Other Yardley labels for Solzhenitsyn are "an elitist" and "a not-very-thinly disguised Czarist."[11] Remarking that Solzhenitsyn "is adroit at self-promotion," the columnist opines, "There is no evidence that he is offended or embarrassed by those who would portray him as the Joan of Arc of the Russian intelligentisia. . . ."[12] In the same vein, Yardley complains that his subject "has accepted his image as a modern saint uncomplainingly."[13]

James Schall, a Jesuit priest, complained that Solzhenitsyn, by focusing on Russia, "seems oblivious to the real needs of the rest of mankind."[14] Because of what Schall takes to be Solzhenitsyn's deficient international consciousness (ignoring what the *Nobel Lecture* says about the need to develop a "worldwide view"), this priest concludes, "In this sense Marxism remains more Christian than Solzhenitsyn's vision, even though he is quite right in his analysis of its performance, its institutions and its procedures."[15] Schall also laments what he considers Solzhenitsyn's "clear anticity, antitechnological bias"; despite what Solzhenitsyn has said about that line dividing good and evil which runs through every human heart, the priest calls him "a true political romantic" who locates "the origin of evil . . . in the city."[16]

William Safire, columnist for the New York *Times*, rushed to declare that he was the first on his block to express reservations about this Russian author. In a column replete with almost all of the distortions catalogued earlier in this chapter, Safire both predicted and contributed to the "flip-flopping" which Solzhenitsyn's literary reputation would undergo in the Western press.[17]

Given these representative reactions to Solzhenitsyn's *Letter*, what shall we make of the letter itself? The first thing to understand about it is that it was intended to be practical advice to those aging men who actually held power in the Soviet Union. *They* were the audience, not Western intellectuals. And Solzhenitsyn was not offering them his "ideal" solutions to the problems of state; rather, he was trying to convince them that they and the state faced grave and mounting dangers and that his proposals were ones they could adopt without compromising themselves and risking the loss of power. He repeatedly acknowledges that he is "talking to total realists," to "realists par excellence."[18] If he has "only the smallest grain of hope" (p. viii) that his auditors will take his advice seriously, he nevertheless has that much. When, after six months, they did not even acknowledge receipt of the letter, Solzhenitsyn chose to let the world see what he had said in private to them. We may only speculate that by doing so he hoped to put increased pressure on the leaders to take his ideas seriously. At any rate, an intelligent reading of this letter absolutely demands recognizing the audience for which it was written; failure to do so opens the door to grotesque distortions.

Perhaps the most intriguing question raised by the letter is what ever brought Solzhenitsyn to think that the Soviet leaders would listen to practical advice from him, by now a target of unequivocal vilification in the official Soviet press. Probably we shall never know the answer to that question. But something—perhaps a sense that he had nothing to lose—impelled him to write. In this one moment of his life, he to some extent abandoned what might be called his prophetic mode and got down to specific cases. Thus, he even implicitly flatters those leaders whose policies he finds repugnant. Early he says, "But this is where the wise differ from the unwise: they heed advice and counsels of caution long before the need becomes overwhelming" (p. 8). He appeals to the leaders' patriotism, reminding them of his "original assumption that you are not alien to your fathers, your grandfathers and the expanses of Russia" (p. 79). He may be trying to establish common ground with the leaders when he criticizes America—for its "turbulent 'democracy run riot' in which once every four years the politicians, and indeed the entire country, nearly kill themselves over an electoral campaign, trying to gratify the masses" (p. 68), as well as for its "weak and undeveloped consciousness" as it "lost" a war to "tiny North Vietnam" (p. 61).

For all his desire to be practical advisor, Solzhenitsyn cannot allow himself to be Machiavellian. He has moral principles he cannot bring himself to violate. He has to say things which can only antagonize his auditors. In his call to recant Marxism, he labels it "rubbishy" (p. 61). He insists on naming Leningrad "Petersburg" (p. 50). He considers Marxism the "tormentor" of _"all religions"_ (p. 77).

These and similar comments inevitably introduce into the letter a mixture of tones which presumably baffled the Soviet leadership and certainly created difficulties for Western readers. Given the apparent fact that the letter did not have the hoped-for effect, at least not in the short run, one can question the wisdom of writing it. What one cannot question is that Solzhenitsyn wrote it out of a deep sense of devotion to duty.

The severe strictures against Solzhenitsyn brought about by the publication of _Letter to the Soviet Leaders_ may be grouped into four categories: that he is anti-democratic and pro-authoritarian, that he is nationalistic, that he is anti-Western, and that he is antitechnological. Since much evidence from other chapters and especially from other sections of this chapter bears on these accusations, we shall in this section limit our attention to the evidence available from the *Letter* itself. It could, of course, be argued that these positions, even if they were his, are not, on the face of it, reprehensible and deserve to be debated on their merits. But the fact is that Solzhenitsyn has been badly misunderstood on each point.

While it is true that Solzhenitsyn makes caustic comments about democracy as it actually operates in the West today, never does he argue for the superiority of authoritarianism. Indeed, as he opens that section of his letter which speaks most directly to the issue at hand, he says to the Soviet leaders,

> . . . you will not allow power to slip out of your hands. That is why you will not willingly tolerate a two-party or a multiparty parliamentary system in our country, you will not tolerate *real* elections, at which people might not vote you in. And on the basis of realism one must admit that this will be within your power for a long time to come.
>
> A long time—but not forever. (p. 67)

This statement certainly does not sound like that of a man who disapproves of democratic elections on principle. Indeed, it suggests both that the writer would, in the abstract, prefer democratic elections to the authoritarian self-perpetuation of the Soviet leaders and that he, in the concrete, thinks that someday the change will be made. It is within the context of that statement that the remarks which he goes on to make must be interpreted.

He notes that in Russia, "for sheer lack of practice, democracy survived for only eight months—from February to October, 1917" (p. 70). Before that time, "for a thousand years Russia lived with an authoritarian order" and still kept "both the physical and spiritual health of her people . . . intact" (p. 71). Therefore, he wonders, "for the foreseeable future, perhaps, whether we like it or not, whether we intend it or not, Russia is nevertheless destined to have an authoritarian order," since "perhaps this is all that she is ripe for today" (p. 72). A writer who loves his homeland yet fears deeply what he considers the almost certain disruptive effects of a revolutionary change—and, further, one who is concerned more for the effects of governance on people's everyday lives than for allegiance to some abstract theory of government—thus willingly suggests a compromise with those rulers who already have a power which they will not let go.

They are of course totalitarian—an extreme form of authoritarianism which he nowhere condones and everywhere condemns. Rather, he seeks—without employing those terms, which, given his audience, would surely negate his moderating intention—to talk them into giving up their totalitarianism and settling for a more benign form of authoritarianism. Further, he cannot refrain from spelling out details which are alien to the leaders' past experience but which are ingredients essential to the fulfillment of his vision for the immediate future of his country. Any future authoritarian government, he asserts, must seek recourse in "the widest possible *consultation* with all working people" (p. 73). Beyond the matter of some sort of (admittedly undefined) popular participation, the leaders must recognize that "freedom is moral" (p. 70). For those thousand years of Russian history which preceded the Bolshevik era, Russia's "authoritarian order possessed a strong moral foundation, embryonic and rudimentary though it was—not the ideology of universal violence, but Christian Orthodoxy . . ." (p. 71). Preferring the steadiness of order to the upheaval of revolution, Solzhenitsyn declares, ". . . *order* is not immoral if it means a calm and stable system. But order, too, has its limits, beyond which it degenerates into arbitrariness and tyranny" (p. 70). That is to say, given the realist's recognition that Russian democracy cannot be built in a day, Solzhenitsyn would settle for a switch from a totalitarian tyranny to an authoritarianism based on moral principles which call for respecting individual citizens. After all, even in modern times there are nations which do not have multiparty elections yet which seem to offer their citizens a peaceable, stable, not unpopular government. That such governments receive widespread approval in the West is apparent. (One might cite some one-party African states.) For offering a similar form of government for his traditionally nondemocractic homeland, Solzhenitsyn is castigated in the Western press. Yet his carefully worded proviso, distinguishing as it does between totalitarianism and authoritarianism, must be kept in mind: "Everything depends upon *what sort* of authoritarian order lies in store for us in the future" (p. 72). If the leaders wish to stay in control, no one can prevent them; so "let it be an authoritarian order, but one founded not on an inexhaustible 'class hatred' but on love of your fellow men" (p. 76).

The charge that Solzhenitsyn is a nationalist is perhaps more difficult to refute, because of the ambiguity of the term itself. There is no question that he thinks that, through two world wars and the ravages of the Gulag Archipelago, the Russians have "suffered more in the twentieth century . . . than any other people in the world" (p. 37). Thus, he calls on the Soviet leaders, mostly Russians, "to heal our wounds, cure our national body and natural spirit . . . to put our own house in order" (p. 38) before all else. He does advocate that Russia look to those great uninhabited reaches of Siberia in the Northeast as "the center of national activity and settlement and a focus for the aspirations of young people" (p. 40), but this suggestion hardly justifies the charge of nationalism.

At the same time, even while recognizing that China, with its hordes, could pose a direct military threat, Solzhenitsyn calls for "drastic cuts in our military investments for many years ahead" (p. 46). Although passages from works other than this *Letter* refute even more clearly the charge of nationalism, we must hear his inveighing against "the need for any *external* expansion of our power" and his observation that "the peoples who created empires have always suffered spiritually as a result. The aims of a great empire and the moral health of the people are incompatible" (p. 54). At the very least, this *Letter* (always keeping in mind its audience) offers no encouragement to imperialism; rather, it seeks to "encourage the *inner*, the moral, the healthy, development of the people" (p. 75).

There is no gainsaying that Solzhenitsyn is unabashedly a patriot, of course a Russian patriot. He scoffs at the "combination" of Marxism and patriotism as "a meaningless absurdity" (p. 60). And he savagely indicts Lenin for his 1915 statement, "We are antipatriots" (p. 61). But only if the terms _patriotism_ and _nationalism_ are equated is it proper to call Solzhenitsyn a nationalist.

To the extent that Solzhenitsyn's statements give any credence to the charge that he is a nationalist, one should understand what Solzhenitsyn is opposing: the avowedly internationalist ideology of Karl Marx. First, Solzhenitsyn notes that even Stalin abandoned appeals to Marxism when the Russians' national life was on the line, appealing instead to "the old Russian banner— sometimes, indeed, the standard of Orthodoxy" (p. 18) during World War II. His criticism of Marxism is acute and fierce:

> Marxism is not only not accurate, is not only not a science, has not only failed to predict a _single event_ in terms of figures, quantities, time-scales or locations . . . [but] it absolutely astounds one by the economic and mechanistic crudity of its attempts to explain that most subtle of creatures, the human being, and that even more complex synthesis of millions of people, society. (p. 57)

This patriot wishes his leaders would agree with him that this alien ideology "has long ceased to be helpful to us here at home" and is now "a sham, cardboard, theatrical prop—take it away and nothing will collapse—nothing will even wobble" (p. 62). If the government could find it in its heart to relinquish Marxism's expansionist ideology, with "its unattainable and irrelevant missions of world domination" and instead "fulfill its national missions and save us from war with China and from technological disaster" (pp. 74-75), Russia could be a major factor in the affairs of the nations of the world, though no longer as an imperial power.

While we must always keep in mind the audience for this letter when it sounds critical of the West, it is still true that the West hardly escapes unscathed. Solzhenitsyn thinks that the United States is marked by "internal dissension and spiritual weakness" (p. 5) and that "the Western world, as a single, clearly unified force, no longer counterbalances the Soviet Union, indeed has almost ceased to exist" (pp. 7-8). He hopes that "we shall not destroy Russia in the general crisis of Western civilization" (p. 33). However, he does not draw a sharp line between Russia and Western civilization; rather, he remarks that "Russia long ago chose the honor of joining" (p. 21) Western civilization. So he, like most, uses the term *West* in two ways: for the political alliances of modern times and also for what is sometimes called the Great Tradition growing out of the fusion of classical and Judaeo-Christian sources of culture. As he sees the modern bearers of that tradition grow effete, he finds no glee, only sadness. And he gives his historical explanation:

> The catastrophic weakening of the Western world and the whole of Western civilization is by no means due solely to the success of an irresistible, persistent Soviet foreign policy. It is, rather, the result of a historical, psychological and moral crisis affecting the entire culture and world outlook which were conceived at the time of the Renaissance and attained the peak of their expression with the eighteenth-century Enlightenment. (p. 9)

That is, the West has abandoned that very view of man and the world which made it great and which infuses Solzhenitsyn's own writings. One of the new views which developed out of the Enlightenment, namely, Marxism, is that very one which he must hold responsible for all the bloodshed of his countrymen in this century. In other statements, to other audiences, Solzhenitsyn has found occasion to make more extensive comments about his view of the West; and, as we shall see, they include some highly favorable ones. But even when he writes to the Soviet rulers, his declarations about what he perceives to be the weakness of the West are couched in a mood of regret, a regret based on his own identification with traditional Western values.

An examination of the evidence makes astounding the charge that Solzhenitsyn is some sort of romantic primitivist, antitechnological in outlook. He is, of course, himself a physicist and mathematician by training. We have seen his consistent praise of engineers and doctors in his fictional works. Also, he shows himself to be knowledgeable about current discussions of the effects of technology. It is true that he prefers small cities to megalopolises; more and more Americans seem to be "voting with their feet" in the same direction these days. He does fear that we shall use up our natural resources quickly if we continue unlimited growth. He is disgusted with industrial pollution. He accepts the arithmetic done by the prestigious Club of Rome. In our country today, to hold these views is to be considered enlightened, committed to an important human cause. When Solzhenitsyn does so, he is considered a reactionary who wants to veto the twentieth century. Persons of good will can debate just what are the limits of growth. But they cannot in fairness accuse Solzhenitsyn of what in fact he has been accused of on this subject.

Solzhenitsyn's view of modern technology is based on a philosophical-historical position, the same one which underlies his view of the nature of man. He opens his discussion by saying that "if the earth is a *finite* object, then its expanses and resources are finite also, and the *endless, infinite* progress dinned into our heads by the dreamers of the Enlightenment cannot be accomplished on it" (p. 23). A debatable question is just how close mankind is to using up the earth's resources. It is at this point that Solzhenitsyn finds the Club of Rome and their computer calculations persuasive. (He mentions also the Teilhard de Chardin Society.) So he proceeds merely to summarize their conclusions. They advocate "a *zero-growth economy*, a stable economy" (p. 24) and a renunciation of "unrestrained industrial growth" and "the gigantic scale of modern technology" (p. 25). This position does not, however, entail a rejection of technology. (The Club's studies were done on computers!) Instead, it leads to a new and clearly stated purpose for technology: "The chief aim of technology will now be to eradicate the lamentable results of previous technologies" (p. 25). With a note of urgency, he elaborates: "And if mankind is to be *saved*, technology has to be adapted to a stable economy in the next twenty to thirty years, and to do that, the process must be started *now, immediately*" (p. 27).

In the light of what he considers these immutable realities facing future generations, he tells the rulers, Russia is extremely fortunate: it has vast uninhabited spaces with untapped resources in its northeast. If it set its mind to it, it could develop a model social order based on the new awareness of the earth's limited resources. Western ingenuity is "so dynamic and so inventive" that "it is more than likely that Western civilization will not perish," that it will find a way to "ride out even this impending crisis, will dismantle all its age-old misconceptions and in a few years set about the necessary reconstruction" (p. 27). Those underdeveloped nations of "the 'Third World' will heed the warnings in good time and *not take the Western path at all*" (p. 27). But what about Russia, which has already set itself on the course of imitating the West's heavy industrialization? Will it switch in time to "an economy of *non*gigantism with a small-scale though highly developed technology" (p. 49)?

And, he tells his rulers, the result would be a quite pleasant prospect. They could build "*new* towns of the *old* type" (p. 49), a happy change from the huge modern metropolises with their noise and dirt. Transportation within them could be restricted to "horses, and battery-powered electric motors, but not poisonous internal combustion engines" (p. 49). The leaders could "give the country back a healthy *silence* . . ." (p. 48). People could once again live in harmony with the rhythms of nature:

> The urban life, which, by now, as much as half our population is doomed to live, is utterly unnatural—and you agree entirely, every one of you, for every evening with one accord you all escape from the city to your dachas in the country. And you are all old enough to remember our old towns—towns made for people, horses, dogs—and streetcars too; towns which were humane, friendly, cozy places, where the air was always clean, which were snow-clad in winter and in spring redolent with garden smells streaming through the fences into the streets. There was a garden to almost every house and hardly a house

more than two stories high—the pleasantest height for human habitation. (pp. 48-49)

Is such an idyllic setting impossible? Perhaps. In any case, the proposal cannot be interpreted as a rejection of technology. It includes streetcars and electric automobiles. It is premised on diverting money and effort from space exploration to a technology which would thaw out the Siberian permafrost to make these new cities possible. It is offered by a knowledgeable visionary who has his eye trained on the future, even though he is old enough to have a not inappropriate nostalgia for some of the good things of the past.

One might not expect a Soviet subject addressing a government dedicated to dialectical materialism to bring up spiritual and religious matters, but Solzhenitsyn cannot refrain from doing so. All of his suggestions, he explains, are framed in the context of his concern for the moral and spiritual health of the people: "Bearing in mind the state of people's morals, their spiritual condition and their relations with one another and with society, all the _material_ achievements we trumpet so proudly are petty and worthless" (pp. 44-45). He scolds the leaders for their effort at "the eradication of Christian religion and morality" (p. 35). Of their announced "_ideology_ that claims to be a substitute for morality" (p. 51), he alleges, citing Sergei Bulgakov, ". . . atheism is the chief inspirational and emotional hub of Marxism and . . . all the rest of the doctrine has simply been tacked on. Ferocious hostility to religion is Marxism's most persistent feature" (p. 59n). As he pleads that they drop Marxism as a basis for their governmental operations, he boldly states, "I myself see Christianity today as the only living spiritual force capable of undertaking the spiritual healing of Russia. But I request and propose no special privileges for it, simply that it should be treated fairly and not suppressed" (pp. 77-78). However practical he wishes to be, even when he writes to imposing atheists, he can write only within the context of his own religious commitment.

Although very little of what Solzhenitsyn has written has been addressed to Western audiences, a few speeches and interviews have been. Five of those, dating from 1975 and 1976, have been collected in a small volume entitled by the publisher *Warning to the West*.[19] Three of the speeches included were delivered to American audiences, two under the auspices of the AFL-CIO and one to members of the U.S. Congress. The other two pieces are a speech carried by the British Broadcasting Corporation and an interview conducted by Michael Charlton for the BBC's program *Panorama*, subsequently carried by American public television on William F. Buckley, Jr.'s *Firing Line*. Because their content overlaps, we shall treat them as one.

In one of the speeches to the AFL-CIO, Solzhenitsyn is almost apologetic about the role in which he has been cast, about what for him is "the unpleasant and inappropriate role of orator" (p. 82). He adds, "I am a writer, and I would prefer to sit and write books" (p. 82). But he takes on the task of making statements to the West because "a concentration of world evil is taking place, full of hatred for humanity" (p. 82). He speaks out of the conviction that, "by some chance of history," those under Soviet domination "have trodden the same path seventy or eighty years before the West" (p. 101) and that therefore he has a message to bring: "Our experience of life is of vital importance to the West, but I am not convinced that you are capable of assimilating it without having gone through it to the end yourselves" (p. 102). He tells his audience, ". . . you have not yet really suffered the terrible trials of the twentieth century which have rained down on the old continent. You're tired, but not as tired as we are, crushed for sixty years" (p. 82).

The great crisis in the world today, as he sees it, is that the dehumanizing force of Communism is gaining rapidly. There is, it is true, "a process of spiritual liberation in the U.S.S.R. and in the other Communist countries" (p. 83). But this "liberation of the human spirit" (p. 47), explained most fully in *From Under the Rubble*, can proceed only if the Western nations stand fast against the tide of Communism. The problem is that ". . . our movement of opposition and spiritual revival, like any spiritual process, is slow. But your capitulations, like all political processes, move very quickly" (p. 108).

As always, Solzhenitsyn pits the opponents along moral, not political, lines. Specific theories of government are not what are ultimately at stake; the clash is between humanity and anti-humanity. Belittling the term *"anti-Communism"* as "a poor, tasteless locution . . . put together by people who do not understand etymology" (pp. 58-59), because it makes Communism primary and opposition to it only a reaction to its presence, he turns the tables in order that the moral issue be paramount:

> The primary, the eternal concept is humanity, and Communism is anti-humanity. Whoever says "anti-Communism" is saying, in effect, anti-anti-humanity. A poor construction. So we should say: That which is against Communism is for humanity. Not to accept, but to reject this inhuman Communist ideology is simply to be a human being. Such a rejection is more than a political act. It is a protest of our souls against those who would have us forget the concepts of good and evil. (p. 59)

Solzhenitsyn's animosity toward Communism is not against its political or economic theories but against its immorality. "Communism has never concealed the fact that it rejects all absolute concepts of morality. It scoffs at any consideration of 'good' and 'evil' as indisputable categories. Communism considers morality to be relative, to be a class matter" (pp. 57-58).

But Solzhenitsyn knows his moral vision to be unfashionable in the West as well. "In the twentieth century it is almost a joke in the Western world to use words like 'good' and 'evil.' They have become old-fashioned concepts, yet they are very real and genuine" (p. 46). Any why? Because "These are concepts from a sphere which is above us" (p. 46). In the same vein, when he attacks *realpolitik* for its view that the law is what we make it, that law is not answerable to any absolute morality and is therefore higher than morality, he grounds law in the transcendent: ". . . morality is higher than law! Law is our human attempt to embody in rules a part of that moral sphere which is above us" (p. 45).

Within these speeches, again, he offers an historical explanation of the current malaise, as he refers to "the disastrous deviation of the late Enlightenment" (p. 145):

> Once, it was proclaimed and accepted that above man there was no supreme being, but instead that man was the crowning glory of the universe and the measure of all things, and that man's needs, desires, and indeed his weaknesses were taken to be the supreme imperatives of the universe. Consequently, the only good in the world—the only thing that needed to be done—was that which satisfied our feelings. It was several centuries ago in Europe that this philosophy was born; at the time its materialistic excesses were explained away by the previous excesses of Catholicism. But in the course of several centuries this philosophy inexorably flooded the entire Western world. . . . And all this side by side with the outward manifestations of Christianity and the flowering of personal freedom. By the beginning of the twentieth century this philosophy seemed to have reached the height of civilization and reason. . . . In the years which followed the worldwide upheaval of 1917, that pragmatic philosophy on which present-day Europe was nourished, with its refusal to take moral decisions, reached its logical conclusion: since there are no higher spiritual forces above us and since I—Man with a capital *M*— am the crowning glory of the universe, then if anyone must perish today, let it be someone else, anybody, but not I, not my precious self, or those who are close to me. (pp. 127-28, 130-31)

His reading of American history has convinced Solzhenitsyn that America's Founding Fathers understood his cherished principle that all realms of human activity, including politics, are answerable to that transcendent sphere of spiritual reality. He tells an American audience, ". . . the men who created your country never lost sight of their moral bearings. They did not laugh at the absolute nature of the concepts of 'good' and 'evil.' Their practical policies were checked against that moral compass" (p. 80). Such an approach, he adds, turns out to be "the most farsighted and the most salutary" even in practical terms (pp. 80-81).

To a British audience Solzhenitsyn sounds the same note, this time with reference to British history. Whereas "nowadays in the Western press we read a candid declaration of the principle that moral considerations have nothing to do with politics" (p. 110), he reminds his listeners that "in 1939 England thought differently" (p. 110). By capitulating to Hitler's Germany, it could have escaped the suffering inflicted upon it by the war, ". . . but England chose the moral course, and experienced and demonstrated to the world perhaps the most brilliant and heroic period in its history" (p. 110). It acted on the principle that "freedom is indivisible and one has to take a moral attitude toward it" (p. 111). When "Britain assumed a moral stance against Hitler" (p. 134), the result was even to its pragmatic benefit: "A moral stance, even in politics, always safeguards our spirit; sometimes, as we can see, it even protects our very existence. A moral stance can suddenly turn out to be more farsighted than any calculated pragmatism" (p. 134). So he scores that "horrible expression of Bertrand Russell's," in which "there is an absence of all moral criteria": "Better Red than dead" (p. 119). Still thinking of 1939, he asks, "Why did he not say it would be better to be brown [Nazi] than dead?" (p. 119). Solzhenitsyn's own uncompromising view, based on the belief that "between good and evil there is an irreconcilable contradiction" (p. 110), is, "Better to be dead than a scoundrel" (p. 119).

Ever seeking historical understanding, Solzhenitsyn sees modern civilization as facing a crisis: "not just a social crisis, not just a political crisis, not just a military crisis" (p. 145), but a spiritual crisis. And he wonders if we might not be standing at a watershed moment in human history and approaching "an upheaval similar to that which marked the transition from the Middle Ages to the Renaissance" (p. 145). But this time, if voices like those in _From Under the Rubble_ are heard, mankind could give "free rein to the spirit that was breathed into us at birth, that spirit which distinguishes us from the animal world" (p. 146).

These speeches, then, reinforce our understanding of the essentially nonpolitical character of Solzhenitsyn's thought, even when he comments on current affairs. If he scolds the West, as he does, it is never merely for mistaken political maneuverings but always for what he takes to be the moral insufficiency underlying those maneuverings, an insufficiency rooted in a loss of spiritual insight. Only within that context can we understand his comments about current affairs. And in that context we readily perceive how skewed is the charge that he is anti-Western.

Indeed, his own words exhibit quite a different attitude. In his first AFL-CIO speech Solzhenitsyn says that he comes "as a friend of the United States" (p. 22). He considers that "the United States has long shown itself to be the most magnanimous, the most generous country in the world" (p. 27). Even as he decries the seeming inability of the West to stem the tide of Communism, he avers that "the United States, of all the countries of the West, is the least guilty and has done the most in order to prevent it" (p. 26). His travels across the United States following his exile convince him that even today "the American heartland is healthy, strong, and broad in its outlook" (p. 81). He concedes, "In your wide-open spaces even I get a little infected, the dangers seem somehow unreal. On this continent it is hard to believe all the things which are happening in the world" (p. 81).

In the BBC interview, when asked if he accepts the judgment that he is "an impassioned critic" (p. 105) of the West as a whole, Solzhenitsyn complains that "mediocre journalists simply make headlines of their conclusions, which suddenly become generally accepted" (p. 106). Presuming to speak on behalf of his Russian compatriots as well as himself, he responds vehemently: "First I am not a critic of the West. I repeat that for nearly all of our lives we worshipped the West—note the word 'worshipped.' We did not admire it, we worshipped it" (p. 106).

In a similarly highly charged mood he responds to the accusations that he wishes to return to a patriarchal way of life and that he is a nationalist. The rejoinders are laced with sarcasm. As to the first, he says,

Well, as I see it, apart from the half-witted, no normal person could ever propose a return to the past, because it's clear to any normal person that one can only move forward. That means that choice lies only between those movements which go forward and not backward. It is quite easy to imagine that some journalist writing mostly about women's fashions thought up this headline, and so the story gets around that I am calling for a patriarchal way of life. (p. 106)

In the back of his mind, doubtless, is his belief that a spiritual renaissance, as called for in *From Under the Rubble*, is occurring in Russia.

And the charge of being a nationalist equally evokes the ire of this man who has assiduously cultivated a "world-wide view":

. . . take the word "nationalist"—it has become almost meaningless. It is used constantly. Everyone flings it around, but what is a "nationalist"? If someone suggests that his country should have a large army, conquer the countries which surround it, should go on expanding its empire, that sort of person is a nationalist. But if, on the contrary, I suggest that my country should free all the peoples it has conquered, should disband the army, should stop all aggressive actions—who am I? A nationalist! If you love England, what are you? A nationalist! And when are you not a nationalist? When you *hate* England, then you are not a nationalist. (p. 107)

On the other hand, if Solzhenitsyn expresses deep affection for the West, there is something about the West which disappoints him. "I am a critic of the weakness of the West. I am a critic of a fact which we can't comprehend: how can one lose one's spiritual strength, one's will power and, possessing freedom, not value it, not be willing to make sacrifices for it?" (p. 106). He finds in today's West an intersecting of "the loss of courage and the loss of reason" (p. 127), and this condition is incomprehensible to him. Decrying what he considers "the tragic enfeeblement of Europe" (p. 144), he scorchingly charges that Europe today "is nothing more than a collection of cardboard stage sets, all bargaining with each other to see how little can be spent on defense in order to leave more for the comforts of life" (p. 139). Particularly galling to this patriot is the inattention of the Western powers to the plight of his fellow Russians: "Twice we helped save the freedom of Western Europe. And twice you repaid us by abandoning us to our slavery" (p. 136). So bleak is his view of the spiritual health of the West that he asserts that "the West is on the verge of a collapse created by its own hands" (p. 115). In a similar mood, he says, "I wouldn't be surprised at the sudden and imminent fall of the West" (p. 114).

Now, this is gloomy stuff—the stuff, let us say, of the prophet. And there is solid evidence that Solzhenitsyn has been wrong in some of his predictions about the immediacy of decline in the West. For instance, he flatly asserted that Portugal, "at the very westernmost edge of Europe" (p. 67), has, "in effect, fallen out of NATO already. I don't wish to be a prophet of doom but these events are irreversible. Very shortly Portugal will be considered a member of the Warsaw Pact" (p. 69). While the ultimate political fate of Portugal remains to be seen, it is clear that what Solzhenitsyn considered irreversible has not yet proven to be so; indeed, at the moment the opposite seems to be the case. Similarly, he declares, "In 1975 alone four countries were broken off. Four—three in Indochina plus India—and the process keeps going on, very rapidly too. One should be aware of how rapid the tempo is" (p. 75). Here the prophet is at least one-fourth wrong by any calculation. And, in other countries which he does not mention, the outlook for freedom seems today less bleak than it once did.

On the other hand, if Solzhenitsyn, who claims no political expertise, is wrong on certain details, who is to gainsay the real dangers he sees in the overall, global picture? Who can quarrel with him when he scores Franklin Roosevelt for his indulgence of the Soviet Union which allowed it to occupy Estonia, Latvia, Lithuania, Moldavia, and Mongolia and to control the nations of Eastern Europe? What about his prediction that in Vietnam, following the end of the war there, "a million persons will simply be exterminated" (p. 25)? Is his claim indisputably wrong that "a senseless, incomprehensible, non-guaranteed truce in Vietnam was negotiated" (p. 31)? Are we confident that he is mistaken when he says "with certainty" that "the extended ordeal of Vietnam . . . was the least of a long chain of similar trials which awaits you in the near future" (p. 94)? Does the Soviet invasion of Afghanistan encourage us to doubt that "Moscow now takes infinitely less note of the West" (p. 105)?

At the very least, then, we should take Solzhenitsyn's prophetic voice with more seriousness than it has frequently been taken. He has been wrong on some details; that is the risk of sounding a trumpet of warning. But his vision is not without relation to reality, even on most details. If he speaks, as Michael Charlton notes, "from the moral standpoint of a devout Christian" (p. 115), he also speaks as one with considerable knowledge of the world.

It is with both of these points in mind that the reader must approach his strictures against détente as it is currently discussed by the great powers. Contrary to what the Western press has said about him, Solzhenitsyn is not opposed to détente; he has flatly stated, "Détente is necessary . . ." (p. 121). But, he immediately adds, "détente with open hands. Show that there is no stone in your hand!" (p. 121). And he tries to convince his American audience that the Soviets are not playing by those rules: ". . . your partners with whom you are conducting détente have a stone in their hands and it is so heavy that it could kill you with one single blow. Détente becomes self-deception, that's what it is all about" (p. 121). Referring to Soviet naval power, even in the Atlantic Ocean, and especially to the Marxist coup in Angola, he says, ". . . you may call this détente if you like, but after Angola I just can't understand how one's tongue can utter this word!" (p. 120).

The current exercise in détente Solzhenitsyn considers a mere papering over the fact of ongoing ideological hostility: "The most important aspect of détente today is that there is no ideological détente" (p. 116). When the West brings itself to imagine that détente is working, the Soviet view will be quite different: "When there is détente, peaceful co-existence, and trade, they will still insist: the ideological war must continue!

And what is ideological war? It is a concentration of hatred, a continued repetition of the oath to destroy the Western world" (p. 72). Demonstrating again his concern for Soviet peoples, Solzhenitsyn asks, "What does the spirit of Helsinki and the spirit of détente mean for us within the Soviet Union? The strengthening of totalitarianism" (p. 117).

So, calling on the West's remaining reservoir of spirit to withstand the forces of anti-human totalitarianism in our world, he pleads for an accurate understanding of "the nature of Communism" (p. 41), preaches that "only firmness makes it possible to withstand the assaults of Communist totalitarianism" (p. 42), and sets down three characteristics of "a true détente" (p. 39). First, there must be "a dismantling of the weapons of war as well as those of violence" (p. 39). Second, true détente must be based on guarantees that "detente will not be violated overnight," that it will "not be based on smiles, not on verbal concessions, but on a firm foundation. You know the words from the Bible. Build not on sand, but on rock" (p. 39). Third, there must be "an end to ideological warfare": "If we're going to be friends, let's be friends: if we're going to have détente, then let's have détente . . ." (p. 40).

We have seen earlier that as Solzhenitsyn has grown older, his emphasis on spiritual and moral matters has become more overt and pronounced. The pattern holds as he moves from the speeches to Western audiences from 1975-76 to the commencement address delivered at Harvard University in 1978. One of the most interesting aspects of the speech is simply the extensiveness of the press coverage it received. Commencement addresses are seldom the stuff of news; even when Presidents use such forums to make policy statements, they receive no more coverage than Solzhenitsyn did on this occasion. The address is, as the title *A World Split Apart* suggests, an analysis of the current state of the world. It paints an unhappy picture. In this world split apart, the anti-human ideology of Communism is on the offensive, and the West, the bastion of the humanistic tradition, is in retreat. Solzhenitsyn catalogues what he considers examples of the decadence of the West—and this, of course, is what the media took note of, often rather huffily. But the speech culminates in an extended analysis of the underlying cause of the decay—and this key part the press underplayed.

Solzhenitsyn's view of the world situation is not that all evil resides within the West; far from it. But he sets the context for this speech in these words: ". . . since my forced exile in the West has now lasted four years and since my audience is a Western one, I think it may be of greater interest to concentrate on certain aspects of the contemporary West, such as I see them."[20]

As Solzhenitsyn catalogues examples of Western corruption, one of the most interesting things to emphasize once again is that almost everything he mentions has already been common fare for criticism by editorialists and others. For instance, he complains about "today's mass living habits, introduced as by a calling card by the revolting invasion of commercial advertising, by TV stupor, and by intolerable music" (pp. 35-37). He is shocked by "motion pictures full of pornography, crime, and horror" (p. 21). He worries about the rising crime rate. He finds the United States an excessively litigious society. He fears that there has been "a decline in courage" and that it is "particularly noticeable among the ruling and intellectual elites" (p. 11). He is negative toward Europe's recently past practice of colonialism. He wonders whether the American electoral process encourages the triumph of mediocrity. He thinks that it is an excess of freedom when the rights of terrorists and other criminals are valued over the rights of victims. He warns against an attempted alliance with Communist China. If his opinions on these and like subjects are not universally accepted, they are hardly unusual or surprising.

The same may be said for his caustic comments about the press, by which he expressly means all of the mass media, comments obviously not calculated to endear him to the representatives of the media themselves. To this subject he devotes considerable space. As an example, he declares, "Hastiness and superficiality—these are the psychic diseases of the twentieth century and more than anywhere else this is manifested in the press. In-depth analysis of a problem is anathema to the press; it is contrary to its nature. The press merely picks out sensational formulas" (p. 27). There is a skewing of the press in which a coterie keeps the presumably public media from being fully open to the public: "In America, I have received letters from highly intelligent persons—maybe a teacher in a faraway small college who could do much for the renewal and salvation of his country, but the country cannot hear him because the media will not provide him with a forum" (p. 29).

But it must be understood that these and similar specifics are essentially attention-catchers, designed to show that he has put his finger on a real problem, the nature of which needs explicating. That real problem lies deeper than the popular imagination is aware of, and it is toward it that the early parts of the address move. As is true in his fiction and drama, he settles on the issue of the nature of man. To the extent (which Solzhenitsyn would think is considerable) that modern man looks to the surface-level institutions of society to solve problems, it looks to the wrong place. The problems are philosophical. The weakness of the West, in Solzhenitsyn's view, "evidently stems from a humanistic and benevolent concept according to which man—the master of this world—does not bear any evil within himself, and all the defects of life are caused by misguided social systems, which must therefore be corrected" (p. 23).

Solzhenitsyn then returns to his sketch of history, this time fleshing it out a bit more than he had before. If Western civilization has gone awry,

> . . . the mistake must be at the root, at the very foundation of thought in modern times. I refer to the prevailing Western view of the world which was born in the Renaissance and has found political expression since the Age of Enlightenment. It became the basis for political and social doctrine and could be called rationalistic humanism or humanistic autonomy: the proclaimed and practiced autonomy of man from any higher force above him. It could also be called anthropocentricity, with man seen as the center of all. (pp. 47-49)

If it was inevitable that mankind would turn away from the Middle Ages and its "intolerable despotic repression of man's physical nature in favor of the spiritual one" (p. 49), it was a sad thing that the Renaissance "started modern Western civilization on the dangerous trend of worshipping man and his material needs" (p. 49). The process then set in motion a flattening and simplifying of the view of human nature. The new view which developed "did not admit the existence of intrinsic evil in man, nor did it see any task higher than the attainment of happiness on earth" (p. 49). The "ossified formulas of the Enlightenment" (p. 59) have led us to "a harsh spiritual crisis and a political impasse" (p. 51). The real disaster of our times, "a disaster which is already very much with us," is that of "an autonomous, irreligious humanistic consciousness" (p. 57).

It is in the light of this historical shift that we must view Communism. Communism is not simply some economic system carrying within it ramifications for the political order. It is, as Karl Marx said, "naturalized humanism" (p. 53). Communism is a direct philosophical outgrowth of the Enlightenment: "It is no accident that all of communism's rhetorical vows revolve around Man (with a capital *M*) and his earthly happiness" (p. 53). And, since it shares that fundamental position with the modern West, the great division in the world today is not that between the political West and the political East but that between a view of man which is grounded in a consciousness of God and the prevailing view which is not so grounded. "This is the essence of the crisis: the split in the world is less terrifying than the similarity of the disease afflicting its main sections" (p. 57).

If the practical effect of the Enlightenment and the view of man which emanated from it has been devastating for our times, then "we cannot avoid reassessing the fundamental definitions of human life and human society. Is it true that man is above everything? Is there no Superior Spirit above him?" (p. 59). Although Solzhenitsyn's spiritual convictions have earlier been clearly evident, nowhere does he spell them out so explicitly as in this speech to the audience at Harvard, that bastion of secular enlightenment. In a time when, according to his perception, "man's sense of responsibility to God and society has grown dimmer and dimmer" (p. 51), he brings the old message of the Great Tradition of the West that historically "all individual human rights were granted on the ground that man is God's creature" (p. 51). He is saddened by the "total emancipation" which has "occurred from the moral heritage of Christian centuries with their great reserves of mercy and sacrifice" (p. 51). He is a humanist but a Christian humanist—that is, one who believes that human dignity is best safeguarded by seeing that man, though fallen, is also created in the image of God. In the modern vortex of ideas arising out of the Enlightenment, "humanism which has lost its Christian heritage cannot prevail" (p. 55). The real calamity of our times is not simply that an inferior political system is conquering an inherently superior one: "We have placed too much hope in politics and social reforms, only to find out that we were being deprived of our most precious possession: our spiritual life" (p. 57). The real calamity is that in both East and West "we have lost the concept of a Supreme Complete Entity . . ." (p. 57).

The Harvard address ends with a crystallization of Solzhenitsyn's sense that we may now have "reached a major watershed in history, equal in importance to the turn from the Middle Ages to the Renaissance" (p. 61). If one era belittled the physical and the next belittled the spiritual, we may be ready for a revised definition of humanity which, by giving full play to both, restores an ancient sense of wholeness: ". . . we shall have to rise to a new height of vision, to a new level of life, where our physical nature will not be cursed, as in the Middle Ages, but even more importantly, our spiritual being will not be trampled upon, as in the Modern Era" (p. 61).

It is precisely in the hope of helping to bring about such a cataclysmic groundshift of consciousness that Solzhenitsyn and some friends embarked on the project of putting together the essays which constitute *From Under the Rubble*. These eleven essays—three by Solzhenitsyn, three by the famed mathematician Igor Shafarevich, and one each by five other younger authors—are distinctively Russian in content and intended audience. They are in conscious imitation of *Vekhi (Landmarks,* or *Signposts),* a collection of essays by Russian intellectuals dated 1909. That collection, by writers who had been attracted by the siren song of Marxism but had rejected it in favor of a religious vision, pleaded with Russia to turn away from socialism before it was too late. The message went unheeded. Now, after some sixty years of unhappiness with the Russian experiment in Marxism, a new group emerged to signal to their countrymen their hoped-for end to the experiment. These essays were composed before Solzhenitsyn's speeches to the West, including the Harvard speech, but because of their focus on the future, they are reserved for the climactic position in this chapter. Since this study is designed for Western readers, it will forego discussion of those sections which delve into intricate Russian matters and demand more background familiarity than the typical Western reader has. Suffice it to say that those specifics are grounded in the book's general principles, which are universally accessible.

Most of the citations offered here will be drawn from Solzhenitsyn's own essays, with buttressing references drawn from the essays of others as they seem especially helpful in clarifying Solzhenitsyn's point of view. While emphases differ from one essayist to the next, the nature of the volume makes it legitimate to read as a unified manifesto. Incidentally, one myth which this book puts to rest at one stroke is that Solzhenitsyn is a lone voice crying in the wilderness with no support within his own nation.

One purpose of *From Under the Rubble* is to resume the high level of discussion about man and society which characterized Russian intellectual history before the intellectual void of the past sixty years. The authors seek to help their contemporaries overcome the intellectual isolation imposed on a people who have lost connection with their cultural roots. The central question of the manifesto is that of the title of the concluding essay, by Shafarevich: "Does Russia Have a Future?"[21] Because the writers see some possibility that the answer is yes—a slim but nevertheless real possibility—theirs may appropriately be called an exercise in "historical optimism."[22]

The opening essay, Solzhenitsyn's "As Breathing and Consciousness Return," starts with a friendly argument with Andrei Sakharov, a colleague in dissent (recently arrested and exiled) and a man Solzhenitsyn considers noble. Solzhenitsyn disagrees with Sakharov's belief that the introduction into the Soviet Union of a multiparty parliamentary democracy, perhaps through a convergence of East and West, would resolve the deepest problems of the Russian people. Even the West's "unlimited external freedom in itself is quite inadequate to save us" (p. 18). Such freedom "for its own sake" cannot "be the goal of conscious living beings"; rather, it is machinery, "only a framework within which other and higher aims can be realized" (p. 21). Political parties always seek their own welfare, not that of the nation; they cannot admit their mistakes, because to do so would be to the benefit of their opponents. Party struggles are power struggles, "with no ethical basis" (p. 22).

Unlike Sakharov, Solzhenitsyn cherishes the concept of "the vitality of the national spirit" (p. 15). And he makes the objective observation that "in spite of Marxism, the twentieth century has revealed to us the inexhaustible strength and vitality of national feelings . . ." (p. 15). He also notes that "in the long history of mankind there have not been so very many democratic republics, yet people lived for centuries without them and were not always worse off" (p. 23). Particularly, Russia demonstrated in 1917 that it was not ready for democracy, and its readiness "can only have declined still further in the half century since" (p. 23).

So he suggests that perhaps in the foreseeable future Russia might be well advised to settle for an authoritarian (not totalitarian) government, since for centuries it has done so and "did not experience episodes of self-destruction like those of the twentieth century . . ." (p. 23). Solzhenitsyn does not positively advocate authoritarianism, but he seems to fear it less than he does democracy in the immediate Russian context. He is quick

to note that "there are . . . great dangers and defects in authoritarian systems of government . . ." (p. 23). And he certainly does
not equate authoritarianism and totalitarianism; one need only
remember the searing indictment of the latter in *The Gulag
Archipelago*. Doubtless, he would concur with his colleague,
Mikhail Agursky, who writes at one point: "So far I have talked
about the defects of contemporary democracy. But the defects
of totalitarianism are of a completely different order. Democracy's faults pale into insignificance beside the enormities of
totalitarianism. . . ."[23]

And here Solzhenitsyn offers two views of autocracy;
they parallel the two kinds of artists he describes in the *Nobel
Lecture*. Thinking always in the Russian context, he writes:

> The autocrats of earlier, religious ages, though their power was
> ostensibly unlimited, felt themselves responsible before God
> and their own consciences. The autocrats of our own time are
> dangerous precisely because it is difficult to find higher values
> which would bind them. (p. 24)

Against that background, Solzhenitsyn comes to the main
point of *From Under the Rubble*: simply put, politics is not the
primary category of human concern. Like all other earthly
spheres of activity, it is answerable to that higher sphere of
spiritual authority. In a time when politics is given primacy in
both East and West, Solzhenitsyn asserts, ". . . the state structure is of secondary significance. That this is so, Christ himself
teaches us. 'Render unto Caesar what is Caesar's'—not because
every Caesar deserves it, but because Caesar's concern is not
with the most important thing in our lives" (p. 24). He explains
that "the absolutely essential task is not political liberation, but
the liberation of our souls from participation in the lie forced
upon us . . ." (p. 25). At the same time, one who believes in God
may sometimes have to resist the state: "When Caesar, having
exacted what is Caesar's, demands still more insistently that
we render unto him what is God's—that is a sacrifice we dare
not make!" (p. 25). Essayist after essayist in *From Under the
Rubble* echoes this belief. One and all call for a spiritual renewal

in Russia. If that were to come about, whatever particular system of governance were imposed would be humane. "A just and rational system can be built only on a foundation of spiritual and moral values."[24] Spiritual renewal would rule out totalitarian government, though not a benign authoritarianism. "Totalitarian societies are neither eternal nor unshakable" and one "important factor undermining their stability is the revival of religious consciousness, the natural enemy of totalitarianism, which lays claim to total control of the human spirit."[25]

Since every thinking person evaluates all of his (or her) experience in the light of his most deeply held convictions, the religious believer will inevitably evaluate in the light of his faith in God. His world-view is centered in that faith. Thus, his experience is not unassimilated and fragmented but unified, its parts interconnected. This matter must be kept in mind whenever a reader encounters remarks by Solzhenitsyn about political and other mundane affairs. Solzhenitsyn himself, in his essay "Repentance and Self-Limitation in the Life of Nations," speaks eloquently on this subject, as we have seen in the opening chapter; and he moves from the consciousness of the individual to the consciousness of the society:

> The transference of values is entirely natural to the religious cast of mind: human society cannot be exempted from the laws and demands which constitute the aim and meaning of individual human lives. But even without a religious foundation, this sort of transference is readily and naturally made. It is very human to apply even to the biggest social events or human organizations, including whole states and the United Nations, our spiritual values. . . . And clearly, whatever feelings predominate in the members of a given society at a given moment in time, they will serve to color the whole of that society and determine its moral character. (p. 106)

In other words, Solzhenitsyn and his colleagues know that they are not objective observers; no one is. Everyone judges according to his or her developed world-view. Some may not be aware that this is what they are doing; Solzhenitsyn is very much aware.

When Solzhenitsyn brings his religious perspective to bear

on the condition of the Russian nation, he speaks, then, in full recognition that he is applying spiritual categories to social concerns. As the title of this essay indicates, he calls for national repentance—and, following that, national self-limitation. Solzhenitsyn finds in the ability to repent one of the glories of humanity; he speaks of "the gift of repentance, which perhaps more than anything else distinguishes man from the animal world . . ." (p. 107). It is not an easy virtue: ". . . repentance is always painful, otherwise it would have no moral value" (p. 119). Employing his standard analogy between individual and nation, he observes that "a nation can no more live without sin than can an individual" (p. 111). And he cites the biblical acknowledgment that the sins of the fathers are visited upon the children to the third and fourth generation.

Solzhenitsyn brings his call for Russian national repentance down to cases. The established Orthodox Church should repent of its "monstrous punishment of the Old Believers" (p. 116). But the Russian domination of the many peoples within the Soviet Union is the greatest reason for national repentance. No one, he thinks, has suffered so massively under "the stinking swamp of a society based on force and fraud" (p. 117) as the Russians, Ukrainians, and Byelorussians themselves. Something approximating that has been incurred by the natives of the Siberian reaches. At the same time, he does not minimize the need for Russians "to acknowledge our *external* sins, those against other peoples" (p. 128). He singles out for special attention the historic hostility between the Russians and the Poles and calls for mutual repentance. Each citizen of each nation shares in "a community of guilt" (p. 113). Reiterating one of his key thoughts, he comments that

> . . . the universal dividing line between good and evil runs not between countries, not between nations, not between parties, not between classes, nor even between good and bad men: the dividing line cuts across nations and parties, shifting constantly, yielding now to the pressure of light, now to the pressure of darkness. It divides the heart of every man. (p. 108)

It would be a serious error to imagine that Solzhenitsyn's

emphasis on individual responsibility is a manifestation of ascetic or monastic otherworldliness. After all, the focus of this particular essay is on repentance in the life of *nations*. And Solzhenitsyn has explained how the individual, especially the religious believer, must bring his religious commitment to bear on the whole range of human affairs, not excluding politics. Says his colleague Evgeny Barabanov: ". . . the genuine hope of religion, the 'good news' of Christianity about the Kingdom of God, which constitutes the basic content of the Gospel, is not limited to the world beyond the grave."[26] Solzhenitsyn emphatically agrees. Barabanov urges his fellow Christians to resist "that greatest of all temptations": "that of 'simplifying' Christianity, of reducing it from being a teaching about a new *life* to a mere caring for the salvation of one's own soul" (p. 181). Similarly, F. Korsakov[27] inveighs against "the traditional, centuries-old, tried and tested slave armor that openly calls itself the salvation of the individual soul. . . ."[28] Far from being otherworldly in their Christianity, the writers of *From Under the Rubble* agree that Christians must relate their beliefs to the real world in which they live.

Solzhenitsyn's own eagerness to participate in the life of his nation and of the world is everywhere apparent in the subjects about which he has chosen to write. He is a Christian. But he is also a member of the world community and, more immediately, a member of the Russian community. His commitment to Christian beliefs allows him no divorce between Christianity and human culture. Far from it. He must bring into symbiosis his loyalty to that kingdom of God which is beyond this world and his loyalty to one of the nations of this world. The sum of his struggle with this potential conflict of loyalties is not a schizophrenic division of the person but a harmonious melding of a person who is aware of both immanence and transcendence. And in this world, recognizing the evils of a narrowly nationalistic outlook, he declares himself a patriot. He explains:

> As we understand it patriotism means unqualified and un-
> wavering love for the nation, which implies not uncritical
> eagerness to serve, not support for unjust claims, but frank

assessment of its vices and sins, and penitence for them. . . .
no people is eternally great or eternally noble. . . . the greatness
of a people is to be sought . . . in the level of its *inner* development, in its breadth of soul . . . in unarmed moral steadfastness. . . . (p. 120)

Patriot he is; chauvinistic nationalist he is not.

If a nation were to try to follow the generalized advice of
Solzhenitsyn and his compatriots, what kind of civic order would
result? They are seldom specific; after all, their goal is not to
enunciate a particular political strategy. Still, readers wanting
to be down to earth—perhaps especially Western readers, reared
as they are to believe in the primacy of politics—will wish to
know. Mikhail Agursky gets more specific on this subject than
does any of his fellow essayists. He categorically rejects totalitarianism and gives a qualified assent to democracy: ". . . the
society of the future must be democratic, but first, it will need
a high degree of self-discipline. . . ."[29] On the other hand, ". . .
some key aspects of social life will have to be controlled, though
the control must not be of a totalitarian nature" (p. 85). There
will be elections but no political parties; candidates will run as
individuals. Mass media are particularly nettlesome. They must
be freed from the propagandism of the East and the commer-
cialism of the West. "Censorship of the mass media is absolutely
indispensable, but it should be exercised not by bureaucratic
organizations but by elected persons" (p. 86). Censors will have
status akin to that of judges, and similar rights of appeal will
pertain. Although some centralizing of power is inevitable, both
the economy and the structures of government should be as
decentralized as possible. And "it is essential to eradicate the
idea that productivity is the yardstick of a society's progres-
siveness" (p. 81). Further, "the abolition of the gulf between
physical and intellectual labor, as also between industrial and
agricultural work, will be one of the essential features of the
future" (p. 83).

Far from offering the total blueprint of a utopian schemer,
Agursky starts with spiritual and moral values and then sketches
in certain elements of what he considers would be a good so-

ciety. Unlike the utopian, he insists that "any future socio-economic system . . . must be created organically out of existing systems" (p. 87). That is, his sense of history brings him to call for evolution, not revolution. Implicit in all of his speculations is the idea that the state exists to eliminate or minimize external impediments to the fullest spiritual and moral development of its citizens, not to impose virtue. Such a view was once prevalent in Western civilization; it is hardly a novel idea.

Solzhenitsyn never gets as specific about the desired future society as does Agursky. What he does say is that, after the step of national repentance, the next logical step is national self-limitation. He, too, looks to tradition. "The idea of self-limitation is society is not a new one. We find it a century ago in such thoroughgoing Christians as the Russian Old Believers" (p. 136). Such an idea carries within it the moral seeds of genuine freedom.

> After the Western ideal of unlimited freedom, after the Marxist concept of freedom as the acceptance of the yoke of necessity—here is the true Christian definition of freedom. Freedom is *self-restriction*! Restriction of the self for the sake of others! (p. 136)

Accepting this definition of freedom would foster the cultivation of a person's most precious possession, his soul. It would bring about "a new phenomenon in human history, of which little is yet known and which as yet no one has prophetically described in clear and precise forms" (p. 37). If the nations of the earth will adopt the principle of self-limitation, "the turn toward *inward* development, the triumph of inwardness over outwardness, if it ever happens, will be a great turning point in the history of mankind, comparable to the transition from the Middle Ages to the Renaissance" (p. 137).

Without question, this line of thought sounds strange to Western ears, attuned as they are to the Enlightenment doctrine of progress. Yet, surely, the long view of history suggests that someday the hegemony of Western liberal democracy must pass. What *will* take its place? Perhaps a global totalitarianism? But does not the example of Solzhenitsyn, along with his many fellow dissenters in the Soviet Union, indicate that totalitarianism can never attain its goal of total control over human beings? If not totalitarianism, then what? Who is to say that the aspirations of the essayists in *From Under the Rubble* can never be approximately realized? One must always exercise extreme caution in jumping on any bandwagon of futuristic speculation. But these writers combine reasonableness and spirit, and their vision is not necessarily implausible.

It may be a matter of Western pride to imagine that the West will always be the pacesetter in civic affairs. It is a long-standing vision among the Russian intelligentsia that Russia might teach the rest of the world important things. And in a perverse way such has been the case in the twentieth century: Marxism came to power first in the Soviet Union, and its allure has spread throughout the world. Not a few thinkers have perceived the Soviet Union as the future which works. Perhaps again a vision of society will find its genesis in Russia. Perhaps only those who have had the dreadful experience of being under the rubble will be able to point the way for mankind. A. B.,[30] in his essay "The Direction of Change," thinks that a community of religious believers ready to practice self-restriction is already forming among his countrymen. He, along with his colleagues in this manifesto, thinks that this emerging community heralds the proper direction of change; he and they are early examples of it. The good news is that some are indeed crawling out from under the rubble, determined to seek a new way. In a major passage he makes more explicit than does Solzhenitsyn what is certainly a major impelling factor in Solzhenitsyn's sense of mission in life:

> Mysteriously and unsuspected by the busy multitude, Christian consciousness, once almost defunct, is stealing back. In the last few years Christianity's word has suddenly and miraculously evoked a response in the hearts of many whose whole education, way of life and fashionable ideas about "alienation" and the historical pessimism of contemporary art would seem to have cut them off from it irrevocably. It is as if a door had opened while nobody was looking.

Why is this rebirth taking place in our country, where Christianity is attacked particularly systematically and with great brutality, while the rest of the world suffers a general decline in faith and religious feeling? Once again our history over the last fifty years provides a clue to one of the reasons. We have passed through such bottomless pits, we have been exposed to all the winds of Kolyma,[31] we have experienced such utter exhaustion of human resources that we have learned to see the "one essential" that cannot be taken away from man, and we have learned not to look to human resources for succor. In glorious destitution, in utter defenselessness in the face of suffering, our hearts have been kindled by an inner spiritual warmth and have opened to new, unexpected impulses. (pp. 145-46)

He sees a natural linkage between two factors: "the return of Christian consciousness and the presentiment of change" (p. 146). And he states in most forthright terms what many others, he is confident, would agree to: "We are profoundly convinced that Christianity alone possesses enough motive force gradually to inspire and transform our world. . . . Christianity is more than a system of views, it is a way of life" (p. 147). Sharing Solzhenitsyn's view of the great suffering which has been visited upon the Russian people in the twentieth century, A. B. pleads,

We must conserve and assimilate the vast spiritual strength for which we in our country have paid so dearly. We must transform it into an inward fortress of resistance to lies and violence, to the point of laying down our lives if necessary. And this transformation must take place within our souls. (p. 149)

Agreeing with Solzhenitsyn's concern for self-restriction, A. B., in distinctively Eastern Orthodox tones, beckons:

Christianity teaches the concept of "abstinence"—the cleansing of the soul, spiritual repose, the aspiration toward inner simplicity and harmony. We should begin with this, for only to the abstinent spirit is truth revealed, and only truth liberates. There is no need to begin with external solutions. (pp. 149-50)

Like Gleb Nerzhin of *The First Circle*, A. B. brings into symbiosis the individual and community: "Mysterious inner freedom, once achieved, will give us a sense of community with everybody and responsibility for all" (p. 150). And, again with Solzhenitsyn, he expresses disillusionment with the West, yet also the hope that Russia can lead the world to a new and better way:

> But we are confused. In the search for a solution our eyes habitually turn toward the West. There they have "progress" and "democracy." But in the West the most sensitive people are trying, with similar alarm and hope, to learn something from us. They assume, probably not unreasonably, that our harsh and oppressed life has taught us something that might be able to counteract the artificiality and soullessness of their own world—something that they have lost in all their worldly bustle. (p. 150)

So he concludes by urging that we heed "the call of the Vineyard Owner" (p. 150) of the fifteenth chapter of the Gospel of St. John.

F. Korsakov strengthens the case when he notes that among many Russians today ". . . mere fashionable interest and curiosity about religion have been swept away by a genuine and avid demand for the Word of God."[32] That sort of spiritual thirst, Evgeny Barabanov exclaims, is exactly what the world needs: "Today, as never before, a Christian initiative is needed to counter the godless humanism which is destroying mankind, and to prevent humanism from deteriorating into a nonreligious humanism."[33] Scolding his fellow Christians for being "too passive in our attitude to the world," he trumpets: "Christian activism must lead not to a reformation but to a transformation of Christian consciousness and life, and through it to a transformation of the world" (pp. 192-93). Christians have a grave duty: "We must speak of what is beyond modernism and conservatism alike, of what is eternally living and absolute in this world of the relative, of what is simultaneously both eternally old and eternally young" (p. 192).

Solzhenitsyn sounds the same note in his third essay in

the manifesto, entitled "The Smatterers." Is it so thoroughly involved in the internecine struggles of Russian intellectuals, past and present, that it is difficult reading for most Westerners. *Smatterers* is Solzhenitsyn's term of scathing contempt for the modern intelligentsia of Russia; he calls them "the semi-educated estate" (p. 242). But the heart of the essay is not to cast opprobrium on Russian intellectuals past and present but to call for a new intelligentsia ready to meet the challenges of the future. At the moment, he has a higher view of the masses than of the intelligentsia: "... *the people* on the whole *takes no part in the official lie,* and this today is its most distinctive feature, allowing one to hope that it is not, as its accusers would have it, utterly devoid of God" (p. 268). However, far from being anti-intellectual and far from vesting his hopes in the peasantry, he calls for a vanguard movement among the intelligentsia, something he terms a *"sacrificial elite"* (p. 273). He explains, "And I am entirely in accord with those who want to see, who want to believe that they can already see the *nucleus of an intelligentsia,* which is our hope for spiritual renewal" (p. 268). If such a nucleus is in fact developing, it is "not yet a compact mass, as a nucleus should be," but is nevertheless already bound together by "a thirst for truth, a craving to cleanse their souls, and the desire of each one to preserve around him an area of purity and brightness" (p. 271). *From Under the Rubble* is both the firstfruit of Solzhenitsyn's desire for a new intelligentsia committed to spirituality and a call for the further development of such a group. So he pleads with his fellow Russian intellectuals to resist the desiccated ideology of the state and to return to a humanism infused with Christian insight, to place religion over politics:

> When oppression is not accompanied by the lie, liberation de-
> mands political measures. But when the lie has fastened its
> claws in us, it is no longer a matter of politics! It is an invasion
> of man's moral world, and our straightening up and *refusing
> to lie* is also not political, but simply a retrieval of our human
> dignity. (p. 275)

And the first beneficiaries will be the former smatterers themselves; that is the way when inward development takes precedence: "But this path is also the most moral: we shall be commencing this liberation with *our own souls*. Before we purify the country we shall have purified ourselves. And this is the only correct historical order . . ." (p. 277).

Do we, then, through the ordeal of Soviet man and the light shed on it by Solzhenitsyn, see the death of man in our time, or the resurrection of man on the model of those Russians who have endured much at the hands of anti-human totalitarianism? Igor Shafarevich, on the final page of *From Under the Rubble*, puts things into penetrating focus:

> One of religion's most ancient ideas is that in order to acquire supernatural power, one must visit another world, one must pass through death. . . . This is now Russia's position. She has passed through death and may hear the voice of God. But God makes history through men, and it is we, every one of us, who may hear His voice.[34]

NOTES

1: INTRODUCTION

1. Throughout this study, I spell the name according to the most common transliteration of it into English, though I retain variant spellings whenever they are used by the source cited.

2. Dan Jacobsen, "The Example of Solzhenitsyn," *Commentary*, 47 (May 1969), 82.

3. "On Solzhenitsyn," in *Aleksandr Solzhenitsyn: Critical Essays and Documentary Materials*, ed. John B. Dunlop, Richard Haugh, and Alexis Klimoff (New York: Collier, 1975), p. 39.

4. Schmemann, p. 39.

5. Schmemann, p. 39.

6. Published in 1972 and reprinted in English in the above-cited collection by Dunlop, Haugh, and Klimoff, p. 44.

2: NOBEL LECTURE

1. *Nobel Lecture* (New York: Farrar, Straus and Giroux, 1972), p. 3. All further references to this work are cited in the text.

2. Appendix to *Cancer Ward* (New York: Bantam, 1969), pp. 554-55.

3. "Repentance and Self-Limitation in the Life of Nations," in *From Under the Rubble*, ed. Alexander Solzhenitsyn (Boston: Little, Brown, 1975), p. 106.

4. "Repentance and Self-Limitation," p. 106.

5. *The Gulag Archipelago*, I (New York: Harper, 1973), p. 168.

6. *Gulag Archipelago*, I, p. 168.

7. David Burg and George Feifer, *Solzhenitsyn: A Biography* (New York: Stein and Day, 1972), p. 190.

8. *Time*, April 3, 1972, p. 31. Translated by Patricia Blake.

9. Thomas Gray, "Elegy Written in a Country Churchyard," l. 59.

10. "A World Split Apart," *Harvard University Gazette*, June 8, 1978, p. 19. Reprinted in book form by Harper (New York, 1978); see pp. 49-51.

11. Aleksandr I. Solzhenitsyn, *The Gulag Archipelago*, II (New York: Harper, 1975), p. 10.

12. Solzhenitsyn illustrated this point in his 1976 interview for the British Broadcasting Company when he said, of the Russian experience, ". . . we have trodden the path the West is taking 70 or 80 years before the West. . . . Our experience in life is of vital importance to the West, but I am not convinced that you are capable of assimilating it without having gone through it right to the end yourselves" (*The Vision of Solzhenitsyn* [Columbia, S.C.: Southern Educational Communications Association, 1976], p. 2).

13. *Washington Post*, February 18, 1974, p. A26.

3: PROSE POEMS AND STORIES

1. *Stories and Prose Poems* (New York: Bantam, 1971). Page references will be cited in the text of this chapter.

2. *For the Good of the Cause* (New York: Praeger, 1964). References to this work will be from the Praeger edition.

3. For a gloss on some pertinent autobiographical details, see *Gulag Archipelago*, III (New York: Harper, 1978), 406-444.

4. *Prussian Nights* (New York: Farrar, Straus and Giroux, 1977), p. 89.

4: ONE DAY IN THE LIFE OF IVAN DENISOVICH AND THE LOVE-GIRL AND THE INNOCENT

1. Quoted in Giovanni Grazzini, *Solzhenitsyn* (New York: Dell: 1973), p. 91. See also Zhores A. Medvedev, *Ten Years after Ivan Denisovich* (New York: Vintage, 1974), p. 7. Incidentally, it was Tvardovsky himself who suggested the (perfect) title *One Day in the Life of Ivan Denisovich* (Medvedev, p. 7).

2. For the most careful and authoritative treatment of the story of the publication of *One Day in the Life of Ivan Denisovich*, see Medvedev, pp. 4-12. David Burg and George Feifer provide additional information and speculation: *Solzhenitsyn: A Biography* (New York: Stein and Day, 1972), pp. 155-170.

3. See Medvedev, p. 143. For a sampling of the glowing tributes the Soviet reviewers heaped on *One Day*, see *Solzhenitsyn: A Documentary Record*, ed. Leopold Labedz (Baltimore: Penguin, 1972), pp. 40-43.

4. The camp at Ekibastuz, about which Solzhenitsyn writes at some length in _The Gulag Archipelago_, III (New York: Harper, 1978).

5. _One Day in the Life of Ivan Denisovich_ (New York: Bantam, 1963), pp. 202-03. All further references to this translation are cited in the text.

6. This quotation comes from the translation by Ralph Parker (New York: Signet, 1963), p. 34. Max Hayward and Ronald Hingley, translators of the Bantam edition, have it: "When you're cold, don't expect sympathy from someone who's warm" (p. 25).

7. Again, the wording is from the Parker translation, p. 149.

8. From the Parker translation, pp. 43-44.

9. From the Parker translation, p. 148.

10. For an interesting discussion of parallels between this Alyosha and the Alyosha of Dostoevsky's _The Brothers Karamazov_, see Alexander Obolensky, "Solzhenitsyn's Alyosha the Baptist and Alyosha Karamazov," _Cross Currents_, 23 (Fall 1973), 329-336.

11. From the Parker translation, p. 154.

12. From the Parker translation, p. 158.

13. _The Love-Girl and the Innocent_ (New York: Bantam, 1971), p. 35. All further references to this work are cited in the text.

14. Solzhenitsyn frequently rails against the imprisoned thieves, especially in Chapter 16 of _The Gulag Archipelago_, II (New York: Harper, 1975), 425-26.

5: CANDLE IN THE WIND

1. See Keith Armes' Introduction to _Candle in the Wind_ (New York: Bantam, 1974), p. 4. All further references to both the Armes introduction and the Solzhenitsyn play are cited in the text.

2. See, first of all, Armes' splendid introduction to the English version (footnote 1, above), which version he translated; see especially p. 20. Gleb Zekulin notes that this play "helps us to understand the world of ideas that inspires Solzhenitsyn as an artist, that underlies all his works . . ."—"Solzhenitsyn's Play _The Candle in the Wind (The Light Which Is in Thee)_," _Canadian Slavonic Papers_, 13 (1971), 191.

3. _Solzhenitsyn_ (New York: Harper, 1975), p. 94.

4. The 1960 date of composition comes from Keith Armes, p. 4. He adds that the Sovremennik theater in Moscow approved the play for production in 1962, at the height of Solzhenitsyn's acceptability by Soviet officials, but cancelled it after several rehearsals because of its politically sensitive matter. Solzhenitsyn's first wife, Natalya A. Reshetovskaya, says that the play was begun in 1960 and completed in 1964 (_Sanya: My Life with Aleksandr Solzhenitsyn_ [Indianapolis:

Bobbs-Merrill Co., 1975], p. 214). Given Solzhenitsyn's penchant for rewriting, both datings conceivably are correct. In any case, the main point that the play is an early work is incontestable.

5. *Time*, Sept. 27, 1968, p. 26.

6. From a 1967 interview with Pavel Licko, as cited by Armes, p. 10. Other than this early play, it is only in a handful of fairly recent pronouncements that Solzhenitsyn has attempted to speak to the world at large rather than to the Russian people, and one has the sense that he is then responding to what he considers a duty thrust upon him, not to an opportunity eagerly sought.

7. Reshetovskaya, p. 214.

8. In this respect, also, Alex's notions sound like Solzhenitsyn's own: "Own nothing! Possess nothing! Buddha and Christ taught us this, and the Stoics and the Cynics. . . . Can't we understand that with property we destroy our soul?" (*The Gulag Archipelago*, I [New York: Harper, 1973], 516).

9. *Stories and Prose Poems* (New York: Bantam, 1971), pp. 217-18.

10. Zekulin, p. 191.

11. Moody, p. 96.

6: THE FIRST CIRCLE

1. *The First Circle* (New York: Bantam, 1969), p. 9. All further references to this work are cited in the text.

2. According to Giovanni Grazzini, he finished it on Christmas Eve— appropriately enough—(*Solzhenitsyn* [New York: Dell, 1973], p. 135).

3. *New York Times*, April 3, 1972, p. C10.

4. A full book—Olga Carlisle, *Solzhenitsyn and the Secret Circle* (New York: Holt, Rinehart and Winston, 1978)—has now appeared, in which the chief intermediary tells the story of how she and some associates were involved in the novel's initial publication. It tells, among other things, of the falling out between Solzhenitsyn and this "secret circle."

5. Cited in an unpublished doctoral dissertation: Wladislaw Georgievich Krasnow, "Polyphony of The First Circle: A Study in Solzhenitsyn's Affinity with Dostoevsky" (University of Washington, 1974), p. 4. Krasnow provides the definitive study of polyphony in *The First Circle*, and my discussion of the subject is heavily indebted to him. His dissertation will appear in revised form as a major chapter of a book on Solzhenitsyn: *Solzhenitsyn and Dostoevsky: A Study in the Polyphonic Novel* (Athens: University of Georgia Press).

6. Licko interview, as cited in Krasnow, p. 4. The "two books" referred to are *The First Circle* and *Cancer Ward*; the "third" is *August 1914*.

7. Krasnow calls Nerzhin "the author's personal hero" (p. 132); this is different from calling him the novel's hero in the usual sense of the term.

8. Lev Kopelev, *To Be Preserved Forever* (Philadelphia: Lippincott, 1977) and Dimitri Panin, *The Notebooks of Sologdin* (New York: Harcourt Brace Jovanovich, 1976).

9. Panin, p. 26.

10. Characters other than these three also were based on real persons; for instance, Panin tells of the peasant on whom Spiridon was based and the professor on whom Chelnov was based (pp. 145, 272). Indeed, nearly all the characters of *The First Circle*, Panin claims, either had living prototypes or were composites (p. 284). Incidentally, Panin has very kind words for Kopelev; he and Solzhenitsyn describe Kopelev (Rubin) similarly. Panin says that he and Kopelev differed mainly on the matter of belief in God (p. 259).

11. Panin, p. 263.

12. See, for example, *The Gulag Archipelago*, I (New York: Harper, 1973), pp. 161-68.

13. Christopher Moody, *Solzhenitsyn* (New York: Harper, 1973), p. 107.

14. The parallel holds even to the matter of age: Stalin wished to live to ninety; the Grand Inquisitor was ninety.

15. This character, Chelnov, writes *zek* instead of *Russian* in the space for nationality on questionnaires. In recent trials, some dissidents have followed his lead.

16. *As You Like It*, Act II, Scene 7, 11. 174-75.

17. The prototype is Solzhenitsyn's first wife, from whom he was later divorced and who has since written an unkind, sometimes scurrilous, book about him—apparently with KGB aid: Natalya Reshetovskaya, *Sanya: My Life with Aleksandr Solzhenitsyn* (Indianapolis: Bobbs-Merrill Co., 1975).

18. Most of Solzhenitsyn's works contain at least one derisive passage scorning the operations of the Soviet literary establishment.

19. *The Infernal Grove*, vol. II of *Chronicles of Wasted Time* (New York: Morrow, 1974), p. 45.

7: CANCER WARD

1. Solzhenitsyn's open letter to the Fourth Soviet Writers' Congress," in *Solzhenitsyn: A Documentary Record*, ed. Leopold Labedz (Baltimore: Penguin, 1972), p. 112.

2. Records of these two meetings are available in English in the above-cited collection edited by Labedz; records of the second meeting are reprinted in the Appendix of the Bantam edition of *Cancer Ward* (see note 8, below).

3. Labedz, pp. 138-39.

4. Labedz, p. 141.

5. Labedz, p. 141.

6. Labedz, p. 144.

7. Labedz, pp. 152-53.

8. *Cancer Ward* (New York: Bantam, 1969), p. 88. All further references to the novel are cited in the text.

9. "As Breathing and Consciousness Return," in *From Under the Rubble*, ed. Alexander Solzhenitsyn (Boston: Little, Brown, 1975), p. 14.

10. Appendix to *Cancer Ward*, p. 554.

11. See Appendix to *Cancer Ward*. One Soviet critic called the novel "an anti-humanitarian work" (p. 551). Another opined, "*Cancer Ward* is too gloomy and should not be printed" (p. 552). A third announced, "It is downright nauseating to read. . . . I always strive to write only about joyful things" (p. 552).

12. *The Gulag Archipelago*, I (New York: Harper, 1973), 591-92.

13. Appendix to *Cancer Ward*, p. 555.

14. *The First Circle* (New York: Bantam, 1968), pp. 117, 127.

15. Appendix to *Cancer Ward*, p. 554.

16. Describing his own tumor, which was "the size of a large man's fist," Solzhenitsyn comments, "What was most terrifying about it was that it exuded poisons and infected the whole body." Then he notes immediately, "And in this same way our whole country was infected by the poisons of the Archipelago. And whether it will ever be able to get rid of them someday, only God knows" (*The Gulag Archipelago*, II [New York: Harper, 1975], 632).

17. Another translation of the novel's final line has it, "Just for the hell of it" (Labedz, p. 147).

8: AUGUST 1914 AND LENIN IN ZURICH

1. "An Author's Appeal," *New York Times*, June 16, 1971, p. 45.

2. Thus, Jeri Laber saw Solzhenitsyn as venerating Tolstoy, engaging him in dialogue, and even assuming his identity ("Muted Echo of a Masterpiece," *New Republic*, October 7, 1972, p. 27). Mary McCarthy entitled her review "The Tolstoy Connection," though at least she realized that Solzhenitsyn argues against Tolstoy's philosophy of history rather than for it (*Saturday Review*, September 16, 1972, pp. 79-96).

For a lengthy discussion detailing Solzhenitsyn's anti-Tolstoyan bias in *August 1914*, see Wladislaw Krasnow's soon-to-be-published *Solzhenitsyn and Dostoevsky: A Study in the Polyphonic Novel* (Athens: University of Georgia Press).

3. William Pritchard, "Long Novels and Short Stories," *Hudson Review*, 26 (Spring 1973), 225.

4. Herbert Gold, "Solzhenitsyn: Question of Life vs. Art," *World*, 1 (September 26, 1972), 54-57.

5. Laber, "Muted Echo," p. 29.

6. McCarthy, p. 80.

7. "Indictment of Soviet Terror," *New Republic*, October 19, 1968, pp. 32-34.

8. "The Real Solzhenitsyn," *Commentary*, 57 (May 1974), 35.

9. "The Real Solzhenitsyn," p. 34.

10. "The Real Solzhenitsyn," pp. 33-34.

11. "The Selling of Solzhenitsyn," *Columbia Journalism Review*, 13 (May-June 1974), 5, 7.

12. *August 1914* (New York: Bantam 1974), p. 11. All further references are to this readily available paperback edition and are cited in the text.

13. "An Author's Appeal," *New York Times*, June 16, 1971, p. 45.

14. "Solzhenitsyn's open letter to the Fourth Soviet Writers' Congress," in *Solzhenitsyn: A Documentary Record*, ed. Leopold Labedz (Baltimore: Penguin, 1972), p. 112.

15. "Author's Preface," *Lenin in Zurich* (New York: Farrar, Straus and Giroux, 1976). All further references to this volume are cited in the text.

16. From *August 1914*, chapter 22; from *October 1916*, chapters 38, 44, 45, 47, 48, 49, 50; from *March 1917*, chapters 1, 2, 3.

17. ". . . the book is neither a caricature nor a political broadside. Solzhenitsyn's Lenin is solidly researched. After reading serveral volumes of Lenin's letters dating from the period, I can testify to the care with which Solzhenitsyn has reproduced Lenin's speech and thought patterns" (review of *Lenin in Zurich* in *New York Times Book Review*, April 25, 1976, p. 7).

18. "Pursuit in Zurich," *Worldview*, 19 (July-August 1976), 50.

19. Review of *Lenin in Zurich* in *New Republic*, April 10, 1976, p. 23.

20. Conquest, p. 24.

21. Conquest, p. 24.

22. "Nearing the Finland Station," *Saturday Review*, April 3, 1976, p. 22.

23. Feifer, p. 22. I must acknowledge here my awareness that Solzhenitsyn denounced an early biography about him of which Feifer was a co-author, a work which—I am now guessing—was considered by its authors to be a labor of love and respect.

24. Feifer, p. 23.

25. Interview conducted by Michael Charlton for the British Broadcasting Company, in Alexander Solzhenitsyn, *Warning to the West* (New York: Farrar, Straus and Giroux, 1976), p. 113. Solzhenitsyn adds that, for purposes of his trilogy, he "thought of Lenin as one of the central characters—if not *the* central character."

26. Conquest, p. 24.

9: THE GULAG ARCHIPELAGO

1. *The Gulag Archipelago*, III (New York: Harper, 1978), 28. All further references to this volume are cited in the text.

2. Zhores A. Medvedev, *Ten Years after Ivan Denisovich* (New York: Vintage, 1974), p. 199.

3. *The Gulag Archipelago*, I (New York: Harper, 1973), 352. All further references to this volume are cited in the text.

4. Zh. Medvedev, p. 204.

5. "Exiled Solzhenitsyn Arrives in West Germany," *Denver Post*, Feb. 14, 1974, p. 16.

6. Solzhenitsyn has explained his frame of mind as he worked on Gulag:

> I do not expect to see it in print anywhere with my own eyes; and I have little hope that those who managed to drag their bones out of the Archipelago will ever read it; and I do not at all believe that it will explain the truth of our history in time for anything to be corrected. In the very heat of working on this book I was struck by the greatest shock of my life: The dragon emerged for one minute, licked up my novel [*The First Circle*] with his wicked rough red tongue, and several other old works—and retired behind the curtain for the time. But I can hear his breathing, and I know that his teeth are aimed at my neck, that it is just that my time is not up yet. And with devastated soul I am going to gather my strength to complete this investigation, so that it at least may escape the dragon's teeth. In the days when Sholokhov, who has long since ceased to be a writer, journeyed from this country of harried and arrested writers to receive a Nobel prize, I was trying to win time for my clandestine, panting pen to complete this very book.

See *The Gulag Archipelago*, II (New York: Harper, 1975), 214. All further references to this volume are cited in the text.

7. From Author's Note (unpaginated) introducing vol. I of _The Gulag Archipelago_.

8. Quoted from _The Times_ (London), January 22, 1974, in Christopher Moody, _Solzhenitsyn_ (New York: Harper, 1975), p. 27a.

9. See also _Letter to the Soviet Leaders_ (New York: Harper, 1975), pp. 38, 64.

10. "Repentance and Self-Limitation in the Life of Nations," in _From Under the Rubble_, ed. Alexander Solzhenitsyn (Boston: Little, Brown, 1975), p. 119.

11. Joseph Alsop, "Solzhenitsyn's Warning," _Washington Post_, January 2, 1974, p. A19.

12. Cf. this example from _The First Circle_: "The free employees . . . had a great many rights, among them the right to work. However, this right was limited to eight hours a day and also by the fact that their work was not creative but consisted of surveillance over the zeks. The zeks, to compensate for being deprived of all other rights, enjoyed a broader right to work—for twelve hours a day" ([New York: Bantam, 1969], p. 27).

13. "A Poem We Need Today," _Commentary_, 65 (March 1976), 68.

14. For this idea I am indebted to a lead from Professor Philip Reiff of the University of Pennsylvania, who made this connection in passing in a speech on a different subject. The elaboration of the idea is mine.

15. "On Solzhenitsyn's _The Gulag Archipelago_," in _Aleksandr Solzhenitsyn: Critical Essays and Documentary Materials_, ed. John B. Dunlop, Richard Haugh, and Alexis Klimoff (New York: Collier, 1975), p. 474.

16. R. Medvedev, p. 475.

17. R. Medvedev, p. 474.

18. R. Medvedev, p. 476.

19. _Underground Notes_ (Kansas City: Sheed Andrews and McMeel, 1976), p. 176.

20. R. Medvedev, p. 470.

21. "Solzhenitsyn in Zurich: An Interview," _Encounter_, April 1976, p. 12.

10: POLEMICAL WRITINGS

1. _Nobel Lecture_ (New York: Farrar, Straus and Giroux, 1972), p. 32.

2. _A World Split Apart: Commencement Address Delivered at Harvard University, June 8, 1978_ (New York: Harper, 1978), p. 25.

3. If my many conversations with "ordinary" people can be trusted, this particular matter has widespread credence. As best I can trace the matter down, it stems from a single, widely distributed, quite unkind, column, syndicated by the *Chicago Tribune* and written by a columnist who has demonstrated no authoritativeness on the life and works of Solzhenitsyn: Charles Leroux, "Solzhenitsyn makes freedom a prison," *Des Moines Register*, December 17, 1976, pp. 1A, 12A. If my research is accurate, this is a textbook case of the shoddiness of the press which Solzhenitsyn alleges.

4. "Lenten Letter: To Patriarch Pimen of Russia," reprinted in the readily available collection, *Aleksandr Solzhenitsyn: Critical Essays and Documentary Materials*, ed. John B. Dunlop, Richard Haugh, and Alexis Klimoff (New York: Collier, 1973), p. 554. All further references to this "Lenten Letter" are taken from this source and are cited in the text.

5. *New York Times*, March 3, 1974, p. 26.

6. *Des Moines Register*, March 17, 1974, p. 1A.

7. "Solzhenitsyn 'contemptuous' of the U.S.," *Des Moines Register*, March 17, 1974, p. 1A.

8. Astrachan, p. 1A.

9. Astrachan, p. 1A.

10. "Solzhenitsyn—a dispassionate look at a modern 'saint,' " *Des Moines Register*, June 23, 1974, p. 6A.

11. Yardley, p. 6A.

12. Yardley, p. 6A.

13. Yardley, p. 6A.

14. James V. Schall, "Solzhenitsyn's Letter," *Worldview*, 17 (July 1974), 29.

15. Schall, p. 29.

16. Schall, p. 28.

17. "Solzhenitsyn Without Tears," *New York Times*, February 18, 1974, p. 25.

18. *Letter to the Soviet Leaders* (New York: Harper, 1975), pp. 10, 11, 67. All further references are cited in the text.

19. *Warning to the West* (New York: Farrar, Straus and Giroux, 1976). All further references to these speeches and interviews are taken from this readily available collection and are cited in the text.

20. *A World Split Apart*, p. 9. All further references to the address are cited in the text. The edition interpaginates the Russian original and the English translation.

21. *From Under the Rubble* (Boston: Little, Brown, 1975), p. 279. All further references to the volume are taken from this edition. Authors, essay titles, and page numbers are either footnoted or cited in the text, as appropriate.

22. Mikhail Agursky, "Contemporary Socioeconomic Systems and Their Future Prospects," p. 87.

23. "Contemporary Socioeconomic Systems and Their Future Prospects," p. 79.

24. Agursky, "Contemporary Socioeconomic Systems and Their Future Prospects," p. 81.

25. Agursky, "Contemporary Socioeconomic Systems and Their Future Prospects," p. 79.

26. "The Schism Between the Church and the World," p. 181.

27. A pseudonym used to protect the author from government harassment.

28. F. Korsakov, "Russian Destinies," p. 168.

29. "Contemporary Socioeconomic Systems and Their Future Prospects," p. 85.

30. A pseudonym used to protect the author from government harassment.

31. The location of some of the harshest of Soviet prison camps.

32. "Russian Destinies," p. 153.

33. "The Schism Between the Church and the World," p. 192.

34. Igor Shafarevich, "Does Russia Have a Future?", p. 294.

INDEX